THE
EARLY IRISH STAGE

JOHN OGILBY

Founder of the Irish Stage

THE
EARLY IRISH STAGE

THE BEGINNINGS TO 1720

BY

WILLIAM SMITH CLARK

GREENWOOD PRESS, PUBLISHERS
WESTPORT, CONNECTICUT

Library of Congress Cataloging in Publication Data

Clark, William Smith, 1900-
   The early Irish stage, the beginnings to 1720.

   Reprint of the 1955 ed. published by Clarendon Press,
Oxford.
   Bibliography: p.
   1. Theater--Ireland--History. I. Title.
[PN2601.C6 1973]   792'.09415   73-9262
ISBN 0-8371-7004-4

Originally published in 1955 by the Clarendon Press, Oxford

This reprint has been authorized by the Clarendon Press Oxford

Reprinted in 1973 by Greenwood Press,
a division of Williamhouse-Regency Inc.

Library of Congress Catalogue Card Number 73-9262

ISBN 0-8371-7004-4

Printed in the United States of America

PREFACE

IRELAND, in proportion to her human resources, has enriched the art of the stage and the screen in the twentieth century more than has any other segment of the English-speaking world. Her extraordinary contributions have been the outgrowth of dramatic traditions which date back at least five centuries. These traditions, though dominated by English influence until the last years of the nineteenth century, none the less effectively cultivated the theatrical temperament of the island's inhabitants, and formed an indispensable preparation for the conspicuous flowering of Irish stage genius under nationalist impulses after 1900. The present volume encompasses the initial period of Ireland's accomplishments in dramatic art, a period which may be considered to have ended in 1720 with the death of her first outstanding actor and director, Joseph Ashbury. The colour and the significances in the story of this period have yet to be fully appreciated in Ireland as well as abroad.

Numerous histories of Irish theatrical activity have appeared since William Rufus Chetwood brought out the original and still invaluable account in 1749. All of these histories, however, pay relatively little attention to events before 1720, in large measure because the evidence is scarce, fragmentary, tedious to uncover, and difficult to piece together for an appealing tale. The most readable and the most scholarly recital of pre-Victorian activity, Miss La Tourette Stockwell's *Dublin Theatres and Theatre Customs (1637–1820)*, concentrates upon matters between 1730 and 1820, and treats the century previous to 1730 in rather sketchy fashion. The most recent study, *The Irish Theatre* by Peter Kavanagh, adds some interesting details about seventeenth-century Jesuit dramatics, but it too focuses upon the later eighteenth and the early nineteenth century without equalling the clarity or the scope of Miss Stockwell's narrative.

That distinguished Irish historian of the English stage, the late William J. Lawrence, dreamed of publishing a thorough record of Irish theatricals from the seventeenth century onward and assembled a large body of notes to that end. This dream Dr. Lawrence bequeathed to me as his pupil at the same time that he disposed of his notebooks to the University of Cincinnati Library, where they could be immediately accessible for my research. The materials of peculiar value in Dr. Lawrence's three notebooks for the years before 1720 are his transcripts of documents bearing upon Irish stage affairs and formerly existing in the Public Record Office, Dublin. The originals perished in the burning of the priceless archives at the Four Courts in 1922. In addition to the Lawrence transcripts I have drawn from a considerable number of manuscripts and printed sources heretofore either not known or not utilized. Appendixes A and B contain two independent series of papers which in greater portion have never before been published and which have yielded information of the highest importance.

This record of the childhood and adolescence of the Irish stage seeks to place the theatrical developments in relation to the contemporary social scene with a continuity and a detail not undertaken by preceding historians. Two other new emphases may also be observed: careful discussion, at appropriate intervals, of staging methods in Dublin, and constant attention to the composition of the acting troupe at the Dublin Theatre Royal. Appendixes C and D offer as complete a listing as possible of its repertoire and personnel from 1637 to 1720. A great many fresh facts are presented on both of these subjects. Finally, this narrative stresses, with a precision which it is believed no earlier attempt approaches, the phases of change through which theatricals in Ireland passed from their beginnings to their coming-of-age, so to speak, around 1720.

To a very large company of persons on both sides of the Atlantic I am deeply grateful for aid in connexion with my present undertaking, but, so great is the number, I cannot completely enumerate the indebtedness. The works of my recent predecessors, Miss Stockwell and Mr. Kavanagh, have been freely consulted and have in certain respects pointed the way. Any conscious borrowings of materials from their research I have tried to acknowledge in the chapter notes. My fellow scholars in theatrical history—Dr. Giles Dawson and Dr. James

MacManaway of the Folger Shakespeare Library; Professor
Allardyce Nicoll of the University of Birmingham; Professor
Allan Stevenson of the Illinois Institute of Technology; Dr.
William Van Lennep, Curator of the Harvard Theatre Collection—not only have given expert friendly counsel but have
called to my attention important items of evidence. The late
Mr. Joseph Bouch of the National Library, Dublin, guided my
exploration of the historical remains and archives in Ireland's
capital, and introduced me to many fresh sources of information. Mr. Michael Breen, also of the National Library, has
generously assisted me as a skilful investigator and copyist.
Mr. Patrick Meehan of the Muniment Department of the
Dublin City Hall, the Reverend W. J. McCreery of St. Werburgh's Church, Mr. Hubert Carr of the King's Inns Library,
and Mr. E. H. Alton of Trinity College, Dublin, permitted me
to examine original documents of inestimable value, which
were under their charge. Dr. F. S. Bourke, Dr. T. Percy Kirk-
patrick, Lord and Lady Longford, Mr. Lennox Robinson, all
of Dublin, and Mrs. J. B. Arbuthnot of Myrtle Grove, Youghal,
provided unforgettable hospitality as well as all kinds of advice.
The following institutions and their staffs have extended to me
indispensable help: the King's Inns Library, the National
Gallery, the National Library, the Pearse Street Library, the
Royal Irish Academy, the Trinity College Library, Dublin;
the Bodleian Library, Oxford; the British Museum; the
Victoria and Albert Museum; the Harvard College Library;
the Folger Shakespeare Library; the Library of Congress; and
the University of Cincinnati Library.

Despite the widespread co-operation of individuals and
institutions I could never have accomplished the research and
travel requisite for an historical project of this sort without
financial subvention from benevolent sponsors. The University
of Cincinnati granted me in 1939 leave of absence to pursue
my investigations in England and Ireland. Towards that same
end the John Simon Guggenheim Foundation honoured me
with one of its annual fellowships, and the Charles Phelps
Taft Memorial Fund, University of Cincinnati, awarded
me a grant-in-aid. The Taft Memorial Fund also purchased
on my behalf the William J. Lawrence collection of books and

manuscripts relating to the Irish stage as well as much other relevant material.

May my host of benefactors, named and unnamed, experience their compensation by finding in this book at least an iota of the fascination that rightfully belongs to its subject.

W. S. C.

CONTENTS

LIST OF ILLUSTRATIONS

CHAPTER I

The Beginnings

IRELAND is a country of many names. Over the centuries it has been variously called the Watering Pot of the Planets,[1] the Land of Ire or Heaven's Wrath,[2] the Land of Poets,[3] the Island of Saints.[4] Yet none of these labels highlights the passionate individualism which from the distant past has characterized Ireland's inhabitants to the despair as well as the delight of herself and her friends. 'Every day within her borders men are doing mad things . . . most often of all for the stark fascinating insanity of the thing itself.'[5] Thus the Irish have always lived peculiarly absorbed in the projection of their individual dreams and fantasies. No people ever have so consistently and so richly demonstrated the truth of Shakespeare's famous metaphor that 'all the world's a stage, and all the men and women merely players'.[6] This innate love of the dramatic led an eighteenth-century English observer to style Ireland 'the Hot-Bed for Actors'.[7] Here is perhaps the most distinctive of all the epithets which have been coined to describe that country of many names.

It is, however, an outstanding paradox among the numerous paradoxes in the history of the Irish that their extraordinary flair for acting did not produce a native theatrical tradition. This failure may be explained in part by the unsettled condition of Irish life for more than a millennium after the break-up of the Roman Empire. The chronic internecine strife under the rule of the Five Kings was followed after the Anglo-Norman invasion of the twelfth century by recurrent anarchy and military violence

---

[1] *A Brief Character of Ireland* (London, 1692), p. 2.
[2] *A Trip to Ireland* (Dublin, 1699), p. 3.
[3] Mario M. Rossi, *Pilgrimage in the West* (trans. J. M. Hone, Dublin, 1933), p. 1.
[4] Ibid.
[5] *My Countrymen. By an Irishman* (Edinburgh and London, 1930), p. 7.
[6] *As You Like It*, Act II, sc. 7.
[7] *An Answer to the Memoirs of Mrs. Billington* (London, 1792), p. 33.

for over 400 years, until the English had completed the sub-
jugation of the island. Although these continual disturbances
severely hindered the progress of Irish artistic effort, it was at
bottom the exclusively rural pattern of Gaelic culture which
prevented the growth of an indigenous formal drama. Such
drama everywhere has been the product of communal living,
has been a town art supported by fixed patronage. Now the
Irish never founded a town. Even villages of the English or
Continental kind did not exist in the original Irish civilization.
The towns and cities of Ireland are of Danish, Norman, or
English descent. And it was in these communities that regular
dramatic entertainment arose out of immigrant English influence. Hence the history of the stage in Ireland is the account
of alien forces slowly moulding and developing the natural
theatrical instincts in the Irish genius.

Early Irish historians mentioned in connexion with the kings
of Ireland *Druidth Righeadh*, a phrase which has been translated
as 'royal comedians'.[1] The persons so designated are not to be
thought of, however, as stage-players; they were professional
jesters and gleemen, the customary merrymakers attendant
upon ancient and medieval rulers all over western Europe. The
great fairs of Ireland, rather than the royal courts, may have
provided occasional pastimes with tentative dramatic elements.
The Tailtenn, held mid-way between Navan and Kells, or the
Carman at Wexford, had elaborate and varied exhibitions of
prowess in addition to the marketing of craft and produce.[2]
Their programmes included not only athletic and equestrian
games, but also dancing, music, poetic recitations, and the performances of jugglers, tumblers, mountebanks, minstrels, and
buffoons. These last perhaps at times put on humorous imper-
sonations. The fairgrounds contained large and carefully levelled
greens. The group hymn singing on the greens seems to have
possessed a striking similarity to the dithyrambic chorales on
the *orchestra* of the Athenian theatre in the sixth and fifth
centuries B.C.

Whatever the fairs may have brought forth in the way of
dramatic expression, the wakes eventually provoked the Irish

[1] Charles Vallancey, *Collectanea de Rebus Hibernicis* (Dublin, 1770–1804), iii. 531.
[2] P. W. Joyce, *A Social History of Ancient Ireland* (London, 1903), ii. 438 ff.

folk to rude skits with traces of religious symbolism, both Christian and pre-Christian, in their action.[1] The practice of playing at wakes evolved some basic themes with conventional bits of dialogue and business, but with the greater portion of the material impromptu. Two very popular scenarios, which survived until within the last century, were called 'The Building of the Ship' (the story of Noah and the Deluge) and 'The Defense of the Fort (Castle)'. In the latter the players entered as masked warriors, bearing fantastic spears and shields, and broke into opposing factions for battle. Then ensued a duel between the champions of the two sides. One champion was killed, but was revived by the incantations of a herb doctor. Finally the whole group of warriors assembled in triumphal procession and marched out.

The custom of miming spread from wakes to weddings and other festive occasions. Then the representations contained wholly secular and humorous action, often interspersed with songs or dances, or both. Favourite subjects became 'the marriage act', 'the servants serving their lord at table', 'the fulling or thickening of cloth', and, above all, 'Sir Sop (Wisp) the Knight of Straw'.[2] In this last there were two principal actors: an Irish chieftain named after the highest Irish family in the neighbourhood, and clad in the finest appropriate clothes obtainable; an English chieftain, called Sir Sop, dressed in straw with a straw helmet on his head. These two, accompanied by retainers, lined up opposite each other and engaged in altercation, which at last led to combat. Sir Sop felled his rival. A surgeon treated the latter's wound. Both champions retired only to reenter and fight again. Sir Sop was mortally hurt and borne off the field. The Irish chieftain brandished his sword in triumph, strode about, offered thanks to Heaven in a flowery speech, and departed. Throughout the action the officers and servants on both sides functioned like a Greek chorus.

The pieces of mumming which the English settlers brought over from the fifteenth century onward, gradually coloured and

---

[1] Henry Morris, 'Irish Wake Games', *Journal of the Folklore of Ireland Society*, viii (1938), 121–41.

[2] Joseph C. Walker, 'An Historical Essay on the Irish Stage', *Transactions of the Royal Irish Academy*, ii (1788), 75 n.

enriched the Irish folk mimes, especially in the south of Ireland. The Sir Sop play, as it came to be given in West Kerry on St. Stephen's Day at the 'Hunting of the Wren', developed into an elaborate group pageantry and action, with several songs, but still with little plot or dialogue.[1] The principal actors expanded in number to four: (1) the Irish chieftain, a tall man with green coat, yellow buttons, gold braid, white breeches, black knee-boots, three-cornered hat with a bird's wing, white gloves, leather belt and scabbard, sword in right hand; (2) Sir Sop in a straw suit; (3) Sean Scot, an antic; (4) the Wren Man with a large purse at his waist and, in his hand, a high stake surmounted by a holly bush, in the middle of which lay a dead wren. The supporting players, all masked, included male and female clowns as well as men in fantastic clothes with swords, shields, and helmets. Some of these warriors wore rye or wheat-straw costumes and had conical headgear which entirely covered both the head and the face. Musicians with flutes, pipes, and drums accompanied the troupe. The high point of action continued to be the mock battle of the rival factions, a battle waged with wooden swords and inflated bladders tied to the end of sticks.

By the late seventeenth century mumming plays of mixed English and Irish matter had become of frequent occurrence, especially on May Day and Christmas, in County Cork and County Wexford. Saints and devils plus Oliver Cromwell and a Doctor usually constituted the chief dramatis personae. A sketchy but vivid description of the typical stage business is given in an unpublished report of the mummery on the city green at Cork during the Christmas season of 1685:

Last evening there was presented the drollest piece of mummery I ever saw in or out of Ireland. There was St. George and St. Denis and St. Patrick in their buffe Coats, and the Turke was there likewise and Oliver Cromwell and a Doctor, and an old woman who made rare sport, till Belzibub came in with a frying pan upon his shoulder and a great flail in his hand threshing about him on friends and foes, and at last running away with the bold usurper Cromwell, whom he tweeked by his gilded nose—and then came a little Devil with a broom to gather up the money that was thrown

[1] D. J. O'Sullivan, *Journal of the Irish Folk Song Society*, xxvi. 87–89.

to the Mummers for their sport. It is an ancient pastime, they tell me, of the Citizens.[1]

The 'little Devil with a broom' mentioned here was called 'little Devil Doubt' in eighteenth-century Wexford. He entered saying:

Here I am, little Devil Doubt,
If you don't give me money I'll sweep yous all out;
Money I want, and money I crave
If yous don't give me money I'll sweep yous all into the grave.[2]

The irregular riming dialogue and the quaint touches of Irish brogue are more fully recorded in an early nineteenth-century Wexford play:

Enter a Boy dressed as a Punch or a clown, waving his bauble.

BOY.   Room, room, brave gallants,
             Come give us room to rhyme,
             For I'm come to show my mirth
             And activity in Christmas time.

             Active young and active age,
             The like was never acted on a stage;
             And if you believe not what I say,
             Enter in, St. George, and boldly clear the way.
                                                        [*Exit.*

Enter St. George in red sash, knee-breeches tied with red ribbons, large buckles on his shoes, a feathered hat with rim looped up in front, a wooden falchion with a basket-hilt; makes six broadsword cuts, and salutes.

ST. GEORGE. Here am I, St. George;
             From England have I sprung,
             One of these noble deeds of valour to begin.
             Seven long years in a close cave have I been kept,
             And out of that upon a prison leapt;
             And out of that upon a rock of stone,
             Where I made my sad and grievous moan.

[1] Manuscript description of Cork in 1685 as quoted by Thomas C. Croker in 'Recollections of Cork', Trinity College, Dublin, MS. 1206, chap. 9, pp. 11–12.

[2] P. J. M'Call, 'Irish Mumming Plays', a paper read before the National Literary Society, Dublin, in the 1890's, and quoted in an unidentifiable newspaper clipping in the W. J. Lawrence Irish theatre collection, University of Cincinnati.

Many a joiant I did subdue;
I run the fiery dragon through and through;
I freed fair Sabra from the stake;
What more could mortal man then undertake?
I fought them all courageously,
And still have gained the victory.
For England's right and Ireland's nation
Here I draw my bloody weapon.
Show me the man that daares me stand;
I'll cut him down with my courageous hand.

Enter St. Patrick attired similarly to St. George, but with sash, ribbons, and feathers colored green; throws himself into fighting attitude, making broadsword cuts.

ST. PATRICK.   Here, I'm the man that daare you challenge,
                 Whose courage is great;
                 And with my sword I make dukes and earls quake.
ST. GEORGE.   What are you, St. Patrick, but St. George's boy?
                 He fed his horse seven long years on oats and hay,
                 And afterwards he run away.
ST. PATRICK.   I say, St. George, you lie, sir,
[*enraged*]   Pull out your soord and thry, sir.
                 Pull out your purse and pay, sir.
                 I'll run my rapier through your body, and make you
                     run away, sir.
                                  [*They fight; St. George falls.*
ST. PATRICK.   A docthor, a docthor!
[*in a fright*] Ten pounds for a docthor!
                 Is there ne'er a docthor to be found,
                 To heal the prince of his deep and deadly wound?

Enter Doctor wearing a large red nose, black clothes, three-cornered hat, and carrying a cane and pill-box.

DOCTOR.   Here I am, a doctor pure and good,
                 And with me soord I'll staunch his blood.
                 If you wish this prince's life to save,
                 Full fifty guineas I must have.
ST. PATRICK.   Doctor, doctor, what can you cure?
DOCTOR.   What can't I cure?
                 I can cure the plague within, the plague without,
                 The palsy, small-pox, and the gout;
                 And if the Devil was within, I'd surely rout him out.

Moreover, if you bring me an old woman of three-
score and ten,
And the knuckle-bone of her hip be broke, I'll set
it to rights again.
[*Here St. George rises and retires.*
And if you believe me not in what I say,
Enter in, Oliver Cromwell, and boldly clear the way.
[*Retires as Oliver enters.*

*Enter Oliver Cromwell wearing a very red nose, a truculent look, black stock,
buckskin-breeches, jack-boots, and armed with a yeomanry-cavalry helmet and
sword.*

CROMWELL. Here am I, Oliver Cromwell, as you may suppose.
I conquered many nations wid me copper nose.
I made the French to tremble an' the Spaniards for
to quake,
An' I beat the jolly Dutchmen till I made their
hearts to ache.
And if you don't believe what I say,
Enter in, Beelzebub, and clear the way.
[*He flourishes his sword and withdraws.*

*Enter Beelzebub wearing a black wig, a red vizard, a hump on his back, and
carrying a club in one hand, a frying-pan in the other.*

BEELZEBUB. Here am I, Beelzebub,
And over my shoulder I carry my club,
And in my hand a dripping-pan;
I think myself a jolly old man;
And if you don't believe what I say,
Enter in, Devil D'Out, and clear the way.
[*Knocks the pan with the club, and exit.*

Enter Devil D'Out, wielding a broom and annoying the persons nearest to him.

DEVIL D'OUT. Here I am, little Devil D'Out,
If yous don't give me money, I'll sweep yous all out.
[*Broom wielded.*
Money I want and money I crave,
If yous don't give me money I'll sweep yous to the
grave.
Finis[1]

[1] Patrick Kennedy, *The Banks of the Boro: a Chronicle of the County of Wexford*
(Dublin, 1875), pp. 227–9.

These Irish folk plays of diverse origins remained sporadic, improvised, and, for the most part, rural activities. They cultivated no certain audience and established no theatrical tradition. Formal dramatics in Ireland, as in England and on the Continent, got their start through the town churches where the clergy, in order to enliven religious instruction, began by the thirteenth century to sponsor simple representations of Biblical story. At first the representations were dumb shows inserted at the appropriate point in the service of the day, notably on Christmas, Good Friday, and Easter. Then short dramatizations with the dialogue sung in Latin were woven into the liturgy. One such liturgical play of the fourteenth century, given at Easter in the Church of St. John the Evangelist, Dublin, has survived.[1] Six characters, effectively costumed, composed the cast: the Three Marys, with veils, surplices, silk copes, and boxes of ointment; St. John, with unembroidered alb, white tunic, bare feet, and a palm branch; St. Peter, with unembroidered alb, red tunic, bare feet, and keys; the Angel (no directions as to dress). The action follows that commonly found in surviving English and French manuscript versions of the Easter Office. The Three Marys enter separately, lament the death of Christ in a hymn, proceed together toward the tomb, meet the Angel, learn of Christ's resurrection, enter the tomb, draw back in joy and wonder on finding it empty, and start to go to inform the disciples. Hereupon they meet John and Peter, tell them the news, and walk aside. The two disciples hasten to the tomb, John outrunning Peter. They find the tomb empty, return to the Marys, and announce the glad news. The choir breaks into a joyful chant and closes with the *Te Deum* while the actors withdraw.

The Irish churches, like the English and the Continental, soon introduced more elaborate dramatizations of both Biblical and legendary material, which were performed apart from any service. Probably most of these miracle plays, as they were termed, came from abroad because of the scarcity of native

---

[1] Marsh's Library, Dublin, MS. Z. 4.2.20. An incomplete text is printed in J. M. Manly, *Specimens of the Pre-Shakespearean Drama* (Boston, 1897), i. xxii–xxvi. E. K. Chambers, in *The Mediaeval Stage* (Oxford, 1903), ii. 315–18, prints a later manuscript.

playwrights. The two specimens which have been preserved in Ireland, *Abraham's Sacrifice* and *The Play of the Sacrament*, are both fifteenth-century copies of English manuscripts, and may never have had an Irish production.[1] *The Play of the Sacrament* is quite distinctive in its miraculous theme, namely, the desecration of the Blessed Sacrament by five wealthy Jewish merchants of Aragon, and their conversion to the Christian faith.

There has been found written on the back of account sheets of the Priory of the Holy Trinity (later Christ Church), Dublin, a fragment of an early fifteenth-century morality, probably the oldest example of the genre in the English tongue.[2] This fragment, entitled by its modern editor *The Pride of Life*, affords evidence that the play was originally composed in England, though it has never turned up in English archives. The canons of the Holy Trinity Priory may well have copied the text from one in the possession of an English visitor and subsequently may have acted the play. The Prologue of *The Pride of Life*, which outlines the whole plot, indicates that, like so many of the moralities, this one too deals with the salvation of the human soul threatened by death. Rex Vivus (the King of Life) has two knights, Health and Strength, and a herald, Mirth, together with a Queen and a Bishop. Each of these five in turn tries to save the King's soul from Death. When at the last Mirth is overthrown by Death in combat, the King's lost soul is rescued by the intercession of the Virgin. Other moralities probably made their way into Ireland; *The Pride of Life* is, however, the only one of which even a fragment has been discovered.

Though almost no details of church theatricals in Dublin or elsewhere in Ireland exist, there are stray references to indicate that such theatricals stirred up controversy and opposition by reason of their allegedly profane effects. An Irish poem of the late thirteenth century, *The Land of Cokaygne*, chastises in satire

[1] Trinity College, Dublin, MS. D. IV. 18 and MS. Madden F. IV. 20: both printed in *Non-Cycle Mystery Plays*, Early English Text Society, civ (1909). A better edited text of *The Play of the Sacrament* is in J. Q. Adams, *Chief Pre-Shakespearian Dramas* (Boston [1924]), pp. 243–62.

[2] *Account Roll of the Priory of the Holy Trinity, Dublin, 1337–1346, with the Middle English Moral Play 'The Pride of Life'* (from the original in the Christ Church Collection in the Public Record Office, Dublin). Edited with translation, notes, and introduction by James Mills, *M.R.I.A.* (Dublin, 1891), pp. 126–42.

the friars of Kildare near Dublin for their dumb shows portray-
ing Biblical incidents, especially the Crucifixion.[1] During the
following century dramatic spectacles under church auspices
multiplied apparently to such an extent that they came to be
viewed by many of the religious as ungodly distractions. An
ecclesiastical council of Dublin Province, meeting in 1366 at
Kilkenny under Archbishop Thomas Minot, passed the following resolution:

We distinctly order all parish priests of our diocese and province to
announce publicly in their churches that no one is to presume to
hold dances, wrestling-matches, or other disgraceful games in our
churches and cemeteries, especially on the vigils and feasts of the
saints. . . . [They must also forbid] such theatrical games and
frivolous spectacles by which the churches are dishonored, and the
aforesaid priests must warn them [i.e. the offenders], under pain
of suspension, and order them in future to abstain from such acts
and cease from them, under pain of greater ex-communication.[2]

This severe prohibition certainly did not become a long-con-
tinued official policy in the province. The only extant dated
record of church theatricals shows that St. Patrick's Cathedral,
Dublin, in the early sixteenth century, was giving miracle plays
at Whitsuntide (approximately seven weeks after Easter). An
entry in the cathedral accounts for 1509 lists a payment of four
shillings and seven pence to the 'Players, with the great and the
small angel and the dragon, at Whitsuntide'.[3] This brief item
marks the tantalizing end to present knowledge of the course
which dramatic entertainment in the Irish churches followed.

The church plays in due time whetted the appetite of Dublin
citizens for further stage spectacles. During the latter half of
the fifteenth century the city corporation in association with the
trade guilds undertook, after the custom of the large towns in the
north and west of England, to celebrate the Corpus Christi
festival (observed in either late May or early June) with an
elaborate procession. Dublin was by now a bustling port and

---

[1] St. John D. Seymour, *Anglo-Irish Literature: 1200–1582* (Cambridge, 1929),
p. 115.
[2] English translation of resolution no. 7 in Durham Cathedral MS. Roll 5822,
printed without note of source in Aubrey Gwynn, 'The Origin of the Anglo-Irish
Theatre', *Studies* (Dublin), xxxviii, no. 110 (June 1939), p. 268.
[3] John T. Gilbert, *A History of the City of Dublin* (Dublin, 1854–9), i. 37.

metropolis, the capital of the English Pale and the main base of English operations against the unconquered Irish. Its medieval walls and six gates enclosed on the south bank of the River Liffey an irregular quadrilateral sixty odd acres in area[1] and somewhat less than two miles in circuit.[2] Comparable in appearance and size to Chester and York, the Irish city possessed very narrow unpaved streets lined mostly with half-timbered houses of plaster or brick, but with a few gabled buildings of stone. The High Cross at the junction of the High Street and Skinners' Row marked Dublin's central square.[3] On its south-east corner stood the stone Tholsel or city hall, the site of all civic ceremonies. The Corpus Christi processional doubtless started near the middle of the city and first passed before the Tholsel where such notables as the mayor and the King's Lord Deputy for Ireland were assembled. The order and nature of the guild *tableaux vivants* or dumb shows seem not to have varied much as the years went by. The processional at an early period was composed of the following pageants and sponsors:

1. 'Adam and Eve, with an angel following bearing a sword' = the Glovers.
2. 'Cain and Abel, with an altar and the offering' = the Shoe-makers.
3. 'Noah, with his ship' = the Mariners, Vintners, Ship-carpenters, and Salmon-takers.
4. 'Abraham and Isaac with their altar and a lamb' = the Weavers.
5. 'Pharaoh, with his host' = the Smiths, Shearmen, Bakers, Cooks, and Masons.
6. 'The body of the Camel, and Our Lady and her child well apparelled, with Joseph to lead the camel, and Moses with the Children of Israel, and the porters to bear the camel' = the Skinners, House-carpenters, Tanners, and Embroiderers; the Stainers and Painters 'to paint the head of the camel'.
7. 'Three Kings of Cologne [i.e. the Wise Men], riding worshipfully, with the offerings, with a star before them' = the Goldsmiths.
8. 'The Shepherds, with an Angel singing *Gloria in excelsis Deo*' = the Coopers.

[1] An estimate based on the Dublin parish survey of 1851.
[2] An estimate based on John Speed's map of Dublin, 1610.
[3] See Speed's map for topographical details of early Dublin.

9. 'Christ in his Passion, with Three Marys, and angels bearing tapers of wax in their hands' = Corpus Christi Guild.

10. 'Pilate, with his fellowship, and his lady and his knights' = the Tailors.

11. 'Annas and Caiaphas, well arrayed' = the Barbers.

12. The Twelve Apostles = the Fishers.

13. The Prophets = the Merchants.

14. 'The Tormentors [i.e. Executioners] with their garments well and cleanly fixed' = the Butchers.[1]

By 1498 two representations had been added to the foregoing array:

15. 'Arthur, with [his] knights' = the Cutlers.

16. The Nine Worthies [i.e. Joshua, David, Judas Maccabeus, Hector, Alexander, Julius Caesar, Arthur, Charlemagne, Godfrey of Boulogne] 'riding worshipfully, with their followers' = the Mayor and Bachelors of the Bull-Ring (an organization of unwedded youth elected yearly by the citizens, which acted as a civil guard and took its name from the quaint custom of having every bachelor on his wedding day after the ceremony kiss the iron ring in the Cornmarket where the bulls to be used in bull-baiting were tied).[2]

The Dublin corporation in 1498 took the festival programme so seriously that it instituted the heavy penalty of forty shillings to be levied upon any guild which did not perform its part.[3]

An especially memorable performance of the Corpus Christi pageants took place in June 1541, when the festival became the occasion for celebrating what the corporation records termed 'the triumph of peace'[4]—namely, the public observance of the action of the Irish Parliament, composed of Anglo-Norman and Irish lords, in recognizing the English monarch Henry VIII as King of Ireland.[5] After this historic celebration the annual pro-

---

[1] *Calendar of Ancient Records of Dublin* (ed. John T. Gilbert, Dublin, 1889–1922), i. 241; Walter Harris, *The History and Antiquities of the City of Dublin* (Dublin, 1766), chap. 7. The descriptions of properties and business are quoted from these two sources or from the 1498 list in *Cal. Anc. Rec. Dublin*, i. 239–40. The spelling in the quotations has been modernized.

[2] *Cal. Anc. Rec. Dublin*, i. 239–40.   [3] Ibid.

[4] 'Treasury Book of the City of Dublin: 1541–1612' in the Muniment Room, City Hall, Dublin.

[5] Sir James Ware in his *Rerum Hibernicarum Annales* (Dublin, 1664), p. 161, speaks of *epulas, comoidias, et certamina ludicra* as given on this occasion.

cession of tableaux continued regularly well into Queen Elizabeth's reign. Surviving fragments from the accounts of the
Tailors' Guild contain expenditures for their representation of
Pilate and his court as late as 1569, and include a few amusing
details about the yearly arrangements.[1] In 1554 and again in
1556 the guild paid Stephen Case (or Cass) two shillings Irish
'for playing Pilot on Corpus Christi Day'. The remuneration
went up to three shillings within a couple of years. Pilate, more
often referred to in the guild accounts as 'the Emperor', wore a
painted headpiece or crown; fancy shoes and gloves, which cost
respectively eightpence, and ninepence or a shilling; and a
sword, for the 'scouring' (polishing) of which the cutler in 1554
received sixpence, just half the charge of the new weapon purchased in 1560. Pilate's wife, called 'the Empress', wore a crown
and fancy gloves costing the same as her husband's. In 1567 the
painter who refurbished her crown and also the 'paganette' or
pageant wagon on which she rode with Pilate, was paid two
shillings for that labour and twopence additional for his 'drink'.
Breakfast and dinner each year were supplied to 'the Emperor
and Empress' at the expense of the guild.

Not content with the pageantry on Corpus Christi Day, the
Dublin corporation in conjunction with the social and religious
Guild of St. George inaugurated, toward the close of the fifteenth
century, a similar, though less extensive, processional on St.
George's Day (23 April) to St. George's Chapel, located a little
outside the city walls to the south-east of the Castle.[2] The only
known particulars as to the dumb-show accompaniment appear
in a corporation ordinance of 1564, which specified that the
responsibilities for outfitting the 'Pageant of St. George's Day'
should be apportioned as follows:

(a) The Emperor, attended by two doctors; and the Empress,
    attended by two Knights, and by two maidens 'to bear up
    the train of her gown' = the Mayor of the previous year.
(b) 'St. George a-horseback' = the present Mayor.
(c) Four horsemen and horses to bear the pole-axe, the standard,
    and the swords of the Emperor and St. George = the Bailiffs.

[1] 'Extracts from Old Books of Accounts, Tailors Guild, Dublin', in MS. De
Rebus Eblanae 80 (Gilbert Collection, Pearse Street Library, Dublin), i, ff. 120–3
(A.D. 1554–69).   [2] Gilbert, iii. 182–3.

(d) 'A maid well apparelled to lead the Dragon' = the Elder
Master of St. George's Guild.

(e) 'A good line for the Dragon' = the Clerk of the Market.

(f) Four trumpeters = the Elder Warden of the Guild.

(g) King and Queen of 'Dele' [Dole, or Grief] with two knights
to lead the Queen and two maidens to bear up the train of
her gown, the group of six to be 'wholly in black apparel' =
the Younger Warden.[1]

As for the Dragon, the Haggardmen and the Husbandmen for
over a half-century were assigned 'to bear the Dragon, and to
repair the Dragon' on St. George's Day and also on Corpus
Christi,[2] although in 1560 the city treasury paid for the Dragon's
mending and painting.[3] In the 1570's, when St. George's Chapel
fell into decay,[4] the colourful procession on St. George's Day
was abandoned.

These guild celebrations with their elaborate pageantry ultimately merged with the ancient Dublin custom of 'riding the
franchises'. The new festivity took the form of a city-wide per-
ambulation of the trade guilds under the leadership of the
mayor and aldermen on horseback. The processional was carried
out in August every third year (perhaps yearly at first) during
the seventeenth and eighteenth centuries. Gaudy cars, drawn
by richly caparisoned horses and fitted with large high-canopied
platforms, preceded each trade group and bore not only living
figures costumed to portray each calling's historic patron, but
also pantomimes of an allegorical or humorous sort to illustrate
each trade activity.[5]

Most inexplicably, however, the guilds of the Irish capital
never moved on from these processional shows to develop, as
did the guilds in the comparable English cities of Chester and
York, a series of religious and legendary plays for performance
on Corpus Christi or other holidays. Indeed, until well after the

[1] *Cal. Anc. Rec. Dublin*, i. 242 ff. The spelling in the quotations has been modernized.

[2] Ibid. i. 240; ii. 3–4.

[3] 'Treasury Book of the City of Dublin: 1541–1612.'

[4] Gilbert, iii. 183–4.

[5] For further colourful details on this Dublin celebration see John O'Keeffe,
Recollections of the Life of John O'Keeffe (London, 1826), i. 39–42; Jonah Barrington,
Personal Sketches of His Own Times (London, 1827), i. 257–63; J. D. Herbert, *Irish
Varieties* (London, 1836), pp. 71–72.

beginning of Queen Elizabeth's reign, the stage entertainments, by the guilds or by other groups, which the city officials from time to time sponsored in honour of the English viceroys, appear to have been no more than dumb shows, though in the scattered records by later Dublin historians they were spoken of as 'plays'. Thus the Dublin corporation was reported to have entertained in the Christmastide of 1528 the then Lord Deputy, Piers Butler, Earl of Ossory, with the following programme of 'plays', staged on a platform erected east of the city wall in Hoggen Green (now College Green), the usual site of the formal reception of a new viceroy:

1. 'The Tailors acted the part of Adam and Eve.'
2. 'The Shoemakers represented the story of Crispin and Crispianus.'
3. 'The Vintners acted Bacchus and his story.'
4. 'The Carpenters, that of Joseph and Mary.'
5. The Smiths, 'Vulcan and what related to him.'
6. The Bakers, 'the comedy of Ceres, the goddess of corn.'
7. 'The Priors of St. John of Jerusalem, of the Blessed Trinity, and of All-Hallows, caused two plays to be acted: the one representing the passion of our Saviour, and the other, the several deaths which the Apostles suffered.'[1]

The foregoing description of the entertainments suggests that they were none other than the Biblical or the emblematic pageants which the respective trade and religious bodies were accustomed to present at the popular festivals. Likewise, the performances of the 'Nine Worthies' which in 1557,[2] and again in 1561,[3] were said to have been given under the patronage of the mayor in honour of the Lord Deputy, Thomas, Earl of Sussex, may be presumed as mere repetitions of Dublin's favourite Corpus Christi dumb show.

The first certain notice of a secular performance of regular drama in Dublin appears during the viceregency of Sir Henry Sidney. With his arrival in 1566 the efforts to conquer and pacify Ireland were much intensified. While the countryside

---

[1] Robert Ware, 'The History and Antiquities of Dublin Collected from Authentic Records and The Manuscripts Collection of Sir James Ware' (wr. c. 1678), MS. De Rebus Eblanae 74, f. 173: printed in Gilbert, iii. 3–4. Chambers, ii. 365, accepts this record and the two following as those of 'actual plays'.

[2] Walker, p. 80.   [3] James Ware, p. 161.

throughout the island was being systematically laid waste, Dublin as the centre for the expanding activities of war and colonization prospered under a steady influx of English settlers, soldiery, and camp followers. The currents of Renaissance England flowed more and more vigorously into the formerly provincial Irish metropolis, so that it advanced in material attractiveness and in culture despite the surrounding ruin. Its progress took a momentous turn in 1590 when the city fathers allocated the old monastic precincts on the east side of Hoggen Green as a site for Ireland's first institution of higher learning, Trinity College, which opened its doors in 1592. Long before this date, however, Sir Henry Sidney, a typical Elizabethan patron of public works and the arts, had given impetus to the improvement of the capital by renovating the fabrics of Christ Church Cathedral and the Castle, and beautifying their interiors.

Before taking up residence in Ireland, the Lord Deputy and his family, which included the later renowned poet and critic Philip Sidney, had been accustomed to enjoy a rich variety of pastimes.[1] Presumably, therefore, on coming to Dublin Sir Henry encouraged the acting of plays, a mode of amusement which under Elizabeth's hearty approbation was fast growing to be the most fashionable in England. Thus Sidney may well have been very instrumental in accelerating the laggard development of Dublin's theatricals. Whatever the case, in the fall or winter of 1569 the city corporation entertained the Lord Deputy at the newly-finished banquet hall of the Tholsel with a play and the refreshing accompaniment of wine toddy.[2] Here, in a room accommodating 300 or so persons and equipped with a temporary wooden platform at one end, dramatic performances under official patronage came to be not uncommon, though irregular, events. Sometimes they were to celebrate a public holiday, as in 1583 when the schoolmaster David Duke

---

[1] Great Britain. *Historical Manuscripts Commission: Report on the Manuscripts of Lord De l'Isle and Dudley Preserved at Penshurst* (London, 1925–42), i and ii *passim*.

[2] 'Treasury Book of the City of Dublin: 1541–1612', f. 240. This entry and certain others hereafter quoted were included in MS. De Rebus Eblanae 67, 'An Antient Treasury Book of the City of Dublin Transcribed in 1867 for Sir John Gilbert', but this treasury book was neither accurately nor fully transcribed. Miss La Tourette Stockwell in *Dublin Theatres and Theatre Customs* (Kingsport, Tenn., 1938), xv, printed from the Gilbert Collection transcript.

got up a production for Black Monday (Easter Monday)—then so called at Dublin in commemoration of the massacre of 500 festive Dublin citizens by a troop of Irish outlaws in 1209. Duke was paid by the city the very generous sum of twenty-six shillings and eight pence 'for his pains in playing an interlude',[1] but he perhaps had to share this remuneration with his cast. Or again, the performances in the Tholsel were to honour the Lord Deputy, as in 1584 when Sir John Perrott occupied that office and the city paid his musicians forty shillings to do a play for their master's entertainment.[2]

Eventually Dublin attracted the attention of the acting troupes who strolled about England outside of London. In the summer of 1589, when for the first time in years the waters around Ireland were cleared of Spanish warships by reason of the English victory over the Armada, two such provincial companies joined forces to brave the often rigorous passage by sail across the Irish Sea and to try their fortunes in what was for their profession virgin territory. These two, the Queen's Players and the Earl of Essex's Players, after acting in Lancashire during July, probably reached the Irish capital early in August, for they were reported back in Lancashire in September.[3] Their several performances, and indeed their very presence in town, must have proved an exciting experience for Dublin's citizens, who had never before seen professional actors and productions. The comment of the city's treasury book in recording payment to these visiting troupes reveals the enthusiasm and appreciation of the populace. One of the two entries baldly states 'To ye Queen and Earl of Essex players—4£', but the other elaborates: 'Payd to ye Queenes players,—coming to this Cittie,—requital of their go[o]dness in shewing their sporte in this Cittie, by warrant of commandment signed by the mayor and aldermen— 4£.'[4]

During the next half-century strolling actors out of England doubtless made occasional trips to Dublin, though the visit of

---

[1] 'Treasury Book', f. 364. [2] Ibid., f. 375.
[3] John Tucker Murray, *English Dramatic Companies: 1558–1642* (London, 1910), ii. 296–7.
[4] 'Treasury Book', midsummer 1589. Summarized, but not transcribed fully, in MS. De Rebus Eblanae 67. This strolling troupe of the Queen's Players is not to be confused with the famous London company of the same name.

1589 is the first and the last on record. Certainly in the reigns of James I and Charles I English companies travelled to the south coast of Ireland with some frequency to play at Youghal, a thriving walled seaport of three to four thousand inhabitants. Here, after the Armada battle, Sir Walter Raleigh had settled in the town's principal residence, a large gabled grey-stone manor-house, where Edmund Spenser the poet sojourned and perhaps wrote parts of *The Faerie Queene*. In Youghal, as in Dublin, the strollers acted in the Tholsel or town hall under the patronage of the city officials. Sometimes the players were favoured with the presence and bounty of Sir Richard Boyle (later titled the 'Great Earl of Cork'), who was Youghal's leading citizen and lived in the Raleigh house. On 11 February 1615/16, Sir Richard viewed the acting of Prince Charles's Men, a well-known provincial troupe of the period, and bestowed upon them twenty-two shillings.[1] The same troupe pleased him again with their performance on 8 April 1619 and received another twenty-two shillings as reward.[2] Early in the following February these players, or a like group, drew so many spectators to the Tholsel that some unruly citizens 'to come in hither to see the said play do break and batter the windows and glass there'.[3] In consequence of this riot, the town council quite sensibly did not move to prohibit further theatricals, but rather it took steps to protect the town against the costs of similar damage in the future. It resolved to confer the privilege of 'freeman' upon a certain glazier, William Durant, on condition that he would glaze all the Tholsel windows, fit iron bars into the windows, paint the king's arms, whitewash the walls, and keep the windows in order during his life.

Youghal enjoyed so high a reputation for its interest in dramatics that some five years later, when the plague was raging in London and the theatres therefore were closed, the leading London company, the King's Players, got a royal

---

[1] *Lismore Papers*, 1st series (ed. A. B. Grosart, London, 1886), i. 100. The Raleigh–Boyle manor-house, now called Myrtle Grove and owned by descendants of Sir Henry Blake, Victorian official and diplomat, has been splendidly preserved.

[2] Ibid., p. 215.

[3] *The Council Book of the Corporation of Youghal* (ed. Richard Caulfield, Guildford, Surrey, 1878), p. 64. Stockwell, p. xvi, has followed *Lismore Papers*, i. xix, in misprinting and hence misinterpreting the passage.

licence to travel abroad[1] and proceeded to honour Youghal with a visit during the fall of 1625. Richard Gough, the mayor, 'in company with some of the aldermen', made up a purse of five shillings to express their gratification to the actors.[2] During the next decade, local opposition to stage amusement grew so intense that on 5 October 1635 the town council agreed 'that no Mayor or Bayliffes shall give license to stage players, or any other of that kind, to make use of the Town Hall, and whatsoever officer shall do contrary to this By-law shall forfeit £10 to be recovered by the Mayor'.[3] This unhappy prohibition brought a cessation of theatricals in Youghal for an indefinitely long period.

Meanwhile, in seventeenth-century Dublin, a city of 20,000 or upward, and of rising affluence now that the English 'pacification' of Ireland had been achieved, the acting of plays became an established form of entertainment among all sorts of citizens. High society, centring around the Lord Deputy and the Castle, had taken up dramatics as a modish recreation. During Lord Mountjoy's régime, which comprised the last three years of Elizabeth's reign, amateur performances were said to have occurred often at the viceregal residence, probably in either the dining hall or the state audience chamber. On the queen's birthday, 7 September 1601, the gentlemen of the Castle put on at night the old tragedy of *Gorboduc*, because they doubtless thought its theme of a divided kingdom most appropriate to the present crisis of Essex's plotting against the queen. The only detail of this birthday production that has been preserved is the high cost for lighting the show. Twenty-one shillings and two pence were spent for candles of the best quality, namely, wax tapers.[4]

The Dublin tradesmen, too, entertained themselves with plays on festive occasions. The Tailors' Guild in 1612 had a dramatic performance after its Midsummer Day banquet in the Tailors' Hall on Winetavern Street, which led from Christ Church to the Liffey quays. Since the actors got in compensation

[1] G. E. Bentley, *The Jacobean and Caroline Stage* (Oxford, 1941), i. 19–20.
[2] *Lismore Papers*, i. xix.
[3] *The Council Book of the Corporation of Youghal*, p. 188.
[4] W. R. Chetwood, *A General History of the Stage* (London, 1749), p. 51.

only the paltry sum of two shillings, they surely must have been members of the Guild.[1]

The students at Trinity College developed the custom of theatricals around Christmastide. On 23 December 1629 the College Register noted that 'the Senior Sophisters [the fourth year men] exercise dominion over the Junior sort [the third year men] this Christmas. A comedy by them [the Seniors] and a play by the Batchelors [the graduate students]'.[2] In the following year the custom of Christmas plays was threatened with extinction by the new provost, Robert Ussher, who was 'no friend to the Levitie of Theatricall Gaieties and Representations'.[3] 'The great solicitation of considerable Persons'[4] finally persuaded the straightlaced Provost to a compromise grudgingly set down in the Register on 29 December 1630: 'It is condescended and agreed that the Batchelors should act their play but not in the Colledge.'[5] Perhaps the necessity to stage their performances of that year outside the college precincts cooled the ardour of the Trinity players. At any rate the Register contains no subsequent hints of university dramatics.

Dublin's other student group of that period, the apprentice lawyers, also now and then indulged in theatrical amusements. These young men resided on the north side of the Liffey near the Old Bridge in handsome stone dormitories with a cloister, the whole called 'The Inns'. In their large dining-hall they celebrated every term the 'grand day', when choice beverages accompanied the dinner and a special programme followed. On occasion a dramatic production would constitute the special programme, as in January of Hilary Term, 1631, when 'ye players for ye grand day' performed, and received two pounds for their services.[6]

Dublin and Youghal were not the only communities in Ireland to lay the foundations of a stage tradition before the 1641 Rebellion. Since the middle of the previous century the old walled town of Kilkenny, seventy miles south-west of Dublin, had been fostering the regular production of plays. A county

---

[1] MS. De Rebus Eblanae 80, f. 134.
[2] Trinity College Register (Muniment Room, Trinity College, Dublin), p. 26.
[3] Robert Ware, MS. De Rebus Eblanae 75, f. 328.
[4] Ibid.   [5] p. 34.
[6] 'The Black Book of Kings Inns', Library of King's Inns, Dublin, MS. 38, f. 27.

seat with a population of four to five thousand, and the market centre for one of Ireland's most fertile regions, Kilkenny early gained distinction for its attractive environment. In the 1600's a popular saying praised it thus: 'Fire without Smoke, Water without Mud, Air without Fogg.'[1] The town was described by an Elizabethan traveller as 'scituate in a pleasant valley, and upon a fresh ryver [the Nore] . . . with delightfull orchards and gardens, which are somewhat rare in Ireland. The houses are of grey marble fayrely builte, the fronts of theyr houses are supported (most of them) with pillars, or arches, under which there is an open pavement to walke on. At one end of the towne is a large cathedrall, at the other end, a high mounted castle appertayning to the Earles of Ormond and overlooking the ryver.'[2] The High Street which connected these two ends ran past the Tholsel and through the main square where the Market Cross stood.[3]

It was at this cross on 20 August 1553, the day of celebration for Queen Mary's accession, that Kilkenny's first known dramatic performances took place. Young men of the town 'in the forenoon played a tragedy of God's Promises in the old law . . . with organ, playings, and songs very aptly. In the afternoon again they played a comedy of Saint John the Baptist's Preachings, of Christ's Baptising, and of His Temptation in the Wilderness; to the small contention of the Priests and other Papists there.'[4] The author of these dull miracle plays, which, he assured the spectators, 'shall your inward stomach cheer',[5] was the Englishman John ('Bilious') Bale (1495–1563), the new bishop at Kilkenny and a notorious anti-Catholic, who had previously written for the Protestant cause two other dramatic works, *Three Lawes* and *Kynge Johan*. Bishop Bale undoubtedly sponsored the Kilkenny theatricals in 1553 as propaganda to offset

---

[1] John Dunton, *The Dublin Scuffle* (London, 1699), p. 376.

[2] Luke Gernon, 'A Discourse of Ireland', Stowe MS. 28, f. 5, as quoted in C. Litton Falkiner, *Illustrations of Irish History and Topography, Mainly of the Seventeenth Century* (London and New York, 1904), p. 354.

[3] John G. A. Prim, 'Olden Popular Pastimes in Kilkenny', *Transactions of the Kilkenny Archaeological Society*, ii (1852–3), 219.

[4] *The Vocation of John Bale to the Bishopric of Ossory in Ireland* (London, 1553), reprinted in the *Harleian Miscellany* (London, 1808–10), vi. 450. Bale's spelling has been modernized.

[5] Prologue to *God's Promises*.

the accession of a Catholic queen. They may well have marked
the initiation of his flock to that form of public entertainment. In
any case, the citizens three years later were reported to have
been so absorbed in watching dramatic performances on Corpus
Christi Day that the town treasurer of Cashel was able to steal
away without difficulty the body of the former Archbishop of
Cashel from his tomb in the Kilkenny Cathedral.[1]

For more than eighty years thereafter the Kilkenny corporation supervised and supported on Corpus Christi, and also on
Midsummer Day, a series of plays based on the stories of the
Temptation, the Resurrection, and the Nine Worthies. The
town fathers, predominantly pro-English and Protestant, followed Bishop Bale's lead and looked upon their community
drama as an important medium of religious persuasion. They
therefore arranged that the children of the 'natives', the pure
Irish residents of Catholic faith, should be duly prepared for
understanding the contents of the festival plays. As late as 1631
William Cousey was granted three pounds three shillings and
four pence per year 'for teaching to write and read and for in-
structing the children of the natives for the play on Corpus
Christi Day'.[2] Though the corporation in 1637 paid Christopher
Coyne ten Irish shillings 'for coppying the book of Corpus
Christi plays, which book was sent to Dublin',[3] not a fragment
seems to have survived.

The corporation records suggest the general scope of the play
material but offer few details as to contents or presentation.
They mention, over the span of many years, the roles of Christ,
John the Evangelist, 'Mary Mother', the Three Marys, Michael
the Archangel, Hector, Joshua, Caesar, Charlemagne, Godfrey,
Satan, and the archdemon Belphegor, who 'goeth about in
stacions',[4] that is, frolics about at the various acting spots. This
last part evidently resembled, except in name, the comic 'devil'
or 'vice' in some English miracle and morality dramas. Doubling
of roles in the casting of the Nine Worthies was practised in

---

[1] John Lynch, 'De Historia Ecclesiae Hiberniae', Trinity College, Dublin, MS.
K. 6.15.16, ii, f. 467.
[2] Prim, p. 328.
[3] 'Kilkenny Corporation Records', *Journal of the Royal Historical and Archaeological
Association of Ireland*, 4th series, vi (1883–4), 241.
[4] Ibid., p. 240.

certain years. Therefore the lives of these heroes must have been presented in separate episodes which would permit actors time to change make-up. Thomas Lucas in 1593 took the parts of Charlemagne and another 'Conqueror';[1] Matthew Hickey in 1637, the parts of 'two Conquerors';[2] and William Lawless in the same year, the parts of Hector and Godfrey. As for the costuming of the characters and their properties, Christ, John, and the four Marys in the Resurrection scene wore gloves, and the women had lace decoration on their dresses. In 1588 John Bussher received fourteen shillings 'for setting forth of the Maryes'; sixteen pence for six pairs of gloves; seven pence 'for two pareles [rope or iron bands] for the Sepulcre'; six pence 'for pins'.[3] Michael was outfitted with wings, coronet, and a banner. When Thomas Daniel in 1637 was to furnish these items for the archangel at six shillings and eight pence, the mayor took care to assure the fulfilment of the contract by a formal order: 'Lett this warrant be paid upon receipt of the said coronet and banner, not before.'[4]

The manner of staging the Corpus Christi Day plays at Kilkenny appears to have been modelled after the method of presentation on the Continent rather than in England. Each play was acted on a raised wooden platform, on which, in some cases at least, were mounted one or two significant 'props', such as the Sepulchre known to have been used in the Resurrection play. These simple stages were set out according to the order of performance and placed at convenient intervals on spots termed 'stations' either in the market square or along the High Street. Railings 'for keeping out horses and the mob' ran around the 'stations' and provided a reserved space 'for placing strangers at the place where the interlude shall be plaid'.[5] Thus Kilkenny showed special courtesy to the visitors at its dramatic festivals. If the site of a 'station' blocked off a shopman's door and trade, the authorities permitted him to set up shop elsewhere, as in 1632 when 'the north side of the market cross was granted to two persons for shops during the fair time of Corpus Christi, in regard their shops are stopt up by the stations and play of

---

[1] Ibid., p. 239.
[2] Ibid., p. 241.
[3] Ibid., p. 243.
[4] Ibid., p. 241.
[5] Prim, p. 327.

Corpus Christi'.[1] Just as in Chester or York a trumpeter heralded the start of performance. William Courcy got ten shillings in 1584 'for acting and playing the trompetors part, Corpus Christi day and Mid Sumer Eve'.[2] When the trumpet sounded at the outset of the day's programme, the spectators gathered about the first 'station' for the opening play. At its conclusion they moved to the second 'station', and so onward, 'station' by 'station', until they had seen the entire series of plays acted.

To assemble promptly on the festival morning the young men who were the actors, the corporation engaged one of the towns-women, presumably a good cook, to serve the players with breakfast. In the 1630's Mary Roth was paid twenty shillings for her breakfasts to 'the young men that acted uppon the stage uppon Corpus Christi day'.[3] Their acting fees as set by the corporation exhibit many puzzling variations. Simon Archer in 1600 received only ten pence 'for playing a Conqueror on Midsummer Eve',[4] though the usual compensation of a 'Conqueror' at the period was, for one performance, six shillings and eight pence. The actor who took the part of Belphegor, the itinerant 'Devil', was paid in 1602 eleven pence, but in 1603 five shillings.[5] In 1637 William Lawless for acting two 'Conquerors' at Corpus Christi and Midsummer got twenty shillings and eight pence; Matthew Hickey, for the same roles, twenty shillings; James Barry, for one 'Conqueror', thirteen shillings and four pence; and John Purcell, for the same part, six shillings and eight pence.[6] Experience and seniority may explain at least some cases of apparent disparity.

Since the last notice of Corpus Christi plays at Kilkenny is for 1639,[7] it is clear that the turmoil in the country both before and after the Rebellion put an end to the custom. Yet the taste for theatricals had been too deeply instilled in this vigorous and fashionable town to be extinguished forever. Before the close of the century Kilkenny was again seeing plays. First, however, a great change had to come in the system of production. The dramatics so far recorded for the Irish towns consisted of

---

[1] Prim, p. 328.
[2] 'Kilkenny Corp. Rec.', p. 242.
[3] Ibid., p. 241; Prim, p. 328.
[4] 'Kilkenny Corp. Rec.', p. 239.
[5] Ibid., p. 240.
[6] Ibid., pp. 240–2.
[7] Ibid., p. 242.

amateur performances by private or community groups, or of sporadic presentations by strolling professionals from England. Neither type of production could supply the proper basis for a permanent stage tradition. What Ireland now needed was the establishment of a professional playhouse with its own troupe and a regular theatrical programme.

CHAPTER II

Ireland's First Theatre

V ISCOUNT THOMAS WENTWORTH, later Earl of Strafford, came to Dublin as Lord Deputy in the summer of
1633 with two express ambitions: first, to make Ireland
a profitable tributary to the Crown; second, to make her chief
city beautiful and fashionable as befitted the capital of the
English viceroy. To both of these ambitions his energy and fore-
sight brought marked success during his seven years of office.
Dublin flourished under his administration. Sir William Brereton, a wide traveller, reported of the Irish metropolis in 1635
that there had been 'much additions of building lately, and
some of these very fair, stately and complete buildings. . . . There
are divers commodities cried in Dublin as in London, which it
doth more resemble than any town I have seen in the King of
England's dominions.'[1]

Wentworth set about the complete rehabilitation of Dublin
Castle as a viceregal palace; he built new rooms, outbuildings,
and gardens. He introduced more fully than his predecessors
the lavish regimen of a court, including a corps of fifty attendants
in livery. The Castle became a gay place of constant hospitality
and many diversions. A frequent guest there was one of the two
Lords Justices of Ireland, Richard Boyle, Earl of Cork, already
cited as a patron of dramatics at Youghal. On 2 January 1633/4
the Earl of Cork along with the Lord Chancellor, Sir Adam
Loftus, spent a merry day at the Castle, dining, gaming at dice,
supping, and finally seeing 'a play acted by his lordships
gentle[men]'.[2] Again, on 5 January 1635/6, the Earl passed
another similar day at the Castle in company with his son and
several prominent noblemen, dining and playing cards. Then
'we saw a tragedie in the parliament house [the large council

---

[1] Sir William Brereton, *Travels in Holland, The United Provinces, England, Scotland,
and Ireland, 1634–1635* (ed. Edward Hawkins, [London] 1844), p. 144 (12 July 1635).
[2] *Lismore Papers*, 1st series, iv. 6.

hall in the Castle, where the Irish Parliament met in 1635], and which was tragicall, for we had no suppers.'[1] Obviously the Lord Deputy liked theatricals and from the beginning of his Dublin residence saw to it that plays by members of his suite should be an occasional form of amusement.

To take charge of dramatic and other entertainment at the Castle, Wentworth secured from London sometime between 1633 and 1636 a well-known dancing master of Gray's Inn Lane, John Ogilby, and made him a 'gentleman of the household'.[2] This shrewd Scot, born at Edinburgh in 1600, turned out to be a promoter of novel projects and the true founder of the Irish stage. After his arrival in Dublin Ogilby decided that the city with its numerous officials and courtly upper class offered an ideal audience for a professional playhouse such as had not yet been erected outside of London. Obtaining Wentworth's blessing, and perhaps financial support, he undertook, to use his own words, 'great preparations and disbursements in building a new theatre, stocking and bringing over a Company of Actors and Musicians, and settling them in Dublin'.[3] It was a propitious moment to form a resident theatrical troupe in Ireland because the severity of the plague at London wholly closed down the theatres from May 1636 to October 1637. Ogilby therefore could procure experienced and able London actors who were glad to find employment even as far afield as Dublin. He seems to have drawn from several London companies, certainly from those at the Fortune and the Red Bull theatres. From the Fortune he got its three chief performers, Edward Armiger, William Perry, Richard Weekes; and from the Red Bull, William Cooke, who in 1635 had been awarded the sinecure of 'a Groom of the Chamber' to Prince Charles.[4] These four, the only members of

[1] Ibid., pp. 146–7.
[2] John Aubrey, 'Brief Lives', chiefly of Contemporaries, set down by John Aubrey between the Years 1669 and 1696 (ed. Andrew Clark, Oxford, 1898), ii. 101.
[3] MS. S.P. 63, State Papers, Ireland, vol. 345, no. 50, Public Record Office, London. This document is summarized in the Cal. State Papers: Ireland, Addenda, 1669–70, p. 416. The spelling in the quoted excerpt has been modernized.
[4] For biographical details (excluding Irish connexions) concerning Armiger, see Bentley, ii. 350; Perry, ibid., pp. 529–31; Weekes, ibid., pp. 615–16; Cooke, ibid., p. 413. Cooke's Dublin residence on Wood Quay is established by a St. John's parish document of 1638 quoted in Samuel C. Hughes, The Pre-Victorian Drama in Dublin (Dublin, 1904), p. 2. J. T. Gilbert, a far less accurate authority

Ogilby's organization at present identified beyond question,[1] would indicate that the new troupe was worthy of the second city in the kingdom. Perry was the outstanding figure among the Dublin players. He had served as a boy actor in Lady Elizabeth's Company back in 1613, had been made in 1629 'a Groom of the Chamber' to Prince Charles, and had been leading companies in and out of London since 1616. Ogilby sooner or later appointed him deputy and housekeeper; accordingly he lived on the playhouse premises. In 1641 'Mr. Perry at the Playhouse' paid its large parish assessment of five shillings for the poor.[2]

Ogilby wisely located his theatre, in close proximity to the Castle, on St. Werburgh (now Werburgh) Street, which ran south from Castle Street to the Pole Gate, a total distance of only four to five hundred feet.[3] This thoroughfare received its name from St. Werburgh's, a kind of chapel royal for the Lord Deputy. The church was situated on the east side not quite half-way to the Gate. About two score of prosperous residences and shops lined the street. Sir Adam Loftus, Marsh the surgeon, the sadlers Cardiffe and Harding, and Daniel Taylor, who ran a letter office, all resided in the vicinity of the playhouse.[4] Nearby, too, stood the London Tavern, a resort still sufficiently noted

---

on stage history, lists the man as 'Thomas Cooke, player' in *Hist. City Dublin*, i. 39. Neither Gilbert nor Hughes identifies Cooke.

[1] Allan H. Stevenson in his article, 'James Shirley and the Actors of the First Irish Theater' (*Modern Philology*, xl (1942), 152 ff.), suggests that William Allen, Michael Bowyer, Hugh Clark, and William Robins, from the Phoenix Theatre, and Thomas Jordan from Salisbury Court, may have gone to Dublin. Only in the case of the last-named is there any shred of specific evidence: 'Thomas Jordan son to Thomas Jordan' was christened at St. John's, Dublin, on 28 Dec. 1637 (*The Registers of St. John the Evangelist: 1619 to 1699*, ed. James Mills, Dublin, 1906, p. 29). Even though the date is temptingly coincidental, the case for identifying this Thomas Jordan with the London actor is a weak one, because the name was of too common occurrence.

[2] MS. account books for the Poor Cess, 1641–2, St. Werburgh's Church, Dublin.

[3] For topographical details of St. Werburgh Street see the map of Dublin by Charles Brookings, printed in 1728, and John Rocque's far more detailed map printed in 1756.

[4] These names, and that of the London Tavern, appear immediately before or after 'Perry at the Playhouse' on the St. Werburgh Street list of parish ratings for the Poor Cess in the manuscript account books of St. Werburgh's Church. This same list taken in conjunction with the known length of the street provides a pretty accurate basis for computing the number of buildings and households.

after the Restoration to be spoken of in the comedy *Hic et Ubique, or the Humours of Dublin* (1663).[1] The exact location of the playhouse has been the subject of much speculation. One of Ogilby's contemporaries and his first biographer, John Aubrey, wrote down an important clue which has been entirely disregarded. Aubrey, in reporting the fate of Ogilby's theatre after the outbreak of the 1641 Rebellion, stated that it was 'spoyled and a cow house made of the stage'.[2] Now, during the troubled 1640's, the Dublin authorities organized a force called the 'Main Guard' to preserve law and order within the city.[3] The 'Main Guard House' was set up a little to the south of St. Werburgh's Church and several house-lots north of the passage to Hoey's Court, where Jonathan Swift was born in 1667. The Main Guard had its stable, however, in a building somewhat farther down the street on the other (the west) side. This stable-house occupied the lot immediately south of the one that faced the passage to Hoey's Court. For the Main Guard to convert into a stable an empty playhouse close to its station would have been the cheapest and most convenient solution to the problem of housing its horses. Therefore it would seem altogether likely that the Guard stable-house was the remains of Ogilby's theatre and the 'cow house' to which Aubrey referred. If so, the much discussed site at last can be precisely determined: it lies about opposite the twentieth-century entrance to Hoey's Court from Werburgh Street.[4]

The playhouse which Ogilby built was, according to Aubrey, 'a pretty little theatre'.[5] Ogilby had every reason to think his Dublin clientele similar to the restricted audiences of the London 'private' theatres, such as the Phoenix or Salisbury Court. Hence he planned a playhouse of like structural arrangements and small capacity—accommodating, say, three to four hundred

---

[1] Act I, sc. 1, p. 5.   [2] Aubrey, ii. 103 n.   [3] Gilbert, i. 41–42.

[4] 'A Retrospect of the Dublin Stage', an anonymous article in the *Dublin Morning Post*, 18 Oct. 1827, places the site in Derby Square, a court off Werburgh Street to the west. Yet, according to Gilbert, i. 44–45, Derby Square was not built until late in the seventeenth century. John S. Sloane on his 'Map of the Walls of the City of Dublin' in *The Irish Builder*, 1 July 1882, marks the same location for the theatre. A similar map done 'from all available authorities' by Leonard R. Strangways in 1904 puts the playhouse across from the opening to Hoey's Court. Miss Stockwell does not attempt to locate the structure.

[5] Aubrey, ii. 101 n.

people. It may be imagined as a modest rectangular building of timber and brick, containing a roofed sloping pit furnished with benches and lighted by wall candelabra. At the back of the pit (and possibly at the sides) there was perhaps a narrow gallery with one or two boxes for the Castle notables or other 'persons of honour'. The main acting platform had at its rear a curtained inner stage and, over it, a balconied upper room, all three areas equipped with traps and doors. The staging followed the traditional English method of no definite settings and few properties except for infrequent localized scenes, which were 'discovered' on the inner stage by drawing aside the hangings. An elaborate setting of this latter kind, assuredly executed on the St. Werburgh Street inner stage, is the Druid 'temple' with altar and idols in *St. Patrick for Ireland*.[1] The Dublin performances were advertised from day to day according to the London custom of posting bills at various points in the city. In the prologue to one St. Werburgh Street play the speaker makes an amusing allusion to the practice:

> The writs abroad, and men with half an eye
> Might read on every post, this day would sit
> Phoebus himself, and the whole court of wit.[2]

The 'New Theatre in Dublin', as the St. Werburgh Street playhouse was commonly termed,[3] opened in the latter half of 1637. Those of its actors who were drawn from the Fortune Theatre Company had been touring in the English provinces during the winter of 1636–7,[4] and one of them, Edward Armiger, had buried a son at London as late as 6 May 1637.[5] Consequently, at least one of the Fortune recruits could not have reached Ireland before May. Sometime after the following October and before April 1638 Armiger and his fellow player from the Fortune, Richard Weekes, died at Dublin.[6] On 'New-

---

[1] Act I, sc. 1; II. 2; IV. 2.

[2] *The Dramatic Works and Poems of James Shirley* (ed. William Gifford and Alexander Dyce, London, 1833), vi. 493.

[3] See the title-pages to *The Royal Master* (London and Dublin, 1638) and *Landgartha* (Dublin, 1641).

[4] Bentley, i. 282.   [5] Ibid., ii. 350.

[6] Manuscript notes from St. Werburgh's Registry (later burned in the fire of 1754), made by John Lyon (1702–90), Archbishop of Dublin, and preserved as

Year's-Day, at night', 1637/8, the St. Werburgh Street troupe went to Dublin Castle to entertain their patron, the Lord Deputy, and there acted a tragicomedy appropriately entitled *The Royal Master*.[1] From this sequence of events it is obvious that between June and December of 1637 Ogilby had got his company assembled and performing in the new theatre.[2]

Within a few months Wentworth became so pleased and impressed with Ogilby's theatrical enterprise that he boldly resolved, perhaps at Ogilby's instigation, to create a new office without authorization from Whitehall. As the counterpart to a long-famous post in the English royal establishment, the Irish creation no doubt was calculated by its author to add lustre to the Lord Deputy's court. On 28 February 1637/8, according to a subsequent royal document, 'John Ogilby gentleman was . . . by Instrumente of the hand and seale of Thomas . . . Earle of Strafford then deputie of our said Kingdome of Ireland . . . nominated and appointed Master of the Revells in and through our said Kingdome of Ireland.'[3] The sole contemporary reference to this new office is to be found in a supplementary note to *Landgartha* (Dublin, 1641), which certifies that the play was

National Library of Ireland MS. 104. The pertinent section in the list of burials reads:

    1637—Oct.29—Lady Fisher
        N:B: Some Players ab^t this time
            buryed—viz: Armiger—Weekes
    1638—Ap: 11—Ald. George Jones

An imperfect transcript of this list is in MS. De Rebus Eblanae 69, p. 301.

  [1] See epilogue to *The Royal Master* as printed in Shirley's *The Dramatic Works,* iv. 187.

  [2] Stockwell, p. 2, chooses the year 1637 'as the more probable one' for the opening of the theatre, because she believes that it was not erected until after Ogilby had been made Master of the Revels in Ireland, an event which she wrongly places early in 1637 (see n. 3). Hence she hits on the correct year by a lucky inaccuracy. Earlier historians have selected without any specific proofs differing years as follows:

    1634—Thomas Wilkes, *A General View of the Stage* (London, 1759), p. 306; W. J. Lawrence, *The Elizabethan Playhouse*: 2nd series (Stratford, 1913), p. 239.

    1635—Chetwood, p. 51; Robert Hitchcock, *An Historical View of the Irish Stage* (Dublin, 1788–94), i. 11; Hughes, p. 2.

  [3] MS. C. 66/2995 Patent Roll, 13 Charles II, pt. 40, no. 37, Public Record Office, London. See Appendix A. Stockwell, p. 2, forgetting the old style of calendaring in state documents before 1752, mistakenly dates Strafford's grant a year earlier, i.e. 28 Feb. 1636/7.

'first Acted . . . with the Allowance of the Master of Revels'. Though Charles I never sanctioned this appointment of Ogilby to be Master of the Revels in Ireland, the Lord Deputy's warrant carried at Dublin all the authority of a royal patent and stamped Ireland's first theatre as the official godchild of the English Ascendancy.

The London plague of 1636 provided Ogilby with the opportunity not only to recruit a first-rate group of English actors, but also to utilize the talents of the most prominent living English playwright, James Shirley. Born at London in 1596 and trained as a Protestant cleric, Shirley gave up his intended career to embrace the Roman Catholic faith. About 1625 he turned dramatist at London and soon attained popularity. In 1636, when he could not for the time being market his wares in England, he moved to Dublin,[1] but at whose invitation he never indicated. Though he may have had relatives in Ireland (a Sir George Shirley was Chief Justice of the King's Bench in Ireland from 1625 to 1649),[2] that fact in itself would hardly have been a decisive inducement to sojourn there. It seems almost a certainty that either Wentworth, who visited London from June to November 1636,[3] or Ogilby saw the chance to turn to advantage Shirley's predicament and solicited his professional services for the stage venture at Dublin. Whatever the circumstances, Shirley's coming to Ireland resulted in a major contribution to her first theatre. His affiliation brought inestimable éclat to an undertaking which needed as much of that commodity as possible to lure an uninitiated as well as a limited public. His facile pen supplied the majority of the new plays, prologues, and epilogues which the St. Werburgh Street audience enjoyed up to the time of his departure for London in the spring of 1640.[4]

The eight prologues which Shirley preserved in print out of all those he wrote for Dublin performances of plays other than

[1] The date 1636 has been pretty generally accepted by reason of the remark 'two yeare/He has liv'd in Dublin' to be found in Shirley's prologue to a Dublin performance of Middleton's *No Wit: No Help Like a Woman's*, which apparently took place in 1638. See p. 33, n. 2 for further details.

[2] Gilbert, i. 40.

[3] Allan H. Stevenson, 'Shirley's Years in Ireland', *Review of English Studies*, xx (1944), 22.

[4] Ibid., p. 26.

his own, constitute the principal source of information about Ogilby's repertoire. Ben Jonson's comedy *The Alchemist* must have been acted during the 1637–8 season, since Jonson, who died in August 1637, was praised in Shirley's prologue as the recently deceased Poet Laureate.[1] In 1638 or 1639 Thomas Middleton's then unprinted comedy *No Wit: No Help Like a Woman's* was produced from a script to which Shirley had made alterations and added a prologue.[2] He may also have retouched for Dublin acting several of John Fletcher's plays, such as *The Night-Walker, Wit Without Money, The Coronation, Loves Crueltie, The Opportunitie*, which were not printed until shortly after Shirley's return to London.[3] At any rate, two prologues by Shirley to 'Master Fletcher's plays in Ireland' survive, though neither one can be connected with a particular title.[4] In addition, three unidentified dramas, *The General, The Irish Gentleman, The Toy*, were put on the boards at St. Werburgh Street with the speeches of introduction from Shirley's hand.[5]

Many of the eight prologues by Shirley lamented the feeble support accorded to the new theatre by the Dubliners, and the lack of taste which they thereby evidenced. In one instance Shirley observed with gentle remonstrance:

> It is our wonder, that this fair island, where
> The air is held so temperate (if there
> Be faith in old geographers, who dare
> With the most happy, boldly this compare)
> That to the noble seeds of art and wit,
> Honour'd elsewhere, it is not natural yet. . . .

[1] Shirley, *The Dramatic Works*, vi. 491.

[2] Ibid., p. 492. The first printed text (1657) of Middleton's *No Wit:* &c., contains an explicit reference to the year 1638 in Act III, sc. 1, ll. 288–9 (Bullen ed.). Presumably this was the text which Shirley fixed up for the Dublin stage, since Middleton had died in 1627.

[3] For a detailed argument in support of this contention see Allan H. Stevenson, 'Shirley's Publishers', *The Library*, xxv (1944–5), 140–61. Stevenson also thinks it probable that Shirley's *Constant Maid, St. Albans, The Politician*, and *The Gentleman of Venice* were first produced in Dublin. Alfred Harbage, *Annals of English Drama: 975–1700* (Philadelphia, 1940), pp. 110–13, lists *Constant Maid* with Dublin première, but questions the fact for the other three titles.

[4] *The Dramatic Works*, vi. 490, 493.

[5] Ibid., pp. 491, 494, 495. Aubrey, ii. 102, states that Ogilby wrote for St. Werburgh Street performance an unpublished play entitled *The Merchant of Dublin*.

But truce, poetic rage, and let not what
Concerns the country, fall upon a spot
Of it, a few here met to see a play:
All these are innocent; the better they
To tell this fault abroad, that there may be
Some repair done to injur'd poesy.[1]

On another occasion he lashed out with caustic irony:

When he did live in England, he heard say
That here were men lov'd wit, and a good play . . .
This he believed, and though they are not found
Above, who knows what may be underground.[2]

Or again his criticism took a more specific turn and ridiculed
the vulgar recreations of the local populace:

Were there a pageant now on foot, or some
Strange monster from Peru or Afric come,
Men would throng to it; any drum will bring
(That beats a bloodless prize or cudgelling)
Spectators hither; nay, the bears invite
Audience, and bag-pipes can do more than wit.[3]

Shirley's strictures should not be interpreted too literally; they
voiced an exaggeration conventional to playwrights of his day.
The same critical and woeful note can be found in London prologues throughout the century. Nevertheless, his comments reflected the current dilemma of the Dublin theatre. For its full
prosperity it should have attracted the commoners, and yet it
could not do so to any considerable extent, because from its in-
ception it had been too frankly designed as a fashionable resort
for the gentry and the aristocracy and the governmental coterie.

Shirley's *The Royal Master* was acted, as already mentioned,
soon after the opening of the St. Werburgh Street Theatre in
1637; his *Rosania: or, Love's Victory* followed about a year later.[4]

---

[1] *The Dramatic Works*, vi. 491.   [2] Ibid., p. 492.

[3] Ibid., p. 494. Stockwell, p. 7, mistakenly interprets these lines as indicating
bear-baitings in the playhouse.

[4] *Rosania* was first printed at London in 1652 and entitled *The Doubtful Heir*.
The Dublin prologue (*The Dramatic Works*, iv. 278) dates the play by its reference
to the current popularity of such play titles as *Aglaura*, a tragicomedy by Sir John
Suckling, first acted in 1637, and *Claracilla*, a tragicomedy by Sir Thomas Killigrew,
first acted in 1635-6.

These two tragicomedies, laid in Italy and Spain respectively, exhibit no distinct selection of dramatic material to amuse an Irish audience. The prologue to *Rosania* does reveal, however, an unusual variation of an old English stage device. Often in the London playhouses, but not always, a board bearing the title of the day's production was put up before the performance somewhere on the stage within view of the gathering audience. For the presentation of *Rosania* at Dublin Shirley conceived the novel scheme of having the prologue speaker himself bring in the title-board and hold it up to the scrutiny of the spectators while he delivered the introductory address. The *Rosania* prologue opens with

> ROSANIA? methinks I hear one say,
> What's that? 'Tis a strange title to a play

and then, after a dozen lines of explanation about this title, the prologue proceeds in a fresh direction:

> To save this charge of wit, that you might know
> Something i' the title, which you need not owe
> To another's understanding, you may see,
> In honest English there, LOVE'S VICTORY.[1]

As the speaker came to the end of this last line he turned the title-board over and showed the play's sub-title printed on the reverse side. Shirley's quaint innovation was not repeated at the London performance of *Rosania* in 1640,[2] and indeed it may not otherwise have been employed at the St. Werburgh Street Theatre. Once an audience was acquainted with the trick, its stage value greatly diminished.

Sometime in 1639 Shirley gave to the Dublin playhouse a composition that for the first and only time openly disclosed the impact of the Irish environment upon him. For this work he chose as the main theme one of the most significant events in Ireland's entire history—the arrival of St. Patrick and his subsequent conversion of the royal family to Christianity. Shirley's

[1] Ibid.
[2] Cf. the London prologue, ibid., p. 279. W. J. Lawrence first called attention to Shirley's device in *The Elizabethan Playhouse*, 1st series (Stratford, 1912), p. 53. Stockwell, p. 9, mistakenly assumes that the device was a regular convention in the Dublin theatre.

tragicomedy, entitled *St. Patrick for Ireland*, employs, together with many fictitious characters, such historical ones as King Loegarius, his 'provost' Milcho, Milcho's daughter Emeria, and the Irish nobleman Dichu who was St. Patrick's first convert. The play's action includes four miraculous episodes from the ancient lore relating to the saint. The fourth and most bizarre, taking place a little before the finale, must have taxed the skill of St. Werburgh Street stagecraft. Archimagus, the king's magician, summons serpents to attack the sleeping St. Patrick, and in answer 'the creeping executioners' come on stage. Waking all of a sudden, St. Patrick orders the reptiles off, and they glide away obediently.[1] The presentation of the crawling snakes, if carried out in full realistic detail, surely required no little ingenuity in costuming and acting.

Shirley did not inject into the action, the setting, or the characters of *St. Patrick for Ireland* any definitely Irish local colour. The native priests or druids (never so called in the play) officiate in a temple decorated with the statues of Jupiter, Saturn, and Mars, and call upon these Roman gods after the manner which English drama had already conventionalized for priests of classical antiquity. Archimagus, the chief priest, is but a degenerate Prospero with a religious patter of ambiguous origin. The king's 'Bard' behaves just as the typical court jester of the Elizabethan stage, quick at repartee and ready with sentimental or bawdy songs according to the occasion; he exhibits no strain of Gaelic minstrelsy whatsoever. Because Shirley depicted these personages of pre-Christian Ireland as indecent or hypocritical or treacherous, it has been unjustifiably claimed that he meant to disparage the ancient Irish race and culture in order to pander to a prevailing anti-Irish attitude in his theatre patrons.[2] His characterizations, however, merely follow the crude conventionalism of contemporary English literature when it treated of all sorts of pagan folk brought into conflict with Christianity. The virtue of the true faith was supposed to be the better emphasized if its opponents in general were portrayed as, to use Shirley's phrase, 'self-loving natures, prison'd in mists and errors'.[3]

---

[1] *The Dramatic Works*, iv. 440–1.　　　[2] Stockwell, pp. 16–17.
[3] *The Dramatic Works*, iv. 434.

In the case of St. Patrick, Shirley so heavily abbreviated his appearances in the earlier acts of the play that the saint does not emerge the forceful and impressive Christian missionary until the final scene. Then the holy man speaks out in prophecies which should have stirred all true Irish hearts among the St. Werburgh Street playgoers. He accompanies his banishment of the serpents from the island with a vision of Ireland as a divinely favoured land:

> O hide, and bury your deformed heads
> Forever in the sea! from this time be
> This island free from beasts of venomous natures.
> The shepherd shall not be afraid hereafter
> To trust his eyes with sleep upon the hills . . .
> The very earth and wood shall have this blessing,
> Above what other Christian nations boast.[1]

Previously St. Patrick had given his benediction to the young Irish prince Conallus with a promise of his country's future eminence:

> Your crown shall flourish, and your blood possess
> The throne you shall leave glorious: this nation
> Shall in a fair succession thrive, and grow
> Up the world's academy, and disperse,
> As the rich spring of human and divine
> Knowledge, clear streams to water kingdoms;
> Which shall be proud to owe what they possess
> In learning, to this great all-nursing island.[2]

These utterances by the strong man of God were deliberately phrased so that they would appeal to that pride in historic Ireland which Shirley thought most of his Dublin audience shared regardless of class or party or religion. In so doing, Shirley, an Englishman, became the first to cultivate on the Irish stage a patriotic sentiment. And thus *St. Patrick for Ireland* gains the honour of being the earliest formal drama with elements of Irish tradition and feeling.

Shirley was not alone in writing for Ogilby's theatre. At least one Irish-born writer, Henry Burnell, contributed plays to its repertoire. Son and heir of Christopher Burnell of Castleknock near Dublin, he belonged to an old Norman family that had

[1] Ibid., p. 441.   [2] Ibid., p. 438.

been active in the politics of the Pale for several centuries and
had more than once opposed the absolutism of the English
Crown.[1] After writing a first play (now lost) which met with
little success, Burnell saw his second drama, *Landgartha*, 'presented in the new Theater in Dublin, with good applause', on
17 March 1639/40.[2] This tragicomedy, laid in Norway and
Denmark, deals with 'an Ancient story'[3] concerning the con-
quest of Frollo, King of Sweden, by the Danish monarch Reynar
and his ally, Landgartha, an Amazonian warrior of Norway;
the marriage of Reynar and Landgartha; and their ultimate
separation.

   Despite its Scandinavian subject-matter *Landgartha* was considered appropriate entertainment for a St. Patrick's Day celebration at the St. Werburgh Street playhouse because of the
Irish touches which Burnell inserted chiefly into the third act.
The scene is a hall at the Danish court just before the wedding
masque in honour of Reynar and Landgartha. Hubba, 'an
humorous merry Danish Captaine', and Marsisa, 'an humorous
gentlewoman' of Norway, enter. The latter, dressed in *'an Irish
Gowne tuck'd up to mid-legge, with a broad basket-hilt Sword on,
hanging in a great Belt, Broags on her feet, her hayre disshevell'd, and
a payre of long neck'd big-rowll'd Spurs on her heels'*,[4] is plainly intended as good-humoured satire on the native Irish squire,
made the more amusing by representing a supposed female of
the species. Countrified pride and occasional Irish turns of
speech find their way into Marsisa's discourse with Hubba:

HUB.   Y'are Cossen-germain to th' Lady Fatyma?
MAR.   Herselfe dare not deny it, sir.
HUB.   I doe not

---

[1] See Gilbert, i. 296–7, for more details on the Burnell family. Neither he nor
Miss Stockwell specifically identifies the playwright, but *D.N.B.*, iii. 86, does so.
Burnell's cousin, Joseph Bermingham, in a congratulatory poem prefixed to *Land-
gartha*, remarks of Burnell in line 19 that 'thou England never saw'st'.

[2] The Prologue, l. 9, speaks of 'too much spite' toward the author's 'first play'.
The Epilogue, l. 13, states that in 'less than two Moneths time he penned' *Land-
gartha*. A note at the end of the play (I₄ *verso*) reads: 'This Play was first Acted on
S. Patricks day, 1639, with the allowance of the Master of Revels.'

[3] *Landgartha. A Tragie-Comedy*, as it was presented in the new Theater in
Dublin, with good applause, being an Ancient story, Written by H.B. Printed
at Dublin Anno 1641.

[4] E₃. (The pages of the *Landgartha* text are not numbered.)

Onely marke your sweet face, but all things else
About you. Y'have a fine legge. The fashion
Of this Gowne likes me well too; I think you had
The patterne on't from us, as we from Ireland.

MAR. That I know not, but am sure a handsome woman
Lookes as well in't, as in any dresse, or habit
Whatsoever.[1]

The scene between these two comics is soon interrupted by the
entrance of the royal party to watch the masque. At the conclusion of that entertainment, Hubba and Marsisa 'without her
Sword, and her Gowne untuck'd'[2] re-enter. After informing Reynar,
'I have brought a fine friendly dancer with me', Hubba proceeds with Marsisa to 'Dance the whip of Donboyne merrily'.[3] Subsequent to her boisterous Irish folk-dancing, Marsisa makes two
brief reappearances, both in the fifth act, once 'with her Gowne
tuck'd to the midleg, spurs, etc.',[4] and once 'with her Gowne untuck'd
and Sword on'.[5] This Irish-costumed Amazon, though in no way
essential to the plot, gives Landgartha the distinction of being the
first play written by an Irishman with Irish local colour.

The Burnell composition may have been the last new drama
performed at the St. Werburgh Street Theatre before political
violence, so long the island's plague, finally struck Dublin.[6] The
Rebellion broke out there in October 1641. Then, if not prior
to the outbreak, Ogilby's playhouse, on order of the Lords
Justices, Sir William Parsons and Sir John Borelace, was closed[7]
and in due course 'fell to utter rueine by the Calamitie of those
times'.[8] In consequence, its owner—so he later asserted—
suffered 'the damage of Two Thousand pounds at least'.[9] Ogilby
did not get away to England until after he had 'like to have
been blown up at the castle of Refarnum [Rathfarnum] neer
Dublin'.[10] After four years of theatrical activity he had, however,
driven the foundations of a professional stage so deeply into
Dublin's experience that they could not be blasted out of mind

---

[1] E₃ verso.   [2] F₂ verso.
[3] Ibid.   [4] H₄.   [5] I₂.
[6] Chetwood, p. 52, n. 2, asserts, without citing any authority, that Landgartha
was 'the last that was performed . . . before the Rebellion'.
[7] Ibid., p. 52.
[8] MS. S.P. 63, State Papers, Ireland, vol. 345, no. 50. See Appendix A.
[9] Ibid.   [10] Aubrey, ii. 101.

and remained to be built upon when peace and monarchy had been restored.

During the twenty years of the Interregnum, stage performances, though not seen in Dublin, appeared elsewhere in Ireland. Kilkenny, long steeped in the dramatics of its Protestant constituency, became the scene of Catholic school plays after the opening of a Jesuit college in 1642.[1] *Titus: or the Palme of Christian Courage* was 'exhibited by the Schollars of the Society of Jesus, at Kilkenny, Anno Domini 1644'. The sponsors distributed an elaborate bill, somewhat like a modern theatre programme, to advertise the occasion and to enlighten the audience on the foreign subject-matter of the play.[2] The plot, drawn from Father Francis Solier's *Ecclesiastical History of Japan* (1620), treats of a noble Christian, Titus, who refuses to give up his religious faith when the King of the Bungos threatens him with death. His steadfastness so amazes the king that in admiration the latter restores to Titus his wife, children, property, and even freedom of worship. Here indeed was a morality drama eminently fitted to the stress of the times, an impressive *exemplum* for the Irish Catholic faithful to endure the persecutions ahead. These Jesuit performances at Kilkenny had to be discontinued when the protective authority of the Catholic Confederation was brought to an end in 1648 by the Puritan régime.[3]

The severe restrictions which that régime imposed upon popular amusements had been appreciably relaxed by the later 1650's. Then in Ireland just as in England groups of strolling actors began to appear and entertain publicly in town halls or market squares. About 1657 or 1658 William Edmundson, a

[1] Peter Kavanagh, *The Irish Theatre* (Tralee, 1946), pp. 52–53.
[2] The unique copy of this playbill is preserved in the Bradshaw Collection, Cambridge University Library, and is reproduced as a frontispiece in Kavanagh.
[3] There was published at Kilkenny in 1646 an extremely rare quarto with the following title-page: 'A Tragedy of Cola's Furie, or Lirenda's Miserie. Written by Henry Birkenhead, 1645. Printed at Kilkenny, 1645. And are to be sold at the signe of the White Swanne, in Kilkenny, MDCXLVI.' This work by a 'Bristol merchant' is a five-act play in blank verse, but it does not seem particularly designed for stage performance. Written for the most part in a heavy-handed and undramatic form, the composition is intended, above all else, as a political tract which should arouse sympathy for the trials of the Irish in the Rebellion period. There is no evidence that the piece was ever acted anywhere. For further details see La Tourette Stockwell, 'Lirenda's Miserie', *Dublin Magazine*, new series, v (July–Sept. 1930), 19–26.

noted Quaker preacher, encountered such strollers in the north of Ireland at Londonderry, a thriving county town somewhat smaller than Kilkenny. He wrote down his experience with picturesque eloquence:

The next day I came to Londonderry; it was market-day, and there were stage-players and rope-dancers in the market-place, and abundance of people gathered. The Lord's Spirit filled my heart, his power struck at them, and his word was sharp. So I stood in the market-place, and proclaimed the day of the Lord among them, and warned them all to repent. . . . When I found my spirit a little eased, I walked along the street, and the people flocked about me. . . . I stood still and declared truth to them, directing them to the light of Christ in their own hearts, and they were very sober and attentive, but the stage-players were sore vexed that the people left them, and followed me: whereupon they got the mayor to send two officers to take me to prison: so they came and took me; but the sober people were angry that stage-players should be suffered, and a man that declared against wickedness and vanity, and taught the things of God, must not be suffered, but haled to prison. The officers made excuse, saying, they were commanded, and must obey. So they took me to prison. The gaoler put me in a room that had a window facing the market-place, where I had full sight of the people; and my heart being filled with the word of life and testimony of Jesus, I thrust my arm out at the window and waved it, till some of them espying, came near, and others followed apace; so that presently I had most of the people from the stage-players, which vexed them much. Then they got the mayor to cause the gaoler to keep me close; so he bolted me, and locked my leg to a place where he used to fasten condemned persons. There I sat in much peace of conscience, and sweet union with the Spirit of Truth.[1]

Thus for once the forces of Thespis gave the opponent a taste of his own medicine. So daring a reversal of the usual seventeenth-century situation could have happened only in a town such as Londonderry, where there still prevailed the lusty traditions of its English colonization in the reign of James I. The stage-players in question perhaps had come from England, for Londonderry at this time was readily accessible from west-coast ports.

[1] *A Journal of the Life, Travels, Sufferings, and Labour in the Work of the Ministry, of that worthy elder and faithful servant of Jesus Christ, William Edmundson* (3rd edition, Dublin, 1820), section vi.

During the next few years strolling troupes, evidently English, performed around Ireland with some frequency and caused agitation by their jibes at the native residents. At Christmas, 1661, it was reported to George Williamson, Secretary for Ireland, that 'discontents were raised to a great height, because players were allowed to contemn the Irish on their stages'.[1] These nondescript travelling companies doubtless initiated and fostered an acquaintance with formal dramatics in a considerable number of Irish towns, but they contributed not at all to the re-establishment of the professional stage. That development was to depend once again on the interest of English authority rather than on popular demand in Ireland.

[1] *Cal. State Papers: Domestic, 1661–62*, p. 191.

CHAPTER III

The Revival of the Dublin Stage after the Restoration

THE restoration of Charles II as King of England, Scotland, and Ireland in May of 1660 quickly brought about official approbation and support of stage amusements throughout the three kingdoms. On 20 June Sir Henry Herbert assumed his former office of Master of the Revels in England.[1] During August two of Charles's favourite courtiers, Thomas Killigrew and Sir William Davenant, received patents granting them a monopoly in the conduct of theatrical performances within the city of London.[2] By mid-November both patentees had their companies organized and acting.[3]

Back in 1638 Sir William Davenant had won preferment over James Shirley, the mainstay of Dublin's St. Werburgh Street Theatre, for the post of court poet in succession to Ben Jonson. A year later Davenant secured from Charles I a London theatre patent which he never utilized.[4] By 1656, however, he was heavily engaged in theatrical entertainment at London.[5] After the Restoration, finding the prospects too attractive to restrict himself to stage affairs in England, he proceeded to employ his friendship with the king for the purpose of extending his powers to Ireland. The ambitious 'knight' very well knew that John Ogilby, now a prominent London publisher, had prior claim to theatrical authority in Ireland, but even so Davenant did not hesitate about forcing himself into Ogilby's preserve. The latter at present was much occupied with his prosperous book business. He had just elicited praise from court and town for a magnificent

---

[1] A. Nicoll, *A History of English Drama, 1660–1900*: vol. i, *Restoration Drama, 1660–1700* (4th edition, Cambridge, 1952), p. 316.

[2] Ibid., p. 293.   [3] Ibid., p. 294.

[4] Leslie Hotson, *The Commonwealth and Restoration Stage* (Cambridge, Mass., 1928), p. 199.

[5] Ibid., pp. 139 ff.

Bible in royal folio with 'chorographical sculps' by his own hand. As the fall of 1660 passed, he showed no signs of applying to the new sovereign for a confirmation of his rights as Master of the Revels in Ireland, an office which Charles I's viceroy had bestowed upon him twenty-two years before. Taking advantage of Ogilby's dilatoriness, Davenant obtained on 26 November a royal warrant to 'enjoy the authority and office of Master of Revells of Ireland during his life', and to 'erect or provide a Theater in Our Citty of Dublyn . . . noe more Theaters or Play Houses [to] be permitted in Our Citty of Dublin than that One Theater or Play House to be erected or provided by the said Sir William Davenant'.[1]

This coup by Davenant soon stirred Ogilby to present a counter petition, in which he called attention to his 'graunt from the Right Honorable Thomas Earle of Strafford, then Lieutenant of Ireland, for the enjoying and executing the place and office of the Master of the Revells of that kingdome' and humbly requested, 'notwithstanding Sir William Davenets [*sic*] pretences, that your Majestie would bee graciously pleased . . . to confer the said office on him'.[2] Now Ogilby, too, possessed influence at Whitehall Palace; he had been awarded the important responsibility of designing the 'poetical' pageantry with which London was to observe Charles II's coronation on 23 April (St. George's Day) 1661.[3] Through the winter and early spring Ogilby was preparing a series of four large triumphal arches adorned with allegorical paintings, sculptures, and inscriptions, and was also arranging for music and declamations at key points on the processional route from the Tower to Whitehall.[4] These activities naturally promoted his cause with the king. In March 1661 the latter agreed to the justice of Ogilby's claim for precedence over Davenant, and gave orders for a fresh warrant. It revoked 'all Graunts made to other[s] for

---

[1] MS. S.P. 63, State Papers, Ireland, vol. 304, no. 171, Public Record Office, London. See Appendix A for the full text of this and subsequent documents relating to the Office of Master of the Revels in Ireland.

[2] MS. S.P. 63, State Papers, Ireland, vol. 345, no. 50.

[3] *D.N.B.*, xiv. 908.

[4] For full details, see John Ogilby, *The Relation of His Majestie's Entertainment Passing through the City of London, To His Coronation: with a Description of the Triumphal Arches, and Solemnity* (London, 1661).

representing anything' of a theatrical nature in Ireland, and provided that (1) John Ogilby should be granted for life the office of Master of the Revels in Ireland; (2) he should be licensed 'to build upon such grounds by him to be purchased . . . in Dublin or elsewhere in Ireland such Theatre or Theatres as to him shall seeme most fitt . . . and therein to represent Comedyes Tragedyes and Operas and other Enterludes decent and not obnoxious with a prohibition to all persons to performe ye same without License first obteyned from him.'[1] The royal patent issued to Ogilby on May 8 incorporated all the provisions of the foregoing warrant and added the interesting amendment that the office of Master of the Revels in Ireland should be 'exercised and enjoyed' by Ogilby 'or his sufficient Deputie or Deputies for and during his naturall life.'[2]

What the veteran theatre manager at the moment really needed, however, for the revival of his former venture in Dublin was not a deputy, but a partner with enough money to make possible the building of a new playhouse there and the assembling of a troupe. During the summer of 1661 he discovered such a partner in Thomas Stanley, Jr., heir of Thomas Stanley, Esq., of Cumberloe, Hertfordshire. Ogilby's longtime friend, James Shirley, had made him acquainted with this young gentleman. The latter's father, a wealthy poet and scholar, befriended Shirley through the hard days of the Civil War, and in return Shirley wrote some commendatory verses for the senior Stanley's *Poems* (1651). Ogilby found that he could secure capital from young Stanley on the basis of an agreement to share profits from the Dublin theatre, but that to assure the validity of the agreement he must make Stanley co-patentee. Hence Ogilby was compelled to ask for a new royal patent only a few months after he had received his original one. By good fortune he had at hand an excuse which would save him from mentioning any contractual obligations. He had just been appointed Master of His Majesty's Royal Imprimerie—in other words, the King's Printer. Thus faced by added official business, he could

[1] MS. Signet Office Docquet Books, Index 6813, Mar. 1660/1, p. 4, Public Record Office, London.

[2] MS. C. 66/2995 Patent Roll, 13 Charles II, pt. 40, no. 37, Public Record Office, London.

plausibly claim the need of an aide in his theatrical duties. He therefore petitioned that the king would 'graunt the said office of Master of the Revells in your Majesties said Kingdome of Ireland unto your peticōner and some such other person whom hee shall choose for his Assistant, whereby hee may the more freely attend the service of your Majesties Royall Imprimerie'.[1]

On 7 September 1661, His Majesty authorized, upon the surrender of Ogilby's first patent, the issuance of a second to him 'and Thomas Stanley Gent. jointly, to be by them held and enjoyed for and dureing their naturall lives, and ye life of ye longer liver of them'.[2] Ogilby, nevertheless, delayed the surrender of his original patent, perhaps because he had not completed to his satisfaction the financial negotiations with Stanley. By the following mid-winter, when apparently Ogilby crossed to Dublin to get his new theatre project started, the Crown officers had decided that the revised patent should more properly be issued 'under the Greate Seale of that our Kingdome of Ireland' on surrender of the original patent at Dublin. Accordingly, on 23 January 1661/2, a royal warrant was addressed to the Lords Justices of Ireland with instructions to that effect.[3] Ogilby, if in Dublin around the date of this warrant's receipt, still made no move to exchange the patent in force for the new instrument which he had requested six months earlier.

On 21 February Charles II appointed as Lord-Lieutenant of Ireland her peer of highest precedence and most able statesman, James Butler, first Duke of Ormonde. Born at London in 1610 and reared an ardent Royalist, he had served as Commander-in-Chief of the Army in Ireland under the Earl of Strafford in the late 1630's. Presumably Ormonde had met Ogilby at that period and attended performances at the St. Werburgh Street Theatre, for the duke throughout his life took pride in being an enthusiastic patron of learning and the arts. Though loyal to the Stuart monarchy and active on behalf of the Protestant interest in Ireland, he felt none of the English

---

[1] MS. S.P. 63, State Papers, Ireland, vol. 276, no. 62.
[2] Ibid., vol. 307, no. 201.
[3] MS. S.O. 1/5, Signet Office Records, Irish Letter Books, vol. 5, p. 108, Public Record Office, London.

superiority over the people of that country, and worked
zealously for what he conceived to be their cultural as well as their
material advancement. Anything which would bring refinement and dignity to the capital of the Third Kingdom gained
his instant support. Therefore, after he became viceroy, he
offered warm encouragement to Ogilby's plans for reviving the
Dublin stage.[1]

When both of these men were heading for Ireland in the
summer of 1662, another warrant regarding the Irish Revels
Office was dispatched on 13 July to Ormonde as the Lord-
Lieutenant, because he now was to supersede the Lords Justices
as royal agent in Dublin. This latest order directed him, upon
surrender by Ogilby of his original patent, to pass a fresh grant
of the same office 'unto ye said John Ogilby his Executours and
Assignes for by and dureing ye naturall life of him the said
John Ogilby, & of Thomas Stanley Junior . . . and ye life of
ye Longer liver of them'.[2] But Ogilby did not hasten, upon his
arrival at Dublin, to comply with the proviso of the warrant
by turning in the document to be replaced. It was not until the
spring of 1663 that the Lord-Lieutenant could act. Finally, on
5 April, a patent which repeated the provisions of the one
delivered to Ogilby on 8 May 1661 was issued at Dublin to
Ogilby and Stanley jointly.[3] This action brought to an end
almost three years of involved negotiations over the office which
was now denoted, in the revised patent, as 'Master of Revells
and Masques in our Kingdome of Ireland'.

Meanwhile, Ogilby and Ormonde had been settled in Dublin
since July 1662.[4] The latter's assumption of the viceregal office
accelerated the prosperity which the Irish capital had been
experiencing since the first days of the Restoration. English
adventurers, former soldiers, and colonists were streaming into

[1] See in Appendix A the text of the royal warrant of 28 Nov. 1683, *re* William
Morgan.

[2] MS. S.P. 44, Domestic Entry Book, vol. 3, pp. 67–68, Public Record Office,
London.

[3] See Appendix A for the full text. This patent was enrolled on 21 April 1663,
in the Irish Chancery Rolls, Dublin. The original document was destroyed by
the fire at the Public Record Office, Dublin, in 1922. It is summarized in B.M.
Egerton MS. 1773, f. 25, and in *Liber Munerum Publicorum Hiberniae* (London, 1824),
vol. i, pt. ii, pp. 92–93.

[4] Ormonde was inducted into the office of Lord-Lieutenant on 28 July 1662.

the city, either to profit by a widely heralded expansion of the country's economy or to lay claim to the extensive lands confiscated from Cromwellian or Papist holders. During Charles II's reign Dublin's area and population almost doubled—from thirty or thirty-five thousand inhabitants in 1660 to fifty-five or sixty thousand in 1685.[1] The city overflowed beyond its old walls in all directions, most noticeably to the north of the Liffey, and to the east and south-east toward Trinity College and St. Stephen's Green. The mile-long Dame Street from Cork Hill and Dame's Gate to the college rapidly filled up with the large houses of prominent citizens in consequence of Ormonde's moving the seat of Parliament to Chichester House on the north-west side of College Green. Travellers from England on the Bristol, Chester, or Holyhead packets made their entrance into the city through Dame Street after disembarkation at Ringsend, a pleasant bathing resort on a neck of land in the Liffey two miles east of Trinity College.[2] St. Stephen's Green, enclosed by walls and laid out with fine walks between 1666 and 1670, succeeded the inconvenient Oxmantown Green as the Guard's parade ground.[3] The north quays along the Liffey in or near Oxmantown built up fast. There, about 1670, a French visitor observed 'the finest palaces in Dublin'.[4] The ancient Stone Bridge close to the King's Inns soon proved quite inadequate to this northerly settlement. By 1685 four new structures spanned the river, starting upstream with the New or Bloody Bridge which led to Oxmantown Green and ending with Essex Bridge near the Custom House at the foot of Cork Hill.

Vigorous building did not improve the city streets. They continued filthy, badly paved, and so narrow that vehicles had trouble in passing one another.[5] The many sedan chairs and hackney coaches, which constituted the chief means of public

[1] Edward MacLysaght, *Irish Life in the Seventeenth Century: After Cromwell* (London, 1939), p. 187; also C. Litton Falkiner, 'The Phoenix Park: Its Origin and Early History', *Proceedings of the Royal Irish Academy*, 3rd series, vi, no. 3, p. 467.

[2] MacLysaght, p. 196; Weston St. John Joyce, *The Neighbourhood of Dublin* (Dublin, 1912), pp. 1–11.

[3] Falkiner, *Illustrations of Irish History and Topography, Mainly of the Seventeenth Century*, p. 84.

[4] Ibid., p. 414.

[5] MacLysaght, pp. 200, 211.

transport, added to the traffic tangle. No municipal street lighting existed till the close of the century.[1] Candles in house windows or lanterns hung up by front doors afforded but occasional dim illumination. As a result the streets after nightfall saw a good deal of brawling and foul play. Wary foot-passengers hired lantern 'boys' to guide and protect them.[2]

Yet these lingering traces of the provincial in Dublin were quite overshadowed by her advances in urbanity and elegance. In 1684 William Molyneux, founder of the Dublin Philosophical Society, asserted proudly: 'We are come to fine things here in Dublin. . . . Our city increases sensibly in fair buildings, great trade, and splendour in all things—in furniture, coaches, civility, housekeeping, etc.'[3] The Irish metropolis steadily took on more and more of London's aspects and manners. Indeed, the trend toward Anglicization was so intensified by the anti-Catholic troubles at the end of the 1670's that one Anglo-Protestant partisan asserted in a pamphlet: 'The city of Dublin . . . ought ever to be kept a chaste *English* town.'[4] As in Restoration London, coffee-houses, taverns, and bookshops sprang up in great numbers, especially within the old walled city; they came to be meeting-places for the loiterers and the learned alike. The Dublin Philosophical Society, which modelled itself upon the Royal Society, had its beginnings in a Cork Hill coffee-house. London's stylish pastimes of tennis and bowls were introduced by Ormonde. By 1663 a commodious tennis court had been opened in St. John's Lane close to its junction with Winetavern Street near Christ Church.[5] Before 1665 Alderman Tighe built at Oxmantown, just across the Bloody Bridge, a superb bowling green on 'a very large piece of ground well walled in, . . . the walls covered with fruit trees: the south wall with an handsome terrace walk its whole length'.[6] This green, from the first a

---

[1] A system of public lamplights was set up for Dublin in 1697 by act of the English Parliament. See *Cal. State Papers: Domestic, 1697*, p. 440.

[2] MacLysaght, p. 203.

[3] Letter of 12 April 1684, to his brother, Sir Thomas Molyneux. *Dublin University Magazine*, xviii (Oct. 1841), p. 480.

[4] *An Essay on the Present State and Settlement of Ireland* (1679), as quoted in *Cal. State Papers: Domestic, 1679–80*, p. 361.

[5] *Hist. MSS. Commission: Eighth Report*, &c. (London, 1881), Appendix, pt. i, p. 548[b]; Dunton, p. 368.

[6] MacLysaght, p. 203; Dunton, p. 407.

fashionable rendezvous, excelled, according to one English observer, London's noted Marylebone grounds.[1] During Dublin's warmer months it became the mode to promenade beyond Essex Bridge eastward on the Liffey 'Strand', where 'every evening the gentry in their coaches or on horseback make their tours as Londoners do in Hyde Park'.[2] In March or April, and again in September, the ladies as well as the gentlemen of the smart set flocked out to the horse races at 'the Curragh'.[3] This old Irish fairground and race-course on Kildare plain, some twenty-five miles west of the city, developed during Ormonde's régime into the Newmarket of Ireland.

Despite the increasingly complex pattern of Dublin's social life, its fountain head remained the Castle, which was still protected by a medieval moat, drawbridge, and gate. Ormonde transformed the mounting of the guard and the flying of the colours into daily public shows like those at Whitehall Palace.[4] With a loud beating of drums at the Castle gate to signal both his goings and his returns, he made pomp and ceremony out of his every drive into the city. Indeed he set up an establishment the splendour of which completely eclipsed even the celebrated one of Strafford prior to the Rebellion. The court that formed around Ormonde in the summer of 1662 possessed, however, more than outward brilliance; it was also characterized by earnest pretensions to wit and the arts. The Castle coterie included the Lord-Lieutenant's daughter Mary and her husband, Lord William Cavendish; the Lord Chancellor, Sir Maurice Eustace; the Advocate-General, Dr. Pett; the head of the King's Guard, Sir Nicholas Armourer; Commissioners for Settlement of Land Claims, Sir Alan Broderick and Sir Edward Dering; Viscount and Lady Dungannon; Richard Boyle, second Earl of Cork, his wife and two daughters, Anne and Elizabeth; Wentworth Dillon, first Earl of Roscommon, and his wife, Frances, the Earl of Cork's eldest daughter.[5]

The intellectual leadership of this select circle quickly passed to a dynamic untitled visitor from Cardigan, Wales, Mrs.

[1] Dunton, p. 407.   [2] Ibid., p. 379.
[3] Ibid., p. 394.   [4] MacLysaght, p. 403.
[5] Philip W. Souers, *The Matchless Orinda* (Cambridge, Mass., 1931), pp. 156-7, 162-5.

Katherine Philips, who already had attained in England a reputation as letter-writer and poetess under the pseudonym of 'Orinda'. To her new Dublin microcosm she at once introduced a pet interest, the Society of Friendship, the inspiration for which she had drawn from the cult of Platonic love at the court of Charles I.[1] The members of her fellowship addressed one another under assumed names of neo-classical origin, names identical with those in the French pastoral and heroic romances of the mid-seventeenth century. For 'the matchless Orinda' Lady Dungannon became 'the excellent Lucasia'; Lady Anne Boyle, 'the adored Valeria'; Lady Mary Cavendish, 'the bright Policrite'; Sir Edward Dering, 'the noble Silvander'; and so on. Under 'the wise and learned Druyde of Cardigan' the Society mingled the two sexes in an elevated and almost mystical association of souls.[2] Its unique idealism has nowhere been so eloquently presented as in a hitherto unprinted letter from one enthusiastic Dublin member to another soon after the founder's death in 1664:

Orinda had conceived the most generous designe that in my opinion ever entred into any breast, which was to unite all those of her acquaintance which she found worthy or desired to make so, . . . into one societie, and by the bands of friendship to make an alliance more firme than what nature, our country, or equall education can produce: and this would in time have spread very farr, and have been improved with great and yet unimagin'd advantages to the world: for it would have been of great use sure, to show the world that there were satisfactions in vertuous friendship farre transcending all those delights which the most specious follyes can tempt us with; and doubtless many would have quitted the extravagancies of their inclinations for feare of being banish'd so happy a conversaçon, that would have resisted more pressing arguments, and all the instruments of a more rugged discipline.[3]

---

[1] William S. Clark, *The Dramatic Works of Roger Boyle, Earl of Orrery* (Cambridge, Mass., 1937), i. 11–12.

[2] Unpublished letter of 29 Nov. 1662, by Dering to Mrs. Philips. Sir Edward Dering's MS. Letter Book, 1661–1665, letter no. 3, University of Cincinnati Library.

[3] Unpublished letter of 7 Feb. 1664/5, by Dering to Lady Dungannon. MS. Letter Book, 1661–1665, letter no. 47. This letter and many others in the Letter Book refute the contentions of Souers in *The Matchless Orinda*, pp. 44, 58, and elsewhere, that Katherine Philips excluded males as bona fide members of the

The atmosphere of Platonic sensibility engendered by the Society of Friendship permeated fashionable Dublin of 1662 and 1663, affecting among other prominent persons the city's most important literary figure, Roger Boyle, first Earl of Orrery.[1] This outstanding Anglo-Irishman, son of the Great Earl of Cork, had been influential at London in the state councils after the Restoration, had contracted a genuine friendship with Charles II, and then, as the more forceful of the two Lords Justices, had directed the government of Ireland for the year and a half previous to Ormonde's installation.[2] Talented, but over-ambitious and vain, Orrery secretly begrudged Ormonde his superior position in Irish affairs and did all possible to curry greater favour with the king. The latter, before Orrery left London in December 1660 for Dublin, had evinced a desire to see the English practise the French fashion of writing plays in rimed couplets.[3] To please His Majesty, therefore, the Earl during the spring of 1661 at Dublin composed a tragicomedy 'All in Ten Feet verse, & Ryme', and sent this novel piece of drama over to Whitehall where it excited considerable attention around the court and won the hearty approval of Charles.[4] Inspired by this maiden success, Orrery went on to finish, about a year afterwards, a second play of the same kind and posted it to Ormonde at London. These two tragicomedies with rimed dialogue, though circulating only in manuscript, by the summer of 1662 had initiated a fresh dramatic mode and had brought Orrery much fame with the English literary elect.[5] 'Orinda' Philips also caught fire from Orrery's innovation and in July 1662 began at Dublin a rimed translation of Pierre Corneille's famous tragedy, *Mort de Pompée*.[6]

Interest, then, in dramatic and theatrical matters was running high among Dublin's *élite* when Ogilby arrived to furnish them with professional stage amusement, bringing with him as assistant a young relative, William Morgan.[7] Ogilby chose

Society of Friendship and that she did not seriously maintain the Society after the Restoration.

[1] Clark, i. 73–74.
[2] Ibid., pp. 23, 31.   [3] Ibid., pp. 22–23.
[4] Ibid., pp. 23–26.   [5] Ibid., pp. 30–31.
[6] Katherine Philips, *Letters from Orinda to Poliarchus* (London, 1705), p. 61.
[7] The relationship of Morgan to Ogilby has been contradictorily reported ever

PLATE II

THE HEART OF OLD DUBLIN

The site of the Smock Alley Theatre is marked D

for the site of his playhouse a piece of land abutting on the
Blind Quay at the foot of Cork Hill near the Liffey, a location
equally accessible from the Castle, the College, the fashionable
districts across the river, and the well-to-do quarters of the old
city. The selected parcel of ground, known as the 'White House'
lot, measured 150 feet in length, and gradually widened from
58 feet on the Blind Quay at the north to 66 feet on Smock
Alley at the south.[1] An English visitor of the time observed
with amusement that the Dublin playhouse was situated in
'a dirty street, called Smock Alley, which I think is no unfit
Name for a Place where such great opportunities are given for
making of lewd Bargains'.[2] This notorious thoroughfare ran
east and west between Fishamble and Essex Streets, a distance
of only an eighth of a mile. Since at least two houses stood on the
northern portion of the 'White House' lot, Ogilby had to face
his theatre southward. An oblong brick and stone structure,
'very ordinary in its outward appearance',[3] it covered an area
approximately 55 feet wide by 110 feet deep, and fronted on
Smock Alley about mid-way.[4] The same spot continued to be

since the seventeenth century. Aubrey, ii. 104, calls Morgan Ogilby's grandson.
D.N.B., xiv. 909, asserts that Morgan's mother was the daughter of Mrs. Ogilby
by a previous marriage. Morgan's hitherto unexamined petition of 1682 (see
Appendix A for the full text) for a grant of the Office of the Revels in Ireland
stated, however, that Ogilby was his uncle. This petition also certified that Morgan
had been associated with his uncle in the opening of the Dublin theatre.

[1] A patent to Sir James Weymes, dated 15 April 1668, describes the lot thus:
'a house and a large piece of Ground on the Key [i.e. Blind Quay], heretofore
called the White House, late in the possession of Alice Horselin, on part whereof
ye new theatre and a house late in the possession of John Barry is erected.' (*Reports
from the Commissioners . . . respecting the Public Records of Ireland, 1821–25*, p. 147.)
A lease of 1707 gives further details of the same lot: 'All that one messuage or
Tenement and ground now or late commonly called the White House situate on
the said blind Key . . . containing in front in breadth towards the blind Key fifty
eight foot or thereabouts and in breadth backwards towards Smock Alley sixty
six foot or thereabouts and in length from the blind Key towards Smock Alley
one hundred and fifty foot or thereabouts now or late in the possession of Alice
Horslin Widow her assignes or undertenants on part of which said last mentioned
premisses there hath been built and raised a new Theater and several other great
Improvements.' (MS. 56/30/36855, Office of the Registry of Deeds, Dublin.
Printed in Stockwell, p. 311.)

[2] Dunton, p. 340.

[3] Ibid., p. 339.

[4] The length of Smock Alley, the location of the theatre on that street, and the
estimated dimensions of the theatre are based upon the measurements to be derived
from the map of Dublin in 1728 by Charles Brooking.

occupied by a theatre for 150 years.[1] The dimensions of Ogilby's playhouse matched closely those of the Theatre Royal in Bridges Street, Covent Garden, opened by Killigrew the next spring; they far exceeded the 30-foot width and 75-foot length of Davenant's current theatre in Lincoln's Inn Fields.[2]

Partly by reason of size, therefore, 'Orinda' Philips in 1662 could claim to her London friends that the new Dublin theatre was 'much finer than Davenant's'.[3] More especially she must have meant that its interior décor easily surpassed that of Davenant's remodelled tennis court. Smock Alley was, in fact, the first of the Restoration theatres; that is to say, it was the first edifice of the period to have been designed from bottom to top as a playhouse. Ogilby's architectural arrangements in some respects showed the way for the London producers. Oriented toward the north, the building contained a pit filled with rows of cloth-covered benches. Behind and to the sides of the pit there rose what a contemporary described as 'three stories of galleries'.[4] The lowest story consisted of boxes with short benches for seats; the middle and upper galleries differed from the lowest only in that they were not partitioned off. When taking seats in the galleries the Dublin playgoers, like those in London, generally observed the accepted class distinctions. 'Those of the greatest quality sat lowest; those next in quality sat the next above; and the common people in the upmost gallery.'[5] The acting platform at the north end of the hall had a depth of some 30 feet, and was divided by a proscenium arch and curtain into two almost equal areas—a fore-stage or 'apron', and a rear stage.[6] The latter accommodated the 'flats' and side-wings of Restoration pictorial scenery. Both stage areas, and indeed the entire playhouse interior, were crudely lighted from two sources: candelabra fastened along the gal-

[1] In December 1813 the Roman Catholic church of St. Michael and St. John was opened on the former playhouse site.

[2] Hotson, pp. 123, 243.   [3] Philips, p. 78.

[4] Rev. Patrick Adair, *A True Narrative of the Rise and Progress of the Presbyterian Church in Ireland* (Belfast, 1866), p. 303. Adair's account was written before 1694, but remained in manuscript for a century and a half.

[5] Ibid.

[6] These dimensions are based upon the relative measurements for the same areas at the Theatre Royal in Bridges Street, as indicated by the surviving Wren drawings in the Library of All Souls College, Oxford.

leries and suspended in back as well as in front of the proscenium, and a series of oil lamps sunk in a long trough at the edge of the 'apron'.[1] A seventeenth-century attendant at Smock Alley remarked with evident whimsy that all parts of the theatre, 'like other false Beauties, receive a Lustre from their Lamps and Candles'.[2] The lustre must have been a pretty feeble radiance!

Each side-wall of the 'apron' supported two doors, a few feet apart. The downstage one rather closely adjoined the end box of the lowest gallery. The actors made most of their entrances and exits through these four doors, all of which they put to regular use. The geographical layout of the stage at Smock Alley led to the custom of designating the doors as 'East Upper', 'East Lower', 'West Upper', 'West Lower', designations unparalleled among early English playhouses.[3] Over each door, on a level with the middle gallery, was situated a small room provided with a latticed casement window. This compartment soon came to be called in Dublin a 'lattice',[4] a term which apparently originated there and never made its way into London theatrical parlance. The lattices (often spelled 'lettices' in the advertisements) when not required as upper rooms or balconies in the day's production were turned into boxes, especially suitable for 'ladies of quality' because they could adjust the windows either to hide or to advertise their presence.

A different sort of upper room was constructed at the top of the 'house', above the centre of the proscenium, for the Smock Alley musicians.[5] This 'music loft', as it was called, placed the orchestra in a prominent and musically advantageous position. Their playing before and during the performance developed into an important attraction. Smock Alley handbills, 'dispers'd at the Coffee houses, College, and Tholsel',[6] and doubtless at many other points, commonly emphasized the musical features. A prologue to a Smock Alley production of Jonson's

---

[1] See W. J. Lawrence, 'Early English Stage and Theatre Lighting', *Stage Year Book*, 1927, pp. 20–21.

[2] Dunton, p. 339.

[3] See the reproduction between pp. 80 and 81 of two pages from the unique Smock Alley manuscript prompt copy of John Wilson's *Belphegor* (Folger Shakespeare Library MS. 827. 1), which contains such stage directions.

[4] Dunton, p. 339.   [5] Ibid.   [6] Ibid., p. 321.

Volpone: or, The Fox, 'when a consort of haut-boyes [oboes] were added to the musick', reveals the typical form of advertising on the printed fliers:

> 'The Fox,' above, our boasting Play-bills shew;
> 'Variety of Musick' stands below.[1]

Ogilby commenced entertainment at his new theatre around the middle of October 1662, before he had got the scenic machinery in full running order. The time of year, traditionally favourable to playgoing, prompted his hasty opening. The first recorded production at Smock Alley occurred on Saturday, 18 October, when 'Orinda' Philips witnessed there a revival of John Fletcher's *Wit Without Money*.[2] This lively comedy concerns an engaging but eccentric spendthrift of London, by name Valentine, who despises wealth, distrusts women, and insists that a man should live by his wits. Nevertheless, he is finally inveigled into marriage with a rich widow, Lady Heartwell. *Wit Without Money* almost certainly had been in Ogilby's former repertoire at the St. Werburgh Street Theatre.[3] Orinda thought the play 'indifferently well acted'. Her enthusiasm may have been dampened by the unexpectedly bare stage, for 'the Scenes [were] not yet made'.

The performance of *Wit Without Money*, like all Smock Alley performances until near the end of the century, came off in the afternoon. At first the curtain time, as in London, was 3.30, but by James II's reign it had advanced to 4.00,[4] just late enough to permit gentlemanly midday dining at a Dublin tavern or coffee-house. 'For Dinner being ended, away went everyone, according as his Business or his Humour led him: some to the College, some to the Playhouse, others to Court, a few to their Shops.'[5] Though the acting of the usual play still consumed, as in Shakespeare's age, some three hours, it was possible during most of the year to reach home in daylight, a primary consideration with Dublin citizens. Before the rise

---

[1] Harvard College Library MS. English 674 F, p. 14.
[2] Philips, p. 79.   [3] See Chapter II, p. 33, n. 3.
[4] See prologue to John Dryden's *The Wild Gallant* (1663) and the unique Restoration playbill for Beaumont and Fletcher's *A King and No King* on 22 Feb. 1686/7 (*The Library*, 4th series, vol. xi, no. 4, p. 499).
[5] Dunton, p. 321.

of the curtain and during the act-pauses the 'China-orange wenches' strolled, after the London custom, up and down the rows of pit benches, hawking their wares and delighting to overcharge the men of fashion. When John Dunton, the London publisher, visited the Smock Alley Theatre in 1698, he gave the orangewoman 'her own rate for her Oranges; for . . . 'tis below a Gentleman . . . to stand hagling like a Citizen's Wife'.[1]

The original acting company at Smock Alley was evidently gathered by Ogilby from various quarters. The man who soon became its leading performer, Joseph Ashbury, seems to have had no previous stage experience and to have been already in Dublin when for reasons unknown Ogilby recruited him. Born at Covent Garden, London, in 1638 and educated at Eton, Ashbury joined Ormonde's army in Ireland about 1657 and served as a Loyalist soldier until after the Restoration.[2] In 1660 he became a lieutenant in a Dublin infantry company,[3] and then a year or two later entered the King's Guard of Horse, on whose roll in 1667 he was listed as a 'comedian' with 'black hair'.[4] The chief actor next to Ashbury was John Richards, whom Ogilby in the summer of 1662 lured away from Davenant's troupe at the Duke's Theatre. Angered at losing a valuable player, Davenant tried to effect Richards's return by royal warrant,[5] but the latter had gone to Ireland when the order was issued in early August.[6] Richards, considerably older than Ashbury, was born on the Isle of Wight in 1629,[7] and was described as 'not over-happy in his personal appearance',[8] though his 'flaxon hair'[9] must have been a striking adornment. His sister became Ashbury's first wife, but being 'a very infirm woman' she never took up acting.[10] Ogilby secured another

---

[1] Ibid., p. 339.　　　　[2] Chetwood, pp. 79–80.　　　　[3] Ibid.
[4] *Hist. MSS. Commission: Report on the Manuscripts of the Marquis of Ormonde* (London, 1899), ii. 182, 237.
[5] State Papers, Domestic, Charles II, lviii. 15.
[6] MS. S.P. 44/7 S.P. Domestic Entry Book, p. 181, Public Record Office, London. It is summarized in *Cal. State Papers: Domestic, 1661–2*, p. 455.
[7] *Hist. MSS. Commission: Report on the Manuscripts of the Marquis of Ormonde*, ii. 237.
[8] Chetwood, p. 234 n.
[9] *Hist. MSS. Commission: Report on the Manuscripts of the Marquis of Ormonde*, loc. cit.
[10] Chetwood, p. 80. See Chapter IV, p. 84, n. 1, for more details. Stockwell, p. 313, n. 53, confuses Richards's sister with Ashbury's second wife, and refers to the first Mrs. Ashbury as an actress.

experienced recruit in Nicholas Calvert, who as a stroller had played at Norwich in 1660 and a year afterward belonged to George Jolly's famous strolling group.[1] Calvert performed three seasons at Dublin before his death in July 1665.[2] Two other men, noted as 'actors' in the Dublin parish records, may have belonged to the original company: (1) William Moore, who died in October 1667,[3] and (2) a Mr. Yeoghny, whose wife was buried in March 1667/8.[4] These five are the only persons who can be identified with Ogilby's troupe during its early years.

On the same day that this troupe gave its first recorded performance at Smock Alley Theatre, another most important theatrical event took place in Dublin under the auspices of the Earl of Orrery. The Earl was living at the time in Thomas Court, a 'liberty' located on the south-western outskirts of the city and comprising the precincts of the once famous Abbey of St. Thomas the Martyr, which had been confiscated by Henry VIII and bestowed upon the Brabazon family, later the earls of Meath.[5] They had turned the 'House' of the old abbey buildings into a commodious residence and occasionally leased it to the lords deputies or other high officials.[6] In the 'great dining chamber' with its 'forest work hangings of tapestry' Orrery on the evening of 18 October 1662 entertained the new Lord-Lieutenant and many notable personages of Dublin. A sumptuous banquet was followed by the acting of a play from the pen of the host. A brief account of this gala affair found its way into the London newspaper, *Mercurius Publicus*:

Dublin, Oct. 21. On the 18. at evening the Lord Lieutenant and most of the persons of Honor in these parts were entertained by the Earle of *Orery* at *Thomas Court* where his Lordship treated them with a noble Banquet and a Play of his own making.[7]

The drama that Orrery offered to his eminent guests was none other than the tragicomedy which, as his first experiment in

[1] Montague Summers, *The Playhouse of Pepys* (New York, 1935), p. 123.
[2] Mills, p. 138.   [3] Ibid., p. 143.
[4] Ibid., p. 144.   [5] Clark, i. 32.
[6] Rev. Anthony L. Elliott, 'The Abbey of St. Thomas the Martyr', *Journal of the Royal Society of Antiquaries of Ireland*, 5th series, ii (1892), 39.
[7] B.M.E. 195, no. 140, 23–30 Oct. 1662.

rimed verse to please Charles II, he had written at Thomas Court the year before.[1] At this private presentation the play was called *Altemera*, but on its première at the Theatre Royal, London, in September 1664, it bore the title, *The Generall*, and had been so registered in 1663 with the Master of the Revels by Killigrew. Whether Orrery or Killigrew altered the original title as a means of concealing the play's identity is a teasing but insoluble question.

Altemera, or *The Generall*, contains a pseudo-historical plot with a martial background of Mediterranean locale, similar to the plots of Beaumont and Fletcher, Davenant, Carlell, and Suckling, whose plays Orrery had read and also seen in the theatre when he was a sparkling courtier in London before the Civil War.[2] Yet his tragicomedy departs from the pattern of the Caroline specimens in its uniformly serious and gallant tone. There are no scenes in which servants or persons of common station engage in witticism or horse-play. Not only is a humorous vein excluded, as in French tragicomedy, but, like the latter also, *Altemera* lacks roles of lower rank except for the part of Candaces, *confidante* to the heroine. Orrery employs the considerable intrigue and action so characteristic of the earlier English romantic drama, but definitely subordinates these features to the depiction of heroic virtue through the foremost figures in the plot. The usurping King of Sicily; his commanding general, Clorimun; and the leader of certain rebel forces, Lucidor—all three engage in a complicated rivalry for the love of Altemera, a peerless princess, who has promised herself to Lucidor. The emphasis throughout the play falls upon the exposition of the ethical ritual by which the suitors and the princess govern their behaviour. They act in accordance with an extravagant and rigid code of honour in the service of love—a code which smacks strongly of the hyperbolic idealism of the Platonic love cult that in diluted form 'Orinda' Philips introduced to Dublin through her Society of Friendship. Orrery exalted beyond any conceptions of virtuous love to be found among his English predecessors the conduct of his hero Clorimun

---

[1] For complete details about the identity and history of Orrery's first play see Clark, i. 27–28, 101–5.

[2] See ibid., pp. 65–71, for a more complete critical analysis of *Altemera*.

and his heroine Altemera. Persistent argument over the respective obligations of love and honour distinguish their relations with each other and with the lesser characters who are also drawn within love's orbit. These disputations, and indeed the entire dialogue, are couched in heroic couplets.

Thus *Altemera's* heightened love-and-honour situation, exaggerated characterization, lofty ethical argumentation, and riming speech correspond to the basic elements of that unique dramatic species born in the Restoration era. In view of its composition during the early months of 1661 *Altemera* should be designated as the first full-fledged 'heroic play'.[1] Therefore its presentation at Thomas Court on 18 October 1662 under the author's sponsorship constitutes an event of outstanding interest in the history of the Irish stage. Yet the significance has gone unrealized by dramatic historians from that day to the present. The occasion marked not only the first production in Ireland of a Restoration drama but also the maiden performance of an 'heroic play', preceding by a year and a half the pioneer London appearance, that of Dryden and Howard's *The Indian Queen* at the Theatre Royal. Hence Dublin should be accorded the distinction of being both the literary and the stage birthplace of the Restoration 'heroic play'.

There is absolutely no indication as to whether Orrery himself put on *Altemera* at Thomas Court with amateur performers, or hired Ogilby and his players. The latter seems the stronger probability, since the newly-organized Smock Alley Company must have excited much attention and talk around town. In any case, the company almost certainly did not stage at its own playhouse Orrery's tragicomedy or any of his later compositions. The Earl appears to have been the first of a long line of Irish-born playwrights who preferred the éclat of London performance to the encouragement of an independent and fresh dramatic repertoire in Ireland's capital. Their veiled contempt for approbation at home proved for two and a half centuries an insurmountable handicap to the Dublin theatre and, in no inconsiderable measure, accounted for its remaining little more than an imitation of London's stage.

Within a month or so after Orrery's private theatricals

[1] Ibid., p. 30.

Ogilby had completed fitting out the Smock Alley playhouse with the latest form of scenic equipment and had impressed the knowing spectators with the quality as well as the modernity of his productions. At the beginning of December Mrs. Philips wrote proudly to a London friend: 'We have plays here in the newest mode, and not ill acted.'[1] Of course Ogilby's efforts did not always result in an unqualified artistic success. Toward the close of November he grew ambitious and staged *Othello* with all the unhistorical costuming typical of the period, including the bizarre headgear of lofty feathers customarily worn by the principal male characters in tragedy. This Shakespearian venture aroused mixed feelings in Mrs. Philips, who commented:

The Doge of Venice and all his Senators came upon the Stage with Feathers in their Hats, which was like to have chang'd the Tragedy into a Comedy, but that the Moor and Desdemona acted their Parts well.[2]

By mid-winter Ogilby's 'new-mended theatre'[3] in Smock Alley had attained both popularity and prosperity. On 10 January 1662/3 a high official reported to his Whitehall correspondent: 'Mr. Ogilby gets money apace, and his actors reputation.'[4] Dublin stage activity at last had been fully revived, but it continued pretty much as formerly to be the fashionable concern of the strongly Anglicized elements in the Irish capital.

[1] Philips, p. 96.　　　　　　　[2] Ibid.
[3] *Hist. MSS. Commission: Report XI*, Appendix, pt. v, p. 11.
[4] Ibid. Letter of Col. Edward Cooke, a Commissioner of Settlement in Dublin, to Col. William Legge, a Groom of His Majesty's Bedchamber at Whitehall.

CHAPTER IV

Irish Theatricals from 1663 to the Revolution of 1688

THE outstanding production of Ogilby's first season demonstrated in a striking manner the decisive influence which the Dublin Castle coterie at once began to exert upon the Smock Alley Theatre. 'Orinda' Philips, now the leading spirit of that coterie, finished in November or December 1662 her rimed translation of Pierre Corneille's *Pompey*.[1] The novelty as well as the excellence of her poetic accomplishment, which included five original songs for *entr'acte* entertainment, made the Earl of Orrery, who originally had encouraged her in the task, 'resolve to have *Pompey* acted'[2] at the new playhouse. He 'advanc'd a hundred Pounds towards the Expense of buying Roman and Egyptian Habits'[3] so that fresh historical costumes might assure a lavish spectacle.

Mrs. Philips urged various of her friends to exercise their literary and musical talents in support of the *Pompey* production. From the Earl of Roscommon she obtained a prologue, and from Sir Edward Dering, an epilogue.[4] When Dering sent 'Orinda' his contribution, he accompanied it with a witty message of reluctance:

I knew the power you have over me was great but never thought it unlimited before. To write verses at my yeares is allmost an indecencie, but for a judge that is or should be grave to do it, is allmost a prodigy, and this in the midst of so many thousand perplex'd claimes now disquieting my thoughts, that I can hardly judge what is rime when I heare it, and much lesse what is poetrie: And besides I thinke an epilogue the hardest thing in the world to write; I have seen many good prologues but never one good epilogue that I remember. When the plot is discovered and the wedding over, every one is in hast to be gone, and every thing then is tedious, and

---

[1] *Letters*, p. 119.   [2] Ibid.   [3] Ibid.   [4] Ibid.

how certainly will it be so at *Pompey*, and how flat will anything
shew, that comes after your song. So that unfeignedly I thinke it
best to have no epilogue at all. But having this morning some
minuts to spare, my thoughts reflecting upon you as they often do,
I give you this accompt of them, as being pleas'd to give you assur-
ances of my obedience. . . .[1]

'Orinda's' songs for the *entr'actes* and the finale were set to
music by several hands: the first and fifth songs by an unidentified member of her Society of Friendship, 'Philaster'; the
second by a French tutor of Lord Orrery's; the third by the
Advocate-General, Dr. Pett; the fourth by Monsieur Le Grand,
one of the Duchess of Ormonde's retinue.[2] John Ogilby, re-
suming for the moment his old profession of dancing master,
arranged dances to follow three of the songs and also composed
the tunes for the dances.[3]

A colourful *entr'acte* programme, rarely, if ever, paralleled
in Restoration London performances, was finally worked out.
At the close of Act I the drawing apart of the scene flats 'discovers' Ptolomy, the Egyptian king, and Photin, Pompey's
representative, sitting in chairs of state and 'hearkening' to a
song off stage; 'after which an Antick dance of Gypsies is presented'.[4] Act II is followed by the song of 'two Egyptian Priests
on the Stage', but by no dance.[5] At the end of Act III the scene
flats open to 'discover' Pompey's widow, Cornelia, 'asleep on
a Couch', and Pompey's Ghost singing to her 'in Recitative
Air'.[6] After the song there is 'a Military Dance, as the con-
tinuance of her Dream; and then Cornelia starts up, as waken'd
in amazement'.[7] Act IV, like Act II, is followed only by a song,
to which Cleopatra, already on stage, 'sits hearkening'.[8] When
Act V concludes, the two Egyptian priests, as after Act II,
come on stage and sing a duet.[9] Then the scene flats part to
'discover' Caesar and Cleopatra sitting in chairs of state. Before
them 'a Grand Masque is Danc'd' as the finale.[10]

A production with such elaborate pageantry could hardly
be staged so early in the life of the new-born Dublin theatre

[1] Unpublished letter of *c.* Jan. 1662/3. Sir Edward Dering's MS. Letter Book,
1661–1665, letter no. 12.
[2] *Letters*, p. 119.   [3] *Pompey* (London, 1678), p. 64.   [4] Ibid., pp. 12–13.
[5] Ibid., pp. 25–26.   [6] Ibid., p. 37.   [7] Ibid., p. 38.
[8] Ibid., p. 50.   [9] Ibid., p. 63.   [10] Ibid., p. 64.

without some commotion and disagreement. 'The Players fell out about it', the author of *Pompey* reported to a London correspondent and then added in bitter jest: 'Certainly it was conceiv'd in an angry Hour.'[1] Agitation, however, subsided fast. The première went off smoothly on Tuesday afternoon, 10 February 1662/3,[2] and roused loud applause. Yet few in the large and brilliant audience presided over by the Lord-Lieutenant[3] realized that once again within the current theatrical season Dublin had taken the lead over London in an historic stage presentation. *Pompey* marked the first in a long succession of Restoration performances of French plays in English.

So great an interest did the production of *Pompey* excite in both Ireland and England that the play was immediately printed at Dublin and soon afterwards at London.[4] These two printings during 1663 were quickly sold out. A second and quite different aftermath of the performance disclosed that widespread antagonism toward public theatricals existed in Dublin ecclesiastical circles. The difficult *entr'acte* singing in *Pompey* required vocalists from outside the regular Smock Alley Company. Therefore, one of the choristers at Christ Church Cathedral, a Mr. Lee, was called in to assist. When the Christ Church authorities very shortly learned of his participation, they subjected him to severe censure and entered their reprimand of his profane conduct on the church records for 22 February 1662/3:

Mr. Lee, one of the *stipendiarii* of this church, having sung amongst the stage-players in the Playhouse, to the dishonor of God's service and disgrace to the members and ministers of this church, is admonished that he do so no more.[5]

Clearly the Puritan and other Dissenting sects did not constitute the only clerical enemies with whom the Dublin theatre had to contend.

---

[1] *Letters*, p. 159.   [2] Ibid., p. 119.
[3] *Pompey*, 'Prologue for the Theatre at Dublin'. Lines 33–34 are addressed to the Lord-Lieutenant.
[4] *Pompey*. A Tragedy. Dublin. Printed by John Crooke, Printer to the King's Most Excellent Majesty, for Samuel Dancer, next door to the Bear and Raggedstaff in Castle Street, 1663.
Pompey. A Tragedy. Acted with great applause. London, Printed for John Crooke, at the sign of the Ship in St. Paul's Churchyard, 1663.
[5] Gilbert, ii. 68.

In the spring following the première of *Pompey* a notable innovation occurred at Smock Alley. The head of the King's Guard, Sir Nicholas Armourer, decided 'to encourage Mr. Ogilby and his comedians' by paying the expenses of a performance on Saturday afternoon, 9 May, for the entertainment of his troop.[1] Sir Nicholas thereby instituted a practice which was observed by subsequent commanders at least through the reign of Queen Anne. These special days for the Guard became a distinctive custom of the Dublin theatre.

On 3 June Mrs. Philips reported that her copy of London's current stage 'hit', *The Adventures of Five Hours*, a Spanish comedy of intrigue adapted by Sir Samuel Tuke, had been 'snatched from [her] for Mr. Ogilby to have it acted here, almost before [she] had read it over'.[2] There is not, however, any specific record of its production at Smock Alley or of the acting there of another recent comic success in London, *The Cutter of Coleman Street*, a satire of Puritan life by Abraham Cowley, who wrote in the play's preface, dated 1663, that it had been acted 'with good approbation lately at Dublin'.[3] An outbreak of political intrigue and the coming of summer combined to make Dublin theatre business poor in the present June and to hasten the close of the season. Late in the month Mrs. Philips informed her London correspondent:

There is a Plot discover'd here, but what to make of it I know not; and indeed 'tis so unlucky an Age for Plots, that even those on the Stage cannot thrive: For the Players disband apace. . . .[4]

[1] Letter of 9 May 1663 by Armourer to Sir Joseph Williamson at Whitehall. *Cal. State Papers: Ireland, 1663–65*, p. 87.

[2] *Letters*, p. 158.

[3] Stockwell, p. 30, thinks it 'not improbable' that a comedy by Richard Head (?1637–?1686), entitled *Hic et Ubique: or The Humours of Dublin* and printed at London 'for the Author' in 1663, was acted in this same year at Smock Alley. Yet the title-page takes pains to state 'Acted privately, with general Applause' and offers no hint whatsoever of any private performance in Dublin. The play, however, is of some historical significance because it contains one of the earliest stage Irishmen, Patrick, servant to Colonel Kil-tory. Patrick is a voluble, simple-minded character who speaks in an extreme pseudo-Irish brogue.

[4] *Letters*, p. 164. This abortive 'Plot', engineered by the notorious Captain Blood and intended to have come off on 21 May 1663, was to have taken the Lord-Lieutenant captive and to have overthrown the viceregency. Mrs. Philips wrote a poem addressed 'To My Lord Duke of Ormond, upon the late Plot'. *Poems*, London, 1678, p. 150.

And so Smock Alley's first year, though auspicious in its high-lights, ended in an anticlimax.

For the next half-dozen years the fortunes of Ogilby and his playhouse can be no more than haltingly traced. In 1664 he was occupying a house near the theatre on the Blind Quay, where presumably he had lived since his coming to Ireland.[1] He moved farther westward to a larger residence on Wood Quay in 1665.[2] June of that year once more saw a large decline in business at Smock Alley. On Saturday the third, Sir George Rawdon, a theatrical-minded visitor, noted that Dublin's early summer was enticing playgoers to outdoor amusement spots:

The green at Oxmantown is a most noble place, and every evening my Lord Deputy bowls there, and the ladies at Kettle-pins, which spoils the playhouse.[3]

The opening of the autumn season a year later must have been somewhat upset by reason of the fact that the Great Fire of London in early September caused Ogilby to break off his theatre activities and go to England to restore his disrupted publishing business. William Morgan, his Smock Alley assistant, evidently accompanied him, for these two men were soon appointed by the London authorities to the board of four 'sworn viewers' who were to survey the fire-devastated areas, settle boundary disputes, and appraise property damages.[4] Though both Ogilby and Morgan eventually returned to Dublin,[5] Ogilby had become engrossed in new publishing projects and no longer looked upon the Smock Alley enterprise as his primary concern. In 1668 or, at the latest, early in 1669, he left Ireland permanently[6] and turned over his theatrical inter-

---

[1] *Deputy Keeper of the Public Records in Ireland, 57th Report* (1936), p. 563.

[2] *An Enrollment of the Number of Hearths in the City of Dublin, Public Record Office, Dublin, Revenue Exchequer Presentations*, &c., no. 14, p. 20.

[3] Letter of Rawdon to the 2nd Viscount Conway. *Cal. State Papers: Ireland, 1663–65*, p. 589.

[4] *D.N.B.*, xiv. 909.

[5] Ogilby's family remained in Dublin through 1667 and into 1668, for one of his children was buried on 9 Oct. 1667 and another on 4 Jan. 1667/8. See Mills, p. 268.

[6] In 1669 Ogilby published at London an elaborate illustrated folio entitled *An Embassy from the East India Company . . . to the . . . Emperour of China*, &c. *D.N.B.*, xiv. 910.

ests there to Morgan as Deputy Master of the Revels.[1] Because
of this change in management a St. John's parish assessment
'for the Playhouse in Smock Alley' was listed in 1671 under
Morgan's name.[2]

Between 1666 and 1669 the Dublin theatre continued to
function regularly despite Ogilby's absence or absences. Only
a single reference to its repertory during these years has survived, however. John Dancer, a young Irish horsetrooper of
literary attainments, freely translated a French tragicomedy by
Quinault under the title of *Agrippa, King of Alba: or, The False
Tiberinus*. Perhaps through Dancer's acquaintance with the
Duke of Ormonde's son, the Earl of Ossory, the play 'was
several times Acted with great Applause before his Grace the
Duke of Ormond, then [i.e. before March 1669] Lord Lieutenant of Ireland, at the Theatre Royal in Dublin'.[3] At about
this time the Theatre Royal gained considerable notoriety
throughout Britain in connexion with the sensational Ware
case. On Twelfth Night of 1667/8 a certain Sherley of the Irish
gentry met by chance at Smock Alley a Dublin acquaintance,
an heiress, Mary Ware by name. Sherley 'desired to wait on
the said Mary home', was refused, and then proceeded in anger
to abduct and rape the young woman.[4]

In March 1669 the Dublin stage suffered a heavy blow when
its chief patron, the Duke of Ormonde, relinquished his post
as Lord-Lieutenant and went over to England in order to
refute charges against his viceregal conduct. His successor,
John, Baron Roberts, formerly Lord Privy Seal, arrived at the
Irish capital in September. A rigid Presbyterian, he quickly
made himself disliked as 'a public discountenancer of all vice'.[5]
In the words of a sympathetic onlooker, 'the public players he
stopped . . . as well as other vicious persons'.[6] Hence the Smock

---

[1] Stockwell, pp. 33 and 314, n. 71, completely ignores Morgan as Ogilby's
assistant and accepts the erroneous statement of Hughes, p. 4, that Joseph Ashbury
was appointed by the Duke of Ormonde Deputy Master of the Revels in 1662.
Morgan's petition for a new patent to the office of Master of the Revels in 1682
(see the full text in Appendix A) makes clear that he had been sworn in as the one
and only Deputy Master under Ogilby.

[2] Gilbert, ii. 68.

[3] Title-page to *Agrippa*, London, 1675.

[4] *Cal. State Papers: Ireland, 1666–69*, pp. 566–7.

[5] Adair, p. 290.   [6] Ibid.

Alley playhouse had to close and remained shut until its perse-
cutor's welcome departure in the spring of 1670.

The new Lord-Lieutenant, John, Lord Berkeley, a mellow
and tolerant man of rich tastes, completely reversed the policy
of his predecessor toward public amusements as soon as he
reached Dublin on 21 April. Viceregal patronage effected a
speedy reopening of the Smock Alley Theatre. Naturally the
personnel as well as the equipment had lost considerable lustre
because of long idleness. Any defects in production were ob-
scured, however, by the fashionable festivity which surrounded
the performance of Beaumont and Fletcher's popular tragicomedy, *The Loyal Subject*, on Tuesday afternoon, 3 May, when
Lord Berkeley attended the theatre for the first time. His
secretary wrote to Whitehall in enthusiastic terms:

> The house was full of all the Ladyes and Nobility in towne. The
> Actors, most of them, act very well. They want good clothes. But
> his Excellency's bounty and the advantage they will have by his
> countenance will soon make both them and the Scenes very fine.[1]

The Lord-Lieutenant himself was no less pleased, remarking
that it was 'a very good play very well acted' and that 'the
house was exceedingly full of good company'.[2] The revived
Theatre Royal had got off to a favourable start, but rather too
late in the season.

Either before the summer inactivity or after the opening
again in the autumn of 1670 there was given at Smock Alley
a second play by John Dancer, a tragicomedy entitled *Nicomede*,
'translated out of the French of Monsieur [Pierre] Corneille'.[3]
It is highly significant that the only plays known to have
originated on the professional Dublin stage during the first
decade after the Restoration should have been translations of
French drama, then a pet interest of English polite society.
Both the management and the influential supporters of the
Theatre Royal in Dublin looked upon it as an outpost of the
London stage, regularly taking from the latter its cues as to

[1] Letter of 4 May 1670 by Sir Elisha Leighton. *Cal. State Papers: Ireland, Charles II*,
p. 327.

[2] Letter of the same date by Lord Berkeley. Ibid.

[3] Title-page to *Nicomede*, London, 1671. The title-page also states that the play
was licensed for printing on 16 Dec. 1670.

repertory; they never conceived that the Theatre Royal ought to bend its efforts toward stimulating the residents of Ireland to the composition of original plays in order to build up a distinct theatrical bill-of-fare for the country. The sterile notion of the inevitable colonial character of the Irish stage took deep root in the Restoration era among Irishmen of all stations and thenceforth put an effective damper on their creative activity as long as they stayed at home.

In December 1670, at the height of the playgoing season, Smock Alley's operations came to a spectacular halt. On the afternoon of Monday the twenty-sixth, St. Stephen's Day, during a gala holiday production of *Bartholomew Fair*, Ben Jonson's biting satire of the Puritans, the theatre galleries suddenly collapsed.[1] The falling weight of timbers and people, according to an eye-witness, 'hurt a great many and killed a poor girlie, a daughter of Mr. Seaman that lived with my mother, and three other persons, but God be praised the rest had a miraculous escape.'[2] The crash happened, another spectator reported, 'in the 3d Act when the Stocks was brought upon ye Stage to put ye Puritans in'.[3] The Puritan and Nonconformist elements viewed the timing of the catastrophe as no mere coincidence, but as the forewarning of an angry God. An Irish Presbyterian preacher set down a vivid account of this divine chastisement:

And there, among other parts of the play, the poor shadow of a Nonconformist minister is mocked and upbraided; and at last is brought to the stocks, prepared for this purpose, that his legs may be fastened. . . . But behold, when his shadow is brought to the stocks, as an affront upon Presbyterian ministers, and to teach great persons to deal with like severity toward them, down came the

[1] The year date of this occurrence was mistakenly recorded as 1671 in Chetwood, p. 53. The mistake was copied in turn by Wilkes, p. 307; Harris, p. 347; Hitchcock, i. 15; Gilbert, i. 68.

[2] Unpublished letter of 3 Jan. 1670/1, by P. Savage to Robert Southwell. Egmont MSS., vol. 28, Public Record Office, London.

[3] Unpublished letter of 31 Dec. 1670 by Peter Holmes to Robert Southwell. Egmont MSS., loc. cit. There is another letter, dated 27 Dec. to Southwell from Robert Bowyer, about the Smock Alley misfortune, but it sets forth no details which the four accounts cited here do not contain. Stockwell, p. 33, reprints the pertinent portion of Bowyer's letter just as it was printed in *Hist. MSS. Commission: Report on the Egmont Papers* (London, 1909), ii. 24. Both texts reproduce with inaccuracies and omissions the original in the Egmont MSS., loc. cit.

upper gallery on the middle one, where gentlemen and others sat, and that gallery broke too, and much of it fell down on the lords and ladies. . . . Among those that were hurt was one of the Lord Lieutenant's sons, and the Lady Clanbrasil [widely known as 'the Irish Whore'], who, the year before, had caused to be pulled down the preaching house at Bangor [near Belfast]. Such providences, so circumstantial in divers respects, will not pass without the observation of impartial and prudent persons, for surely they [i.e. the 'providences'] have a language if men would hear.[1]

The correspondent of the official *London Gazette* regarded the 'very unfortunate accident . . . at the public Play-house' without concern for God's wrath, but with grave attention to the welfare of top authority:

The upper Galeries on a sudden fell all down, beating down the Second, which, together with all the people that were in them, fell into the Pit and lower Boxes. His Excellency the Lord Lieutenant, with his Lady, happened to be there, but thanks be to God escaped the danger without any harm; part of the Box where they were remaining firm, and so resisting the fall of what was above; onely his two Sons were found quite buried under the Timber; the younger had received but little hurt, but the eldest [*sic*] was taken up dead to all apearance, but having presently been let blood, and other remedies being timely applied to him, he is at present past all danger.[2]

Thus again within the year the Smock Alley Theatre was forced to close. The widespread collapse of its galleries must have necessitated a large amount of rebuilding and prevented any renewal of performances before early spring.

The Theatre Royal at Dublin was not, however, the only stage enterprise in Ireland to be forced to a cessation of activity during 1670. At the market town of New Ross in County Wexford, twenty-five miles down the River Nore from Kilkenny, a Jesuit priest of Belgian extraction, Stephen Gelosse, started a school in 1660 and proceeded to train his students to give moral and religious drama for public audiences. For ten years 'we amused and instructed the people by plays', he informed Rome.[3] Arrested and threatened at intervals, he kept on with his dramatic entertainments through the support of liberal

---

[1] Adair, pp. 303–4.   [2] *London Gazette*, no. 537 (5–9 Jan. 1670/1).
[3] *Letters from Ireland to Rome*, 1670, Hogan Transcripts, f. 787, as quoted by Kavanagh, p. 53, from T. Corcoran, *State Policy in Irish Education: 1536–1816*, p. 82.

Protestants in the town. But popular resentment against him and his labours grew until finally in 1670 he was compelled to close the school and leave New Ross. 'During the month preceding departure four dramatic pieces were presented publicly; and at the last of these the townsfolk and the scholars, even the Protestants, expressed their regret in the sincerest way.'[1] Father Gelosse held firmly to his enthusiasm for stage amusement and many years later he was to restore it for the citizens of New Ross.

Another Jesuit school was founded about 1675 at Cashel, the county seat of Tipperary and a Catholic stronghold. This institution, located in 'a roomy house', was not daunted by the fate of Father Gelosse and began at once to copy his practice of popular stage entertainment. 'The first public result of the school was a notable drama, acted for the Archbishop, Dr. William Burget, who had just come from Rome to the See of Cashel. It was witnessed with great favour by all, even by non-Catholics.'[2] The further history of the Cashel Jesuit plays was never reported.

From the time when Ogilby left Dublin the authority of the Master of the Revels over all professional amusements throughout Ireland was increasingly disregarded. At last the situation grew so confused and derogatory to Ogilby that he felt compelled to appeal for an official reiteration of his powers. On 6 September 1672, exactly a month after Arthur Capel, Earl of Essex, had taken office at Dublin as Lord-Lieutenant in succession to Lord Berkeley, a royal letter ordered Essex to issue a public pronouncement in regard to the Master of the Revels in Ireland. The Lord-Lieutenant complied with a belated proclamation, dated 7 February 1672/3, which reaffirmed Ogilby's powers, as Master of the Revels, to license entertainers of all sorts and complained at the poor observance of his authority, in that several licensed performers, 'men of good behavior travelling with licensed monsters, motions, shows, and other plays and interludes have not been allowed to exhibit in some towns, and afterwards the unlicensed persons, rope-dancers, &c have been tolerated'.[3]

---

[1] Ibid., as quoted by Kavanagh, p. 54, from Corcoran, p. 84.

[2] Hogan Transcripts, f. 751, as quoted by Kavanagh, p. 54.

[3] Folio, Dublin, 1672; reproduced in *Bibliotheca Lindesiana*, vi. Royal Proclamations: 1485–1714 (Oxford, 1910).

This proclamation may have temporarily enabled William Morgan, then the Deputy Master, to secure a broader recognition of the licensing monopoly of the Revels Office. At any rate, he did not long wrestle with the problem of enforcement. In 1675, if not before, he joined the ageing Ogilby in London to assist with the preparation of maps of London and of the English roads. On 5 November Ogilby and 'his kinsman' Morgan received a joint patent as Cosmographer and Geographic Printer to the King.[1] Ogilby, however, never saw his last projects realized, for he died at his house in Fleet Street, Whitefriars,[2] on 4 September 1676, aged seventy-five. Nevertheless, the versatile Scotsman who had twice initiated the professional stage of Ireland did see this, the most important of all his varied projects, crowned with success. Upon Morgan's return to England the management of the Dublin theatre had passed into the hands of its leading actor, Joseph Ashbury. For the next forty-five years Ashbury alone directed the course of the Irish stage, though for nearly a decade he had to wait for a legal share in the patent to the office of Master of the Revels in Ireland.[3]

The Earl of Essex continued to reside at Dublin as Lord-Lieutenant until 1677. Both he and Lady Essex, a most popular hostess, delighted in social entertainment and gay diversions. Hence the Smock Alley playhouse must have prospered, but sole proof of the state of its affairs during the Essex régime comes from a Smock Alley prompt-book, a now dismembered Third Folio of Shakespeare's works.[4] The internal evidence in

[1] *Cal. Treasury Books, 1672–75*, iv. 842. Ogilby had already been made the King's Cosmographer on 28 Mar. 1674. *Cal. State Papers: Domestic, 1675–76*, p. 151.

[2] Letter of 19 April 1673 by Ogilby. *Notes and Queries*, 5th series, xii. 7.

[3] On 30 Sept. 1676 Sir Joseph Williamson took cognizance of Ogilby's recent death and its effect upon the Irish Revels Office by issuing a *caveat* or legal warning that no grant should pass of the office of the Master of the Revels in Ireland without notice to him as Secretary of State. S.P. Dom. Entry Book 45, p. 27; *Cal. State Papers: Domestic, 1676–77*, p. 344.

[4] For a history and description of this Shakespeare folio prompt copy, of which the only known remains are in the Folger Shakespeare Library, see R. C. Bald, 'Shakespeare on the Stage in Restoration Dublin', *PMLA*, lvi. 369–78, and James G. McManaway, 'Additional Prompt-Books of Shakespeare from the Smock Alley Theatre', *MLR*, xlv. 64–65. Bald makes erroneous assumptions about the careers of a few Restoration players and hence about the dates of these Shakespeare prompt texts. For further information on the annotations in the Folger folio frag-

the extant fragments, together with the records of the volume's former condition, reveal that the Dublin theatre possessed in the 1670's an extensive Shakespearian repertoire which was almost equally divided between the tragedies and the comedies: *Hamlet, Julius Caesar, King Lear, Macbeth, Othello, Troilus and Cressida, Henry VIII, 1* and *2 Henry IV, The Merry Wives of Windsor, A Midsummer Night's Dream, Twelfth Night, Measure for Measure, The Tempest,* and possibly *The Comedy of Errors.* Except for the last named, which rarely, if ever, was acted on the Restoration English stage,[1] this Smock Alley selection corresponds to the Shakespeare plays popular with London audiences of the day.

The Merry Wives and *Twelfth Night* were as little cut for Dublin as for London performance. *King Lear, Macbeth,* and *Othello* suffered minor alterations: some for the sake of so-called 'polite' taste, such as the omission of bawdy lines from the Fool's speeches in *King Lear* or from those of the Porter in *Macbeth;* some for economy in casting, such as Banquo's replacement of the Old Man, and of Ross and Angus, in *Macbeth* (II. iv; I. ii, iii), and the omission of the Clown from *Othello.* Other alterations in *Macbeth*—for example, the addition of the witch song and dance in II. iv—suggest the influence of Davenant's operatic version first staged in 1673. The surviving fragment of *Julius Caesar* seems to indicate that this drama was presented according to the version eventually printed in 1719 and attributed at that time to Davenant and Dryden. *Henry VIII* was much shortened, since its chief attraction consisted of the scenes with historical show. The text of *The Comedy of Errors,* though heavily marked for cuts, is so completely lacking in further annotations as to make its performance at Smock Alley very doubtful. As for the remaining seven titles in the Dublin repertoire, little or nothing of the playhouse text is now known.

Those Smock Alley prompt copies which survive provide a unique view of that theatre's scenic resources in the seventeenth century. The Dublin company exercised the same

ments I am indebted to manuscript notes by William Van Lennep, Curator of the Harvard Theatre Collection. He comments briefly on the Folger folio in 'The Smock Alley Players of Dublin', *ELH,* xiii. 216–22.

[1] Nicoll, p. 172.

economy in staging which its London contemporaries pursued. Stock sets appeared over and over again: the 'Court' frequently in *King Lear*, *Macbeth*, and *Twelfth Night*; the 'Towne' in *Macbeth* (IV. iii; V. ii), *Othello* (I. i, ii), and often in *The Merry Wives* and *Twelfth Night*; the 'Grove' in *King Lear* (the heath scenes and Act V entire), *Macbeth* (III. iii; IV. iv), and *The Merry Wives* (II. iii); the 'Castle' in *Macbeth* (V. v–vii), and *Othello* (V. i; II. i, with rear shutter of 'ye shipps' added); the 'Presence' (i.e. a presence chamber with a chair of state) in *Othello* (the Council scene) and *Twelfth Night* (I. i); the 'Chamber' frequently in *King Lear*, *The Merry Wives*, and *Othello*. The numerous sets depicting chamber interiors were carefully differentiated: 'Bed Chamber' in *Othello* (final scene); 'Chamber without ye Bed' in *The Merry Wives* (I. iv); 'Worst Chamber' in *The Merry Wives* (I. iii); 'Anti-Chamber' in *Othello* several times. Other interesting sets included the 'Garden' (*Macbeth*, I. v; IV. ii), the 'Rock' (*Macbeth*, the witch scenes), the 'Tavern' (*The Merry Wives*, scenes at the Garter Inn), the 'Great Forest' (*The Merry Wives*, most of Act V), and the 'Pallace' (*Othello*, *passim*). This catalogue of scenery at Smock Alley proves that, while stock sets formed the backbone of its scenic representation, the array of these on hand by the late 1670's afforded a considerable diversity of stage pictures.

The existing portions of the Shakespeare prompt-book throw almost as much light on the personnel of the Dublin Theatre Royal as on its sets. The playhouse notes contain references by name to eighteen actors and three actresses. The only complete cast preserved, however, is one for *Julius Caesar*. The alphabetical list of the performers, along with their parts, runs as follows:

Ashbury = Cassius	Mrs. Richards = Portia
Baker = Casca	Smith = Antonius
Cotts = the Carpenter	Mrs. Smith = Calphurnia
Cudworth = Caesar	Walmsley = Decius, also Flavius
Lisle = the Cobbler	Williams = Marullus
= the Soothsayer	
Richards = Brutus	

This production could have been seen on the Smock Alley boards not earlier than 1670 and not later than 1676, for only within that period could the three actors Lisle, Richards, and Smith have performed together. Lisle almost certainly was the Jeremiah Lisle who in April 1670 was ordered by the Lord Chamberlain to be arrested for absenting himself from the Duke's Company at Lincoln's Inn Fields, and thereafter disappeared from the London stage records.[1] These circumstances strongly suggest that Lisle left England during the spring or summer of 1670 to take up acting at Dublin. Richards, who was earlier mentioned as a member of the original Smock Alley Company and who remained with it steadily for fifteen seasons, left Ireland in the summer of 1676 and played at Dorset Garden, London, until the union of the London companies in 1682.[2] Henry Smith, who took the important role of Antony, died at Dublin in August 1682 and was then eulogized by the Lord Deputy of Ireland as 'a great pillar of our stage'.[3] Mrs. Smith, his wife and widow, continued to appear at the Smock Alley playhouse into the eighteenth century.

Francis Baker, who impersonated Casca, served his theatrical apprenticeship in Dublin and made a name for himself as Sir Epicure Mammon in Ben Jonson's *The Alchemist* and as Falstaff.[4] A master-paver as well, he 'used to pave with his part pinn'd upon his sleeve and hem [fit the paving stones together] and rehearse alternately'.[5] One day he was rehearsing his Falstaff role with gusto in the presence of two new assistants. He came to the lines uttered by the humorous knight when he saw Sir Walter Blunt lying dead on the ground (v. iii). Baker stared at one of the pavers, who was stooped over, and said audibly: 'Who have we here?—Sir Walter Blunt!—There's honour for you!' The two workmen thought Baker gone mad,

[1] Nicoll, p. 318 n.

[2] John Genest, *Some Account of the English Stage, From the Restoration in 1660 to 1830* (Bath, 1832), i. 194 and *passim*. There is no evidence for Richards on the London stage between 1662 and 1676. On the other hand, he lost a child by death at Dublin in May 1670. See Mills, p. 149.

[3] Letter of 19 Aug. 1682 by the Earl of Arran, Lord Deputy, to his father, the Duke of Ormonde, Lord-Lieutenant. *Hist. MSS. Commission: Calendar of the Manuscripts of the Marquess of Ormonde*, new series, vi (1911), 425. Since Arran's letter speaks of Smith as 'lately dead', the Henry Smith buried on 2 Aug. at St. John's, the Smock Alley parish church, is certainly the actor. See Mills, p. 184.

[4] Chetwood, p. 174.

[5] *The Complete Works of William Congreve* (ed. Montague Summers, London, 1923), i. 73.

bound him hand and foot, and bore him home.[1] Thus he and perhaps a few others among the Smock Alley players during the Restoration period carried on the ancient actor-tradition of a gainful trade off stage. About 1685 Baker went to London and began at Drury Lane an honourable career which lasted long after 1700.[2]

The Williams who did the part of Marullus was probably David Williams, an actor of moderate ability, who, not otherwise recorded in Ireland, first turns up in the London stage records at Dorset Garden in April 1679.[3] Of the remaining three men in the *Julius Caesar* cast, Cotts, Cudworth, and Walmsley, nothing more is known except the fact that the latter two participated in certain Smock Alley productions during the next half-dozen years.

The annotations of the *Macbeth* prompt copy mention Smith as Seyton (v. iii) and three new names: Farlow as servant; Smeton as the Doctor (v. iii); Totterdale as the Messenger (v. v). Smeton eventually left Ireland and joined the company at Drury Lane, where in 1697 he is found cast as an elderly man.[4] John Totterdale (or Totterdell), quite possibly related to Hugh Tatterdell, an actor with the Red Bull Company at London during the 1630's,[5] appeared on the Dublin scene about 1674 or 1675 as a young married man.[6] He was playing at Smock Alley in the early 1680's, but cannot be traced thereafter. These actor references, and the character of the textual revisions already described, date the *Macbeth* production as between 1674 and 1682.

The Smock Alley staging of *Henry VIII* and *Othello* definitely belongs to this same period, because Smith acted the Queen's Gentleman Usher, Griffith, in *Henry VIII* (iv. ii); Totterdale, the Third Gentleman in *Henry VIII* and an officer in *Othello* (i. iii); and Walmsley, a Senator in *Othello* (i. iii). The names of new minor players also occur in the prompt notes: Andrews, a

[1] Chetwood, p. 175.
[2] Genest, i. 440 and *passim*.
[3] Ibid., p. 266 and *passim*.
[4] Ibid. ii. 108 and *passim*.
[5] Bentley, i. 270 ff.
[6] John Totterdale (also -dell, -dall) had three children baptized at St. John's, on 19 Aug. 1675; 9 Sept. 1680; and 28 Aug. 1681 (Mills, pp. 163, 178, 179). It is significant that the first two, both boys, were called Hugh and John respectively. No other family of this name appears in the St. John's records for the period.

gentleman in *Henry VIII*; Barnes, a sailor in *Othello* (I. iii); Kaine, a gentleman in *Henry VIII*; Mrs. Kaine, the Old Lady in *Henry VIII* (v. i). In addition, two rather important figures in the Smock Alley troupe of that era are referred to in the *Othello* text: Freeman in the role of Montano (II. i) and Trefusis in the role of the First Gentleman (II. i). John Freeman obtained his early stage training at Dublin, but finally transferred his activity to London,[1] where he belonged to the United Company by 1687.[2] Joseph ('Honest Jo')[3] Trefusis also first went on the boards in Dublin, stayed at Smock Alley until its closing in 1688,[4] and then, the next year, became a member of the Drury Lane company.[5] After following the leadership of Thomas Betterton to the Lincoln's Inn Fields Theatre in 1695, he came back to Dublin permanently in the fall of 1698.

The surviving half-leaf of the *1 Henry IV* prompt text gives 'Longmo' as the Chamberlain. This name suggests the Mr. Longmore who was a little-known Smock Alley player at the end of the century. If the identity is correct, Longmore's connexion with the Dublin troupe lasted for about two decades, since *1* and *2 Henry IV*, and *The Merry Wives*, must have been staged some years before 1685 to permit Baker's Falstaff to have established, as it had, an impressive reputation previous to his London début.

In addition to Baker, four of his colleagues, Freeman, Smeton, Trefusis, and David Williams, have already been shown to have received their original theatrical experience at Dublin and to have made it a stepping-stone to London careers. Thus, as early as the 1670's, the Irish stage was beginning to function as the great nursery for the London theatres. From the start Dublin actors and playgoers alike seem to have taken for granted this tributary status of the local stage. Their attitude meant that only occasionally would a talented individual, strongly attached to the Irish environment, continue long in Dublin.

During the spring of 1677 the Duke of Ormonde, the original

---

[1] Montague Summers, *The Playhouse of Pepys* (New York, 1935), p. 109, lists him, without evidence, as a member of the company at Dorset Garden before 1682.

[2] Nicoll, p. 332.   [3] Chetwood, p. 169.

[4] Jane, daughter of Joseph and Jane 'Trefuse', was baptized at St. John's in 1684 and buried there in 1687; Sara, daughter of Joseph 'Trefeuses', was baptized on 24 Nov. 1688. See Mills, pp. 192, 204, 209.

[5] Nicoll, p. 333 n.

patron of the Smock Alley Company, decided that it had attained a sufficiently high quality of repertoire and performance to merit a visit to Britain. Again appointed in May Lord-Lieutenant of Ireland to replace the Earl of Essex, Ormonde also held the post of Lord Chancellor of the University of Oxford. He therefore thought to bring honour to both Ireland and himself by having 'his players' from Dublin perform at Oxford during the period of the Act. Calendared to open on the first Monday after the seventh of July, the Act constituted the culmination of the University's academic year and began with the exercises at which the master's and the doctor's degrees were awarded. For the next several weeks town and gown gave themselves over to revelry. To those who then trooped into the city for a summer holiday Oxford offered all the fun of the fair, and the festivities often included plays by one of the London companies. Unfortunately, in July 1674, the King's troupe, according to an Oxford correspondent, 'were guilty of such great rudenesses before they left us, going about the town in the night breakeing of windows, and committeing many other unpardonable rudenesses',[1] that the University had placed a ban upon the future appearance of London players at the Act. But after an absence of professional theatricals in the ensuing two summers the Oxford authorities were more than agreeable to permitting the visitation of a group of performers from Ireland if the Lord Chancellor vouched for them.

The first Irish company to travel abroad, the Smock Alley actors arrived at Oxford in time to start playing on Monday, 9 July 1677, the beginning of the Act. They continued to perform for twenty days afterwards and 'acted much at the same rate the King's and Duke's [companies from London] used to do';[2] that is, twice a day, 'the first play ending every morning before the college hours of dining, and the other never to break into the time of shutting the college gates in the evening'.[3] At

---

[1] Letter of 28 July 1674 by Humphrey Prideaux to John Ellis. *Letters of Humphrey Prideaux ... to John Ellis ... 1674–1722* (ed. E. M. Thompson [London] 1875), p. 5.

[2] Letter of 1 Aug. 1677 by the Rev. Thomas Dixon, a don of Queen's College, Oxford, to Sir Daniel Fleming. *Hist. MSS. Commission: The Manuscripts of S. H. Le Fleming* (1890), p. 139.

[3] Colley Cibber, *An Apology for the Life of Mr. Colley Cibber* (ed. Edmund Bellchambers, London, 1822), p. 402.

their final appearance on Monday, 30 July, the Dublin troupe presented an unusual attraction in the person of Joseph Haynes, the most colourful speaker of prologues and epilogues on the English Restoration stage. As recently as 18 June he had been arrested in London for a slanderous and obscene epilogue,[1] but he cleared himself with the law in time to deliver on behalf of the Irish visitors a valedictory 'Epilogue to the University of Oxford'. Haynes opened with some pungent lines on the diverse aspects of her festival:

> From Ireland, led by Fame, we came to see
> An Oxford Act, England's Epitome,
> The Scholars' Carnival, the Kingdom's Pride,
> The Townsman's Harvest, Cantabrigians' Guide,
> The day of Strangers, the young Students' Grief,
> If from the Parents comes no swift relief;
> Beauty's chief Mansion, Envy of the Court,
> Where, as to Noah's Ark,
> Clean and unclean, all Creatures doe resort,
> Lyons and Monkeys, & our Irish Crew,
> Rope Dancers, Juglers, Jugling Women too. . . .[2]

His epilogue concluded with an amusing reference to the cramped accommodations of Oxford's summer theatre in 1677:

> Methinks you look in this small Spot alone
> Like all th' Apostles in a Cherry Stone.[3]

The playhouse site may have been the yard of the King's Arms in Holywell, or the Guildhall yard, or Robert Wood's tennis court, all three places having housed productions by London companies between 1660 and 1680.[4] Despite the incommodious quarters, the Smock Alley actors won so warm a reception that they 'carried, it is said, 600£ or 700£ clear gains out of Oxford'.[5] The Lord-Lieutenant's confidence in the professional excellence

---

[1] Nicoll, p. 328 n.

[2] Harvard College Library MS. Eng. 674 F, pp. 28–30, 'Epilogue to the University of Oxford 1677—by Mr Jo: Haynes', ll. 1–11.

[3] Ibid., ll. 49–50.

[4] *Life and Times of Anthony Wood* (ed. Andrew Clark, Oxford, 1891–2), i. 405–6 ii. 165, 490.

[5] Letter of the Rev. Thomas Dixon cited on p. 78, n. 2.

of 'his' company had been fully vindicated. Nevertheless, the great success of the Irish troupers on their maiden venture to England aroused among the banned King's Players a smouldering resentment that was to incite them to petty retaliation when the Oxford prohibition was eventually lifted.

For the Dublin Theatre Royal, the next five years marked a high tide of accomplishment and prestige. During the autumn of 1677 the Irish capital teemed with entertainments. To celebrate the marriage of William, Prince of Orange, with the Princess Mary, 'His Grace the Duke of Ormond . . . and all the Nobility and Gentry in Town, met in great Splendor at the Play' on the afternoon of Monday, 19 November.[1] After the performance the Lord-Lieutenant issued 'a general Invitation of all the Company to spend that Evening at the Castle'.[2] In consequence, the city took on a *mardi gras* air for the ensuing night:

And while the Streets were everywhere filled with Bonfires, the Bells Ringing, and all the great Guns of the City Firing round, at the Castle there was Musick and Dancing: (the Ball being ended) there was provided in the Long Gallery a magnificent Banquet for the whole Company, who parted not till Two of the Clock in the morning.[3]

As if this were not enough festivity, the Dubliners three days later welcomed the birth of a son, the Duke of Cambridge, to Charles II by repeating their 'Joy with like Solemnities'.[4] One of the 'Solemnities' repeated must have been another brilliant assemblage at the Theatre Royal.

During the season of 1677–8, or, less probably, early in the following season, the Smock Alley Company staged its first production of an original play, a tragicomedy written in Ireland by an Englishman, John Wilson (1626–?95), Recorder of Londonderry. This event was attended, however, with none of the éclat which surrounded a comparable historic occasion at Smock Alley fifteen years previous when Mrs. Philips's *Pompey* was given. Wilson had first tried playwriting at London after the Restoration and had seen his comedy, *The Cheats*, acted in 1663 with moderate success. Appointed in December 1666 Recorder

---

[1] *London Gazette*, 1677, no. 1257.
[2] Ibid.   [3] Ibid.   [4] Ibid.

The Smock Alley Prompter's Manuscript (p. 45) of *Belphegor* (c. 1677), showing directions about actors, set, and doors

The Smock Alley Prompter's Manuscript (p. 47) of
Belphegor (c. 1677), showing directions about actors, set,
and doors

of Londonderry at the instigation of the Duke of Ormonde, then Lord-Lieutenant, he had come to Dublin in 1667 and been admitted, as barrister, to the King's Inns on 13 January 1667/8.[1] Thereafter he had travelled north to Londonderry and entered upon a stormy decade of office-holding because he could not get along with the Puritan elements in that community. When his patron Ormonde took up residence again at Dublin in August 1677, Wilson, seeking a respite from his small-town wrangles, returned to the metropolis about October to spend the ensuing winter, spring, and summer.[2] Either before or during his Dublin sojourn he completed a tragicomedy, *Belphegor*, based on Machiavelli's story of how the devil Belphegor transformed himself into a husband to test the ill nature of wives. English translations published at London in 1670 and 1676 had recently brought this tale to Wilson's attention.[3] Through Ormonde's good offices, he succeeded in having his play accepted for Dublin performance. A heavy-handed contrivance of Italianated romantic intrigue and farcical trickery, now and then lightened by song, dance, or the weird appearances of devils to the accompaniment of thunder, it proved a failure on the Smock Alley boards. In consequence, one versifying satirist of the time was impelled to remark of the unfortunate playwright:

> For mad hee is, at least hee is possest,
> The fiend Belphegor heaves within his breast.
> Else why should hee Poetick Straine Essay
> Since the sad fate of that unhappy play.[4]

Nevertheless, returning to London in 1682, Wilson saw *Belphegor* favourably received at Dorset Garden eight years later. No doubt he then felt wholly justified in believing what he

---

[1] 'The Black Book of Kings Inns', Library of King's Inns, Dublin, MS. 38, f. 219.

[2] M. C. Nahm, *John Wilson's 'The Cheats'* (Oxford, 1935), p. 24.

[3] The Novels of Don (Francisco de) [Gomez] de Quevedo Villegas . . . faithfully Englished. Whereunto is added, The Marriage of Belphegor, an Italian Novel, translated from Machiavel. (*T.C.*, Nov. 1670.)

The Works of the Famous Nicholas Machiavel . . . Containing . . . 10. The Marriage of Belphegor, a Novel . . . All written originally in Italian, and from thence newly and faithfully Translated into English. (Ibid., Feb. 1675/6.)

[4] MS. poem, 'On Mr Wilson's Admirable Copy of Verses', in a British Museum copy (807. g. 5) of *A Poem to His Excellence Richard Earle of Arran*, &c., *Lord Deputy of Ireland*, Dublin, 1682.

earlier had asserted in Ireland, that London was 'a better place for lawyers and poets' than Dublin.[1]

The Smock Alley manuscript prompt copy of *Belphegor*, which surprisingly enough has escaped destruction,[2] supplements nicely the contemporary Shakespeare prompt-book in throwing light upon the make-up of the Dublin company during the 1670's. Of the nine actors and two actresses named in the prompt notes, four have already been identified among the Shakespearian performers: Barnes, Cudworth, Freeman, and Smeton. In *Belphegor* Barnes took the part of 'a Boy to Sing' (III. i)[3] and was obviously a young vocalist. Cudworth played the Devil's 'Head', which rises out of a stage trap (I. i);[4] Freeman, Beelzebub (IV. iii);[5] Smeton, the third servant (III. ii; IV. i).[6] Three new and otherwise unrecorded players, T. Brown, George Lee, and Mrs. Wall, filled the respective roles of a porter (v. ii), a servant (III. iii), and 'a Woman' (III. iii).[7] The Mrs. Osborn who doubled as an attendant (III. iii) and as the Veiled Lady (v. ii)[8] was probably Mrs. Margaret Osborn who belonged to the Dorset Garden troupe from 1670 to the summer of 1677, then dropped out of London's sight for two years or so, and ultimately reappeared at Dorset Garden about February 1679/80.[9] Finally, and most importantly, the *Belphegor* prompt copy reveals for the first time the fact that three actors who had long interesting careers in the London theatres got their start on the Dublin stage in the 1670's. George Bright, who acted one of the important characters, namely, Marone the bank officer,[10] made his London début at Dorset Garden not later than March 1678/9.[11] William Peer, a servant in *Belphegor*, moved to Drury Lane about the fall of 1679 and eventually assumed the post of property man there.[12] William Pinkiman (or Pinkethman), another servant in *Belphegor*,[13] seems to have remained at Smock Alley until it shut down in 1688. Then, crossing to England, he soon made a place for himself as

---

[1] Letter of 6 Dec. 1682 by the Earl of Arran to Ormonde. *Hist. MSS. Commission: Calendar of the Manuscripts of the Marquess of Ormonde*, new series, vi (1911), 489.

[2] This prompt-book with textual corrections in the hand of the author is now preserved in the Folger Shakespeare Library, MS. 827. 1.

[3] MS. Belphegor, pp. 36, 37.   [4] Ibid., p. 4.   [5] Ibid., p. 63.

[6] Ibid., pp. 40, 42, 55, 59.   [7] Ibid., pp. 45, 75.

[8] Ibid., pp. 45, 78.   [9] Genest, i. 138, 212, 279.

[10] MS. Belphegor, p. 73.   [11] Genest, i. 266.

[12] *D.N.B.*, xv. 675.   [13] MS. Belphegor, p. 69.

a light comedian at Drury Lane, where 'the merry Mr. Pinketh-man' developed into 'the Idol of the Rabble'.[1] The cases of these three men reinforce the evidence from the Shakespeare prompt-book that the Smock Alley Theatre was a fertile breeding ground of Restoration actors even before 1680.

By 1678 the playhouse had taken so strong a hold upon one highborn Dublin citizen, Robert Ware, that he publicly urged more frequent holiday attendance at the Theatre Royal by municipal officers in order to set an encouraging example to the business community. He further argued that the old custom of free holiday amusement for the young apprentices should be revived by giving each one the price of a shilling seat in the upper gallery on special occasions:

The Maior and Aldermen ought to compensate so great a neglect of duty by resorting on [holi]dayes and festivalls to the *Kings Theatre* in their own Persons, and the causing a general resort of Freemen on these times to that place, besides an allowance to every of their Apprentices of twelve pence a piece to recreate themselves at these times at the *Theatre*, in lieu of these sportes this Cittie was bound to entertain them with.[2]

There are no subsequent indications that Ware's bold stand persuaded either the city corporation or the leading tradesmen to undertake any such radical course of action.

Under the patronage of Dublin's gay aristocracy, however, the Theatre Royal flourished well enough. Despite fresh governmental restrictions on their movements the Irish Catholic nobility and gentry were flocking to the city for diversion along with those of Anglo-Protestant persuasion. Lords Dungannon, Clanrickard, and Dillon, for example, would go to the theatre in the afternoon and afterwards visit the Castle to engage the Lord-Lieutenant Ormonde and his son, the Earl of Arran, 'at play till 12, 1, 2, 3 in the night'.[3] Then, passing out of the gates at forbidden hours, 'they did hector the guards'.[4] At the same period the sportive Earl of Ranelagh and his English mistress, 'Cocky', were making 'much discourse in Dublin',[5] probably displaying

---

[1] Genest, ii. 28 and *passim*; Chetwood, pp. 197–8; John Downes, *Roscius Anglicanus* (ed. Montague Summers, London, n.d.), p. 276.

[2] MS. De Rebus Eblanae 74, f. 175.

[3] *Cal. State Papers: Domestic, 1679–80*, p. 72.   [4] Ibid.   [5] Ibid., pp. 272, 375.

themselves at Smock Alley among other prominent spots. The Smock Alley director, Ashbury, by now had found his way into the company of the smart young noblemen about town. One of them, Lord Blayney, reported to the Earl of Arran in the summer of 1679 when the playhouse of course was not operating: 'All the diversions I can find is playing quoits with Joe Ashbury.'[1]

In the following spring Ashbury and his fellow actors felt the urge to repeat their Oxford experience of 1677 and prevailed upon the somewhat reluctant Duke of Ormonde, who was still Lord Chancellor of the University, to take steps for their return. On 16 May 1680 Ormonde wrote from Dublin to the Bishop of Oxford that he had recommended his 'set of players to the acceptance of the University against the Act', but he requested the Bishop to inform the Vice-Chancellor that, because 'the inconvenience they bring with them [was] so great', he was not eager to have his company invited, 'provided no other [company] be admitted'.[2] On 15 May, however, Charles II's Lord Chamberlain, the Earl of Arlington, had written to the Vice-Chancellor and told him that His Majesty wished the King's Company accepted as performers during the Act.[3] Upon hearing of the royal directive, Ormonde's son, the Earl of Ossory, conferred with the Lord Chamberlain and persuaded him not to 'oppose any thing my Lord of Ormond desired, nor . . . any further interpose in this affair'.[4] When apprised of this setback to their cause, the King's Company approached their patron again and obtained a second 'solemn recommendation from His Majesty', which the Lord Chamberlain had to forward to the Vice-Chancellor.[5] That unfortunate official, 'very unwilling to shew any disrespect', finally bowed to royal orders to receive the

---

[1] Letter of 30 Aug. 1679 by Blayney to Arran. *Hist. MSS. Commission: Report on the Manuscripts of the Marquess of Ormonde*, new series, v (1908), 195. By now Ashbury may well have been a widower, for the first Mrs. Ashbury, sister to John Richards the actor, must have died around this year. A persisting series of child deaths occurred in the Ashbury family between 1675 and early 1679, and then ceased altogether. See Mills, pp. 165, 167, 170, 272. Chetwood, p. 80, asserts that the sickly Mrs. Ashbury died soon after her last child.

[2] *Hist. MSS. Commission: Report on the Manuscripts of the Marquess of Ormonde*, new series, v (1908), 320.

[3] Hotson, p. 263.   [4] Ibid., p. 264.

[5] *Hist. MSS. Commission: Report on the Manuscripts of the Marquess of Ormonde*, new series, v (1908), 338.

King's Players to the exclusion of Ormonde's troupe.[1] Still
rankled by the six-year banishment from Oxford and by the
success of the Smock Alley Company there in 1677, the actors
from Drury Lane proceeded to have their chief playwright,
John Dryden, compose a bitter prologue for their Oxford opening at the Act on 12 July 1680. This prologue worked up to an
abusive finale directed against the Dublin visitors of three years
before:

PROLOGUE, TO THE UNIVERSITY OF OXFORD

Discord, and Plots which have undone our Age
With the same ruine, have o'erwhelmed the Stage.
Our House has suffer'd in the common Woe,
We have been troubled with Scotch Rebels too; . . .
But why shou'd I these Renegades describe,
When you your selves have seen a lewder Tribe.
Teg [i.e. the Irishman] has been here, and to this learned Pit,
With *Irish* action slander'd *English* Wit.
You have beheld such barb'rous *Mac*'s [i.e. Irishmen] appear,
As merited a second Massacre.
Such as like Cain were branded with disgrace,
And had their Country stampt upon their Face:
When Stroulers durst presume to pick your purse,
We humbly thought our broken Troop not worse,
How ill soe'er our action may deserve,
Oxford's a place, where Wit can never sterve.[2]

Though the Smock Alley troupe never publicly retorted to
this scurrilous attack, they were not in the least intimidated. In
the very next year they stole a march on their arrogant English
rivals and invaded Scotland in the wake of a London company.
The Earl of Roscommon, who back in 1663 had written the
prologue for the famous Dublin production of *Pompey*, apparently
was persuaded to emulate the example of the Duke of Ormonde
and to sponsor a second trip abroad for the Irish players. Roscommon, now at Edinburgh as Master of the Horse to the
Duchess of York, arranged that they should journey thither to

[1] Hotson, p. 264.
[2] John Dryden, *Miscellany Poems* (London, 1684), pp. 271–2, where the prologue
is not dated. W. J. Lawrence in 'Irish Players at Oxford and Edinburgh', *Dublin
Magazine*, Apr.–June 1932, pp. 49–60, first identified its date and the circumstances
of its presentation.

entertain James, Duke of York, High Commissioner for Scotland, and his entourage. The Dublin company, thirty strong, landed in mid-July 1681 at the west-coast port of Irvine, about forty miles from Edinburgh.[1] Their gorgeous wardrobe caused them to be held up by customs officials for payment of import duty on the rich metal embroidery. They at once appealed to the Scottish Privy Council on the grounds that they planned 'to sett up a playhouse for the diversion and recreation of such as shall desire the same'; that therefore they had 'brought alongst with them cloathes necessary for their employment, mounted with gold and silver lace'; and that such apparel was exempted from customs tax by a parliamentary statute of 1672 which particularly excepted 'comedians, as to the cloaths which they make use of upon the stage'.[2] On 19 July the council approved the entry of the costumes free of duty, but with Scottish canniness it also instructed the collector of customs to inspect the players' apparel 'to see if under colour therof any contraband goods are imported, and to stop the same'.[3] The company, duly inspected, then hastened on to Edinburgh to play before the Duke of York in the tennis-court theatre of Holyrood House. For the gala opening the Earl of Roscommon supplied a prologue, an appropriately extravagant eulogy of the royal prince.[4] The Irish visitors met so enthusiastic a welcome that they prolonged their stay at Edinburgh far into the autumn. During some four months in the city they not only acted for the private entertainment of royalty, but also, in accordance with the purpose which they had avowed to the Privy Council, they certainly 'set up a playhouse for the diversion and recreation' of the public, very possibly in the tennis court on the High Street opposite the Throne Tavern, where stage plays had been given in the recent past.[5]

The Smock Alley Company's continued presence in town in-

---

[1] *Register of the Privy Council of Scotland*, 3rd series, vii (1915), 161.

[2] Ibid., p. 162; James C. Dibdin, *The Annals of the Edinburgh Stage* (Edinburgh, 1888), p. 27.

[3] *Register of the Privy Council of Scotland*, 3rd series, vii (1915), 162.

[4] A contemporary manuscript copy entitled 'Prologue to His Royall Highness the D: of York at Edinburgh, by the late E: of Roscommon' is preserved in Harvard College Library MS. Eng. 674 F, pp. 27–28. The prologue was printed in *Poems by the Earl of Roscommon* (London, 1717), p. 122.

[5] Dibdin, p. 28.

spired the Duchess's ladies of honour to plan a performance of their own in the Holyrood tennis court and to have Ashbury direct it. The ladies chose as their vehicle Nathaniel Lee's *Mithridates*, a tragedy first seen at London two years previously. Ashbury trained with special care the sixteen-year-old Princess Anne (later the Queen of England) for the part of Semandra,the appealing heroine. An eminent Edinburgh lawyer took pains at the time to record the occasion of these unusual court theatricals, but he did so with a matter-of-fact brevity which proved him no stage historian:

15 Novembris, 1681, being the Quean of Brittain's birth-day, it was keeped by our Court at Halirudhouse with great solemnitie, such as bonfyres, shooting of canons, the acting a comedy, called Mithridates King of Pontus, before ther Royall Hynesses, &c, wheirin Ladie Anne, the Duke's daughter, and the Ladies of Honour ware the onlie actors.[1]

Soon after this memorable celebration the Smock Alley Company brought its Scottish sojourn to a close. Twice in four years it had invaded Britain to show its quality before audiences also entertained by the London troupes, and both times it had come away with much honour and reward. No other acting organization from Ireland was to approach that record for two centuries.

Dublin and its Theatre Royal had now arrived at the height of their seventeenth-century prosperity. As a symbol of affluence the city completed in 1681 a new Tholsel and Exchange[2] on the site of its ancient predecessor. The new building was an oblong brick-and-stone structure of two stories, possessing an ornate façade surmounted by a globe with gilded weathercock.[3] Broad stone steps ascended from Skinners Row to a railed portico with

---

[1] Sir John Lauder of Fountainhall, *Historical Selections from the MSS.*, Vol. I: *Historical Observations, 1680–1686* (Edinburgh: printed for the Bannatyne Club, 1837), p. 51. Chetwood, p. 84 n., states that 'Ashbury was Prompter, and conducted the Whole', and that the performance, for which he gives no date, was 'in the Banqueting-House, Whitehall'. Hitchcock, i. 35, follows Chetwood in this manifest error as to the site.

[2] A letter of 14 May 1681 refers to the Tholsel as the 'New Hall'. *Cal. State Papers: Domestic, 1680–81*, p. 281. William Molyneux in a letter of December 1683 reported that it had now been 'arrogantly named' the Royal Exchange. *Dublin University Magazine*, xviii (Oct. 1841), 475.

[3] For these and other interesting details of the interior see Dunton, p. 326; MacLysaght, p. 398.

a front of three arches in square stone, supported on two stone pillars. Over the portico a large balcony, ornamented above by two niches with stone statues of Charles I and Charles II, afforded a splendid view of the metropolis and environs. The most magnificent Restoration edifice in the capital, the new Tholsel made the playhouse in Smock Alley look more unimpressive than ever. Not for this reason, however, did the theatre's prestige and business commence to fall off in the spring of 1682. The departure of its most eminent and most devoted patron, the Lord-Lieutenant Ormonde, removed from its performances a great attraction. The company also needed some new blood, as Ashbury came to realize by summer. The death of Henry Smith, one of his leading actors, at the beginning of August led him to decide to cross over at once to London in search of fresh talent. He knew that a number of good experienced performers had been thrown out of employment by the union of the two London troupes in the preceding May. The Earl of Arran, now Lord Deputy in his father's absence, eagerly supported Ashbury's mission and appealed to Ormonde at London in urgent terms: 'Your encouragement and assistance will be necessary or else the playhouse will fall.'[1] The mission encountered at least a measure of success, for six weeks later Arran reported to Ormonde with some satisfaction that Ashbury had returned from London with 'a recruit of players, which I hope will afford us some divertisement this winter'.[2] The Smock Alley manager brought back with him his brother-in-law, John Richards, and the latter's actress wife. Richards during his six years at Dorset Garden had developed a considerable reputation as a clownish and blustering valet, if this tribute from a contemporary epilogue is to be believed:

> Here's Blundering Richards is my Huffing Esquire,
> Damm me, the best in Englande for't, d'e hear.[3]

Ashbury's only other recruit on record was the veteran Marmaduke Watson, who had played in the King's Company at

---

[1] Letter of 19 Aug. 1682 by Arran to Ormonde. *Hist. MSS. Commission: Calendar of the Manuscripts of the Marquess of Ormonde*, new series, vi (1911), 425.

[2] Letter of 3 Oct. 1682 by Arran to Ormonde. Ibid., p. 458.

[3] Epilogue to *Like Father, Like Son* by Aphra Behn, first printed separately in 1682 and then reprinted by G. Thorn-Drury in *A Little Ark* (London, 1921), p. 44.

London since 1661.[1] Watson's affiliation with the Dublin theatre after the union of 1682 has come to light with the discovery of a manuscript cast of actors in a copy of *The Night-Walker*,[2] a comedy of middle-class London life in the reign of Charles I, written by John Fletcher and James Shirley. This copy of the comedy was prepared for an intended performance at Smock Alley during the 1684–5 season.[3] The alphabetical list of the actors, along with their parts, runs as follows:

Ashbury = Tom Lurcher	Mrs. Ashbury = the Nurse
Baker = Justice Algripe	„ Hardican = a woman
Doggy = the Boy	„ Richards = the Lady, mother
Lisle = Toby	„ to Maria
Richards = Jack Wildbraine	„ Smith = the Mistress
Totterdale = the Sexton	„ Walmsley = a woman
Walmsley = a gentleman	Millicent Yoe = Mistress Newlove[4]
Watson = a servant	

Baker left Dublin in 1685; all the others stayed at Smock Alley until the theatre closed down in 1688. Longmore, Pinkethman, Smeton, and Trefusis also belonged to the Dublin company during the 1680's.[5] Over and beyond these eighteen players, however, a goodly number of the company's personnel at that

[1] Hotson, pp. 264–5; Nicoll, pp. 295, 332.

[2] The Inderwick copy in the Folger Shakespeare Library, a quarto published by Thomas Cotes, London, 1640.

[3] The text contains cuts and slight revisions, but no annotations for scenery and no prompt warnings for entrances, exits, or stage business. It is most doubtful, therefore, that the play was really produced at this time.

[4] The manuscript names of the actors, added on the outside margin of the page which prints the dramatis personae, have been badly mangled by the cutting of the page in binding. The present state of the list reads as follows:

	Women
[As]hberry = Tom Lurcher	[Ri]chards = Lady, Mother to Maria
[Ri]chards = Jack Wildbraine	[ ]lkison = Maria
[blank] ⎫ = Gentlemen	[A]shberry = Nurse
[W]almesley ⎭	[M]illisent Yoe = Mistress Newlove
[Ba]ker = Justice Algripe	[Wa]lmsley ⎫ = Women
[ ]ter = Frank Hartlove	[a]nd Hardican ⎭
[Lis]le = Toby	[Sm]ith = Mistress
[Wa]tson &c. = Servants	
[Tot]terdale = Sexton	
[blank] = Bell-Ringers	
[D]oggy = Boy	

[5] See biographical details in the preceding discussion of the Shakespearian performers.

time still remain unaccounted for, if it maintained anything like the roster of thirty which it had on its tour to Scotland in 1681.

The name of greatest interest in *The Night-Walker* cast is 'Doggy', listed as the Boy. The unusual diminutive surely can be the nickname of none other than Thomas Doggett,[1] Dublin-born comedian renowned in London at the century's end, 'a little lively man',[2] praised in his hey-day as 'the only Comic Original now Extant'.[3] In 1690 he was taken into the Drury Lane Company, so it was recorded, 'from being a stroler'.[4] Now it turns out that he first went on the stage as a young hireling in his home city. Doggett's is, therefore, one more name to be added to the imposing array of talented Smock Alley graduates who sooner or later abandoned what they thought to be a side-show stage for a place in the main arena.

The Mrs. Ashbury assigned the role of the Nurse in *The Night-Walker* was the theatre manager's second wife. After remaining a widower for some years, Ashbury 'fixed his eyes upon a blooming young gentlewoman'[5] and asked her hand in marriage. The match must have attracted no little attention. The Consistory Court of Dublin issued the licence, and the Reverend John Pooley, Dean of Kilkenny and Prebendary of St. Michan's, performed the ceremony. On 7 October 1684 'Joseph Ashbury, Gent., married Ann Darling, spinster, daughter of the Reverend Mr. Darling, Dean of Emly, at St. Michans'.[6] The leader of Dublin's stage had found for himself a mate not only of social position but, what is more surprising, of similar professional interest. Though a clergyman's daughter, the second Mrs. Ashbury evidently had the desire and ability to act, because her husband lost no time in putting her on the boards at Smock Alley. In due course she became a prominent member of the company.

Ashbury's marriage was only one of several happenings which made the year 1684 eventful for him. In this year he also obtained, though as a joint holder, the office of Master of the

---

[1] Allan H. Stevenson first made this identification, and also first called my attention to *The Night-Walker* annotations.

[2] Downes, p. 275.   [3] Ibid., p. 52.

[4] Nicoll, p. 378.   [5] Chetwood, p. 80.

[6] Trinity College, Dublin, MS. 674, f. 1ᵛ, 'The Principal Christenings and Burials in Dublin in the Seventeenth Century'.

Revels in Ireland. When he had visited London in 1682, he had undertaken more business than the recruiting of players. He had conferred with William Morgan, who was still Deputy Master of the Revels in Ireland under the patent issued in 1663. Sometime in 1682 Morgan petitioned the king for leave to make over the joint patent of Ogilby and Stanley to 'his own name, in the stead of Mr Thomas Stanley's Name'.[1] In connexion with this petition he had set forth that he 'togeather with His said Unkle [Ogilby] was at great Charge in building a Theatre, Raising and Setling a Company of Actors at Dublin'; that he had been 'sworn your Majesties Servant as Deputy of ye Revells, and Executed the said office, during the life of His said Unkle, by Assignment'; and that he had been 'left very much in Debt by the said Mr Ogilby'. But Ashbury had evidently demanded that he should have a share in the new patent which Morgan was seeking to acquire, since for years, on behalf of Ogilby and then of Morgan, he had successfully conducted the Theatre Royal in Dublin. Morgan, having then agreed to a joint patent, revised his petition before mid-March 1683, and elaborated it in several important respects, begging that (1) the king bestow upon the Dublin company 'the title of Servants to your Majesty and your Royall Consort', (2) 'the priviledges conteined in Mr. Killigrews patent as Governor of your Majestys Comedians here' be included in the new patent for the Irish office, (3) the powers of the Master of the Revels in Ireland be equal to those exercised by the Master of the Revels in England, and (4) the new patent be granted for life to Morgan, Joseph Ashbury, and his son, Charles Ashbury.[2]

Morgan's petition was referred on 27 March 1683 to the Lord-Lieutenant of Ireland, the Duke of Ormonde, for an official opinion. The latter at Hampstead near London expressed to the King by letter of 2 June his approval.[3] Next, Thomas Stanley, who in twenty years as joint patentee appears to have kept discreetly in the background, surrendered on

---

[1] MS. S.P. 63, State Papers Ireland, vol. 343, no. 77 B, Public Record Office, London. See Appendix A for the full text. This petition, though undated, is filed among papers of the year 1682 and listed in *Cal. State Papers: Domestic, 1682*, p. 621.

[2] MS. S.O. 1/11, Signet Office Records, Irish Letter Books, vol. 11, pp. 234–8, Public Record Office, London. See Appendix A for the full text.

[3] Ibid.

10 November his patent rights.[1] Accordingly, on 28 November, the king issued an order to the Earl of Arran, Lord Deputy of Ireland, to accept Morgan's surrender of the Ogilby and Stanley patent, and to prepare a new patent, granting the office of Master of the Revels in Ireland to Morgan, his executors and assigns, for three lives—his own, and Joseph and Charles Ashbury's—and for the longest liver.[2] This royal warrant, enrolled at the Signet Office on 5 January 1683/4, was then forwarded to Ireland. On 20 January Morgan dispatched to Edward Corkery of Dublin a power of attorney for surrendering the old patent.[3] Finally, after two years of negotiation and legal processing, the joint patent to Morgan and the two Ashburys was issued at Dublin on 11 August 1684.[4] It confirmed both Morgan's title to the Theatre Royal in Dublin and the monopolistic powers of the Master of the Revels over theatre building and performance in Ireland. It also added three interesting provisions which echoed those in the London patents granted to Davenant and Killigrew: first, the Theatre Royal in Dublin may take from the public such payments 'as shall be reasonable in regard of the great expence of scenes, musick, and such new decorations as hath not formerly been used'; second, women's parts may be played by women so long as nothing scandalous is performed; third, actors engaged by the patentee are not to act elsewhere save by his permission—if they desert, they do so at their own peril and may not be engaged in London.[5] How long after the issuance of this new patent Morgan's formal connexion with the Irish stage lasted cannot be exactly stated. He was living in 1689, for he advertised himself on the title-page of his *Pocket Book of the Roads* (fourth edition) as 'Cosmographer to Their Majesties', King William and Queen Mary. By 1701, at any

[1] William Monck Mason, 'Collection for a History of the City of Dublin', British Museum, Egerton MS. 1773, f. 25: a descriptive catalogue of the patents issued for the office of Master of the Revels in Ireland, and of their location at the Rolls Office, Dublin, in the patent rolls which were burned in 1922.

[2] See p. 91, n. 2.

[3] See Appendix A for the full text.

[4] Enrolled at Dublin on 4 Nov. 1684. Excerpts of the original patent in the Public Record Office, Dublin, were transcribed by W. J. Lawrence before the fire of 1922.

[5] This summary of the provisions is based on W. J. Lawrence's notes in his Irish theatre collection, University of Cincinnati.

rate, he had died and left Joseph Ashbury in sole possession of the office of Master of the Revels in Ireland.[1]

Ashbury experienced still another piece of good fortune in 1684 by reason of the Duke of Ormonde's return to Dublin. Accompanied by his son, the Earl of Ossory, and the latter's wife, he landed on Tuesday, 19 August. The first question the Countess of Ossory asked the theatre-loving Lord-Lieutenant as they passed through Dames Gate into the old city was 'the way to the Playhouse'—so Ormonde reported with great satisfaction to her father.[2] After the season had opened at Smock Alley, the Lord-Lieutenant often attended. His presence cheered the actors but did not draw the Dublin citizens to the theatre in any large numbers. The mounting tension between the Protestant and Catholic elements in the metropolis gave rise to feelings of suspicion and insecurity, and as a result, discouraged playgoing. A prologue 'before the Lord Lieutenant and his Lady' voiced the company's plight in a tone of plaintive resignation:

> The Bawling Warden when the Sermon's o're
> Cries with less zeal than we, Pitty the Poor!
> But with much worse success we begg than They,
> For few frequent the Church, fewer the Play:
> Witt nowadaies is in that low condition,
> 'Twill hardly yield as much as a Commission.
> In vain we Plant it here with pains, & Toyle;
> Like Toads, it ill agrees with th' Irish soyle. . . .
> What if again for Scotland we shou'd try?
> We shou'd be there as ill receiv'd, I fear,
> As Bishops heretofore, or Common Pray'r:
> Faith, since this Plott of Strowling will not doe
> Wee'l kindly stay at home & starve with you.[3]

The death of Charles II on 6 February 1684/5 made a bad situation worse, since the Dublin playhouse had to follow the example of the London stage and close down for two months of

---

[1] See a 1701 list of royal patents in Ireland, *Cal. State Papers: Domestic, 1700–01*, p. 480.

[2] Carte Manuscripts, Bodleian Library, vol. 50, f. 348, as printed in Lady Burghclere, *The Life of James First Duke of Ormonde* (London, 1922), ii. 391.

[3] Harvard College Library MS. Eng. 674 F, p. 20, ll. 1–8, 11–15. Van Lennep, pp. 217–22, gives a résumé of the contents of this folio.

mourning.[1] Business apparently did not pick up in the spring or even later. 'Crowded Green and Strand, but Empty Pit' complained a prologue by the Earl of Roscommon,[2] who was now as warmly supporting the Smock Alley troupe at home as he had done at Edinburgh in 1681. This prologue of his prefaced a performance of John Dryden and Nathaniel Lee's tragedy, *Oedipus*, in the presence of the Duke of Ormonde sometime during 1685. The production of another Lee tragedy, *The Rival Queens: or, Alexander the Great*, a current London favourite, celebrated the birthday of James II, on Wednesday, 14 October.[3] The faithful Earl of Roscommon provided the appropriate epilogue of praise for the monarch.[4]

On 9 January 1685/6 the new Lord-Lieutenant, Henry Hyde, Earl of Clarendon, arrived at Dublin. A special prologue greeted him on his first visit to the Theatre Royal,[5] but the play which followed is not known. Around the end of January the Smock Alley Company staged a popular drama of the preceding London season, *The Disappointment: or, The Mother in Fashion*,[6] written by Thomas Southerne. This promising young playwright, born at Oxmantown, Dublin, in 1660, received his early education in dramatic art at Smock Alley, while he was a student in Trinity College between 1676 and 1680.[7] Then he turned his back on the Irish stage to venture his maiden effort in London. Another young Irishman of greater literary capacity, William Congreve, soon imitated Southerne's example. Brought up in Youghal and Kilkenny, he entered Trinity College in the spring of 1686, experienced his first taste of the theatre at Smock Alley, and in 1689 departed for London to make his fortune as a dramatist.[8] Southerne and Congreve were the earliest to follow the fashionable pattern which continued for generations to lead young men of playwriting interests away from Ireland. In consequence, the

---

[1] Nicoll, p. 332.

[2] Harvard College Library MS. Eng. 674 F, pp. 10–12, l. 17.

[3] Ibid., pp. 5–6, 'Prologue to Alexander the Great on the 14th of October 1685'.

[4] Ibid., pp. 7–8, 'Epilogue to the same. By a Person of Honor'. Printed in *Poems by the Earl of Roscommon* (London, 1717), p. 140, and headed 'Epilogue to Alexander the Great, When acted at the Theatre in Dublin'.

[5] Ibid., pp. 1–2.

[6] Ibid., pp. 22–23, 'Prologue to the Mother in Fashion'.

[7] John W. Dodds, *Thomas Southerne, Dramatist* (New Haven, 1933), pp. 2–4.

[8] John Hodges, *William Congreve The Man* (New York, 1941), p. 30.

Dublin stage remained literarily undistinguished for want of Irish-born material.

The prologue which introduced Southerne's *The Disappointment* bewailed the impoverished condition of the Dublin actors:

> Long may you Toure before you meet a Player,
> For they at home both take & feed on Ayre.[1]

Seemingly business at the Theatre Royal had not improved over the previous season. On Monday, 1 February 1685/6, a few days after Southerne's play, a well-known comedy by Thomas Shadwell, *Don John: or, The Libertine*, was acted.[2] During the spring or the subsequent autumn a performance of Thomas Otway's most recent success, *The Atheist: or, The Second Part of the Soldiers Fortune*, occurred.[3] The foregoing records of Smock Alley programming in the 1680's, though very meagre, do nevertheless prove that the Dublin theatre undertook frequent production of modern works. Yet the taste of the Irish audiences of this period betrayed more than a touch of provincial conservatism, and often inclined to the pre-Restoration drama. At least one prologue grumbled at their old-fashionedness:

> You are of late such Antiquaries grown,
> That no regard's to modern writers shown;
> Fletcher & Johnson only will goe down.[4]

Even so, the Smock Alley spectators liked the old plays freshened up a bit, and the management had to satisfy them by tricks of refurbishing, as another prologue confessed:

> We have recourse to ev'ry little Art.
> Sometimes we shift, & interchange a part;
> Sometimes the fallen value to enhance,
> We baite it with a Song, or a Dutch Dance.[5]

By 1687 Ashbury's brother-in-law, John Richards, had become housekeeper of the Theatre Royal, living on the premises

---

[1] Harvard College Library MS. Eng. 674 F, p. 23.

[2] Diary of Sir John Perceval, *Hist. MSS. Commission: The Egmont Manuscripts*, iii (1923), 365.

[3] Harvard College Library MS. Eng. 674 F, pp. 23–25, 'Epilogue to the Atheist'.

[4] Ibid., p. 21.

[5] Ibid., p. 13.

and paying the various parish taxes 'for the Playhouse'.[1] Ashbury himself had occupied for several years past a dwelling somewhere along Smock Alley.[2] The theatre's situation deteriorated steadily after Richard Talbot, Earl of Tyrconnel, and Commander-in-Chief of the Army in Ireland since 1669, assumed the Lord-Lieutenancy on 12 February 1686/7. A proud, fanatical Irish Catholic and a conniving henchman of James II, he had long been biding his time to destroy the Protestant Ascendancy in Ireland and to oppress in turn the oppressors. Now Catholics rapidly took over the higher offices in the military, the trade guilds, and the city corporation. Unrest permeated Dublin, and plundering broke out sporadically. In such a troubled atmosphere the playhouse could not prosper. Furthermore, its old Castle following had scattered and the new head of the government cared not at all for dramatic entertainment. Only the King's Guard still retained their traditional allegiance to the Theatre Royal and their custom of special days there. Either in 1687 or the early part of 1688 'the Captain of a Company of the Regiment of Guards treated them with a Play called *The Jovial Crew*'.[3] This pleasant Caroline comedy, written by Richard Brome and noted for its merry scenes of gipsy life, had enjoyed so popular a revival at London that it had been republished in 1686. Yet, in spite of occasional support by the soldiery, the circumstances of the Smock Alley Company grew increasingly desperate. When it gave a performance on Friday, 14 October 1687, to celebrate James II's birthday, the prologue sounded a truly pathetic note, 'our Poor Broken Troop neglected lyes'.[4]

Early in the next year, just when all stage diversion in Dublin threatened to cease, New Ross experienced a restoration of it. The Catholic dispensation under Tyrconnel made it possible for

---

[1] Mills, p. 278, for poor tax in 1687; Trinity College, Dublin, MS. 1477, no. 195, 'The Valuation Booke of the Parish of St. John's', for parish cess in 1687.

[2] 'The Playhouse', and Ashbury, listed as a Smock Alley householder, each paid to St. John's a separate hearth tax in Aug. 1685. Transcript in the W. J. Lawrence Irish theatre collection, University of Cincinnati, from the Hearth-Money Book of St. John's Parish, destroyed by the fire of 1922 at the Public Record Office, Dublin. Ashbury buried a son at St. John's in May 1687 and a daughter, Ann, in July 1688 (Mills, pp. 203, 209, 210).

[3] Harvard College Library MS. 674 F, pp. 33–34.

[4] Ibid., pp. 3–4, l. 7, 'Prologue on the 14th of Octob: 1687'.

PLATE IV

WILLIAM PINKETHMAN

ROBERT WILKS

Father Stephen Gelosse to open up his old school and to put on once again public theatricals with the aid of students and possibly townsfolk. On this return engagement, as it were, he undertook out-of-doors productions with settings.

He had a tragedy acted in the chief square of New Ross after the manner in use in [Jesuit] Belgian schools. This was done with the unanimous consent of the Protestant officials of the town. The play lasted three hours, and was witnessed by a very large throng of Protestants and Catholics, many of whom came from distant towns to witness the novel spectacle. The acting and scenery were all that could be desired and drew much applause from the spectators.[1]

Here, apparently, was a more ambitious form of stage presentation than had ever been seen in Ireland outside of Dublin, and even there, only at Smock Alley. Perhaps, if Father Gelosse had been permitted, say, a half-dozen years of regular performances, he might have established some sort of community tradition. As it was, the Williamite wars brought a quick end to his efforts. Nevertheless, like the Kilkenny Corpus Christi plays earlier in the century, this Jesuit drama was so far removed from the mundane interests of the Irish people as well as from the conventions of the professional stage in Dublin that it could never have laid the foundations for a secular theatre in any Irish town.

On 5 November 1688 William of Orange landed in England to set up a Protestant monarchy. At this time, if not in the summer previous, playing on the Smock Alley stage had to be indefinitely discontinued by reason of the turmoil in the city.[2] Of course Ashbury and others of his troupe found it hard to abandon all dramatic activity. Hence, though deprived of a public audience, they indulged themselves in one last bout of acting. During the Christmas season of 1688, at Ashbury's house, they put on John Dryden's popular comedy, *The Spanish Friar: or, The Double Discovery*. A young government clerk, Robert Wilks, who had frequented Smock Alley backstage and read cue speeches for John Richards, took the part of the Colonel[3] and thereby

---

[1] Corcoran, p. 83, as quoted in Kavanagh, p. 53.
[2] Chetwood, p. 53.
[3] Ibid., p. 231. Chetwood states that Wilks was born at Rathfarnham in 1670. Daniel O'Bryan, *Authentic Memoirs, or, The Life and Character of That Most Celebrated Comedian, Mr. Robert Wilks* (London, 1732), p. 5, reports, however, that Wilks was born in 1666, the son of a weaver on Meath Street, Dublin. O'Bryan makes

initiated what was to be one of the most brilliant theatrical careers of his generation. But this private performance constituted only a kind of afterpiece. The curtain had already rung down on the main show. For the second time within half a century Irish civil war had closed up the Theatre Royal in Dublin and dispersed its company beyond recall. Yet the harsh cycle of history often leads to healthy change. Never again would that theatre look to the Lord-Lieutenant of Ireland and to Dublin Castle for its primary support. In the future it would secure a broader base of patronage, though it would not disassociate itself from the English Ascendancy which twice had given it birth.

no mention of *The Spanish Friar* performance, but tells of a secret marriage to a weaver's daughter at about the same date.

CHAPTER V

Stage Activity in Ireland under King William III

FROM the landing of James II at Kinsale in March 1689 until his final defeat at the Battle of Aughrim on 12 July 1691, military violence ravaged the face of Ireland at many points. Yet Dublin fortunately never suffered outright attack during the countrywide fighting. The plague, however, struck with great force in the summer of 1689 and again in 1690. By 1691 death and emigration had considerably reduced the city's population. But neither disease nor war could keep the spirits of the Dubliners long subdued. In the fall of 1690 they twice burst out with bonfires, fireworks, and processions to recognize the anniversary of the 1641 Rebellion on 23 October and the birthday of King William on 4 November. A year later, when formal peace had been restored by the Treaty of Limerick on 3 October, Ashbury thought the time at hand to test out the public disposition toward theatrical diversion. He turned for support to the Dublin playhouse's traditional friends, the King's Guard at the Castle, and found the officers eager to serve as actors as well as audience. Sometime during Christmastide the Smock Alley Theatre, after three years of darkness, opened its doors for a free performance of *Othello*.[1] Ashbury played Iago; young Robert Wilks, Othello; probably Mrs. Ashbury, Desdemona; and the Guard's officers, the lesser male parts. The whole production met with great applause; Wilks in particular received such warm praise for his acting that he then and there resolved to go on the stage permanently. After so happy an inaugural Ashbury hastened to form an acting company with his wife, Wilks, and two other pre-war troupers, Longmore and Mrs. Smith, as a nucleus. His former brother-in-law and Smock Alley housekeeper, John Richards, seems

[1] Chetwood, p. 53; Cibber, p. 235.

not to have resumed playing. Within three months Ashbury had completed his preparations so that he could hold the formal reopening of the Theatre Royal in Dublin on Wednesday, 31 March 1691/2, the day appointed for celebrating the end of the Irish War. For so important an occasion, he took no chances on the play and repeated *Othello* with Wilks and himself once more in the two leading masculine roles.[1]

The young ladies and gentlemen of fashion in the city, however, could not wait to taste of stage entertainment until the Smock Alley Theatre got under way. With the blessing of Dr. William King, Archbishop of Dublin, they fitted up one of the large rooms in the Bishop's Palace near St. Patrick's Cathedral and 'with school-house forms a Cockpit made'. Here on Shrove Tuesday, 1691/2, they gave to a delighted audience of high society a twentieth-century-like 'arena' performance of Thomas D'Urfey's London comedy hit, *Love for Money: or, The Boarding School*.[2] This affair scandalized many of the more sober and pious folk, who believed 'the grave old Bishop's house [had] become a Den of Thieves, contriv'd for ranting room'.[3]

Nevertheless, large numbers of the citizenry had a desire for gaiety after the protracted civil and military strife. Aware of their mood, Viscount Henry Sydney, sworn in as the Lord-Lieutenant on 4 September 1692, 'promoted Plays, Sports, and Interludes for the Amusement of the Plundered People'[4]—a refined version of the old Roman policy of 'bread and circuses'. Sydney lasted less than a year as viceroy and was succeeded by Sir Henry Capel, who in turn held office only from May 1695 to May 1696. For the greater part of William III's reign Lords Justices governed Ireland. Dublin Castle, now fallen into bad repair and used but periodically as an official residence, no longer served as the main rendezvous of persons of fashion. Civic institutions such as the Dublin Philosophical Society and Trinity College were beginning to occupy a much larger place in the social and cultural activities of the metropolis. At the same time the Anglo-Protestant Ascendancy predominated

---

[1] Chetwood, p. 53; Cibber, p. 235.
[2] The Lanesborough Manuscripts (Trinity College, Dublin, MS. 879), ii. 329 ff.
[3] Ibid.   [4] *Freeman's Journal* (Dublin), vii, no. 49, p. 196.

more than ever. The Revolution of 1688 had brought in its wake the most severe disabilities for the Irish Catholics, high or low. They were excluded from the franchise, public office, and representation in the Parliament, and their lands were confiscated for the benefit of the Williamite veterans who wished to settle in Ireland. And finally, to add insult to injury, the English Parliament began to enact what was to develop into a long series of penal trade laws which undermined the economy of all Irish residents. In the face of this hateful and stupid policy the habit of admiration for everything English continued unabated. Dubliners still displayed avid concern for the manners and doings of London. In an original Smock Alley play at the turn of the century the smart hero who has just returned from the English metropolis commends himself to the heroine by remarking:

My Pretty Dear Creature, know that I have brought over some New Fashions, New Tunes, and New Plays. I can tell you which House has the Best Audiences, which Player is most Applauded; who the Celebrated Beauty of the Town, who keeps the best Equipage; I can tell you who loves who, and who does worse. . . .[1]

Of course this colonial curiosity and urge to imitation helped materially to advance the Theatre Royal as a popular attraction in Dublin. Though it went on maintaining a close affinity with the viceregal court and the city gentry, it steadily increased its patronage among the tradesmen and the artisans.

Such expanding public interest guaranteed a prosperous future to Ashbury's theatre, but still he moved with caution in building up his organization to its pre-war standards. In 1693 Wilks migrated to Drury Lane Theatre in London on the expectation of bigger income.[2] There, however, he had to start at fifteen shillings per week, whereas he had received from Ashbury twenty shillings per week the first season and thirty shillings per week the second.[3] During the four years following

---

[1] *St. Stephen's Green or The Generous Lovers* (Dublin, 1700), p. 9.

[2] Chetwood, p. 231, says that Wilks at Smock Alley 'went on with great Success for Two Years', i.e. two seasons. The dates of Wilks's movements in the 1690's may be quite accurately worked out by piecing together the diverse information from Chetwood, Genest, O'Bryan, and the St. John's registers.

[3] Chetwood, p. 232; O'Bryan, p. 10.

Wilks's defection Mrs. Ashbury bore three children and hence performed only at irregular intervals.[1] To offset the loss of these two major players Ashbury secured from London for the 1693–4 season Henry Norris (b. 1665) and his wife Sarah, daughter of Captain Ferdinand Knapton of Southampton.[2] Norris, son of London actors, later became the celebrated comedian, 'Jubilee Dicky', a diminutive man with a thin squeaky voice, who, according to the actress Anne Oldfield, 'seem'd form'd by Nature to be a cuckold'.[3]

In the summer of 1694 Ashbury judged conditions ripe for recruiting a goodly number of able performers, since salary disputes had caused heavy dissension at Drury Lane, and numerous London actors felt themselves at loose ends. Ashbury journeyed to England and landed a promising catch of younger talent:[4] Richard and Elizabeth Buckley;[5] Charlotte Butler, a singer of repute;[6] Richard Estcourt (b. 1668),[7] somewhat experienced as a comedian; Hugh and Mary Norton;[8] Robert Wilks and his wife, Elizabeth,[9] sister to Mrs. Henry Norris already in Dublin. Ashbury also induced Wilks to return to Smock Alley by offering him the exorbitant salary of sixty

[1] Mrs. Ashbury bore a son, Boyle, in 1693 (Trinity College, Dublin, MS. 674, f. 1ᵛ); lost an infant daughter in 1694 (Mills, p. 243); and bore a daughter, Frances, in 1697 (Trinity College, Dublin, MS. 674, f. 1ᵛ).

[2] O'Bryan, p. 18. Henry and Sarah Knapton Norris of 'Smoak Alley' had a son, Robert, baptized at St. John's on 5 May 1694; the same parents, denoted as of the 'Playhous', another son, James, on 20 Nov. 1695. See Mills, pp. 222, 227.

[3] Chetwood, pp. 196–7.   [4] O'Bryan, p. 11.

[5] Richard and Elizabeth Buckley of the 'Playhouse' had a daughter, Elizabeth, baptized at St. John's on 4 July 1695. See Mills, p. 225.

[6] Cibber, p. 180.

[7] Ibid. The dates of Estcourt's movements between Dublin and London can be rather closely determined by his appearance and disappearance from the London casts in Genest, ii. The same fact holds true for contemporary and later Smock Alley actors with London stage connexions.

[8] 'Hew' and Mary Norton of the 'Playhouse' had a daughter, Mary, baptized at St. John's on 27 Oct. 1695; another daughter, Elizabeth, on 12 Dec. 1697. See Mills, pp. 226, 245. Norton may have been the son of Mrs. Norton the actress in the King's Company about 1670. See Nicoll, p. 319 n.

[9] Robert and Elizabeth Knapton Wilks 'at ye Play House' had twin daughters, Elizabeth and Mary, baptized at St. John's on 26 Oct. 1694 (Mills, p. 223), and buried on 30 Oct.; another daughter, Frances, baptized on 15 Oct. 1695. See Mills, pp. 226, 244. Stockwell, p. 315, following the erroneous leads of Hughes, *The Church of St. John the Evangelist* (Dublin, 1889), and of the *D.N.B.* article on Wilks, has confused the dates and identities of Wilks's children at this period of his life.

pounds per annum plus a 'benefit'.[1] This agreement with Wilks appears to have marked the introduction of the 'benefit' night to the Dublin stage. London playhouses had long since adopted the custom of designating a performance as in behalf of a specified person, and then of turning over the net proceeds to the person designated. From the actors' point of view the 'benefit' offered the perfect opportunity for friends and admirers to express their esteem in monetary terms.

Wilks had been back at Smock Alley only a little while when Ashbury prevailed upon him, much against his inclination, to attempt a tragic character, that of Alexander in Lee's *The Rival Queens: or, The Death of Alexander the Great.* 'But the dying Scene had such an Effect upon Mr. Wilks, that it flung him into a Fever, under which he continued three Weeks, which put a Stop to the Run of that Tragedy.'[2] Thenceforth Wilks avoided tragedy except for minor parts. Sometime afterwards he more than made amends for this mishap of temperament. Ashbury desired to get up Shakespeare's *Henry VIII* but he did not know

what to do for a young Girl to represent the Princess Elizabeth; Mr. Wilks proposed his Washerwomans Daughter, who was then about three years old, and promised that she should be perfect in her Part as soon as any of the rest. He took a great deal of Pains with her, and when she appeared upon the Stage, all the Audience was most agreeably surprised with her Performance, and a handsome Collection was made for her.[3]

This little girl also played the Page in Southerne's *The Fatal Marriage: or, The Innocent Adultery* during the same season or the next one. Ashbury, it is said, believed her to be Wilks's child and put her on the pay-roll at ten shillings per week.[4]

With a youthful and attractive troupe now at the Theatre Royal the young men of the metropolis 'attended more to the Playhouse than to their studies', so the Archbishop of Dublin reported to London before the end of 1694.[5] One of the playgoing young men was George Farquhar, who entered Trinity College in July of that year at the age of seventeen. At the

---

[1] Chetwood, p. 233.   [2] O'Bryan, p. 12.   [3] Ibid.   [4] Ibid.
[5] Letter by the Archbishop, Dr. William King, to James Bonnell, the Accountant General, at London, as quoted by Gilbert, ii. 69–70.

beginning of 1696 he was in disgrace with the college authorities and had suffered the loss of his scholarship, but on 1 February he regained it.[1] Not long afterward, however, he quit the academic life and, through an acquaintance with Wilks, secured a chance to act on the Smock Alley boards.[2] His opening appearance in the cast of *Othello* 'gained some applause'.[3] During two seasons Farquhar acquitted himself creditably in modest roles: Lenox in *Macbeth*, Lord Dion in Beaumont and Fletcher's *Philaster*, Rochford in John Banks's *Vertue Betray'd*, Young Loveless in Beaumont and Fletcher's *The Scornful Lady*, Careless in Sir Robert Howard's *The Committee*, and Young Bellair in Sir George Etherege's *The Man of Mode*.[4] He brought his acting career to a sudden close by a grievous mistake when he was taking the part of Guyomar in Dryden's *The Indian Emperor*. He was supposed to kill Vasquez, one of the enemy generals, but 'not remembering to change his Sword for a Foil, in the mock Engagement, he wounded the Person that represented Vasquez, tho'' (as it fell out) not dangerously; nevertheless it put an End to his appearing on the stage as an Actor'.[5] Still in love with the theatre, Farquhar then took up playwriting, but, like Southerne and Congreve before him, he would not offer Ireland the first fruits of his labours. Crossing to London about 1698,[6] he soon attained a substantial triumph with his first play, *Love and a Bottle*. Thus London drained away from Dublin the dramatic inspiration which the Irish stage aroused but could rarely utilize for its own enrichment.

Besides Farquhar, two young recruits from England, Benjamin Husband (or Husbands)[7] and Theophilus Keen,[8] joined the Smock Alley Company in 1696 to receive their first pro-

[1] Trinity College Register, p. 335, under the date of 1 Feb. 1695/6, contains the following entry: 'The same day George Farquhair was restored to his exhibition of which he was suspended.'

[2] O'Bryan, p. 13.   [3] Hitchcock, i. 30.

[4] *Works* (Dublin, 1775), 1. iv, states that Thomas Wilkes obtained this list of Farquhar's Dublin roles from 'the late Mr. Husbands who performed at Smock-alley Theatre with Mr. Farquhar'.

[5] Chetwood, pp. 149-50.

[6] *The Complete Works of George Farquhar* (ed. Charles Stonehill, London, 1930), 1. xiv, states without any evidence that Farquhar went to London in 1697.

[7] Chetwood, pp. 168-9.

[8] *Memoirs of the Life of Mr. Theophilus Keene* (London, 1718) asserts that Keen left off strolling in the English provinces about 1696 and crossed to Dublin.

fessional training. The year after their arrival Ashbury ran afoul of the law for the only time on record. He was prosecuted and fined for swearing on the stage.[1] This circumstance, though petty in itself, emphasized how completely English opinion swayed public attitude in Ireland. The campaign against indecency and profanity in the London playhouses, which arose in the early 1690's, reached its culmination in an order of 4 June 1697 by the Lord Chamberlain, 'to prevent the Prophaneness and Immorality of the Stage'. The order required actors to obey the censoring power of the Master of the Revels and 'to leave out such Prophane and Indecent Expressions, as he has thought proper to be omitted'.[2] All this agitation in England about profanity caused quick repercussions in Ireland. The Parliament toward the close of 1697 passed an act dealing strictly with swearing and other improprieties of speech in public. The Recorder of Dublin, Mr. Hancock, was 'a bold and just magistrate, severely putting the law in Execution . . . instances of which are frequently seen in his punishing swearers with 20 shillings for each oath'.[3] No doubt Ashbury had carelessly uttered one or more of the mild oaths common to the dialogue of Restoration drama. That he should have been the sole Dublin actor so victimized is difficult to understand, unless the stern Mr. Hancock simply wanted to single out the Theatre's director for punishment as a warning to the entire company.

During this wave of piety and good manners John Dunton, an eccentric London bookseller who was the uncle of John Wesley the Methodist leader, arrived at Dublin on business. The Irish metropolis in the spring of 1698 impressed him at once. 'Indeed ye Grandeur they live in here', he declared, 'is not much Inferior to what ye see in London.'[4] Dunton went the round of the local amusement places as well as of the

---

[1] William Monck Mason, 'Collection for a History of the Irish Stage', British Museum, Egerton MS. 1763, i, f. 18.

[2] Official London notice as printed in *The Flying Post, or The Post Master*, Dublin, 7 Mar. 1698/9, and reprinted by Stockwell, p. 40. The latter connects Ashbury's arrest with the Lord Chamberlain's order. The Lord Chamberlain, however, had no jurisdiction whatsoever in Ireland.

[3] John Dunton, 'A Tour in Ireland', Bodleian Library MS. Rawlinson D. 71, f. 23.

[4] Ibid., f. 25.

coffee-houses and bookshops. Boisterous Donnibrook Fair on the south-eastern outskirts fascinated him with its bagpipes, 'scrapers' or fiddlers, dances, and ale-drinking.[1] On York Street, leading from Aungier Street to St. Stephen's Green, he stopped in at 'an handsome but not overlarge Tennis Court with a Tavern next door to it, where with ye Juyce of ye generous grape Gentlemen may supply those spirits which they exhausted in tossing their balls'.[2] One day he saw a playbill advertising a performance of Shadwell's famous comedy, *The Squire of Alsatia*, and 'had a great mind to see it'.[3] In the moralistic vein then so typical of the middle-class citizen he set down a description of his approach to the Smock Alley playhouse:

Hither I came in my best cloaths and pouder'd wigg not like a bookseller but a beau, tho not soe much to be seen as to see new faces and new folleys: however ye theater be applauded by a modern Gentleman for ye representation of those things which so mightily promote both Religion and monarchiall Government, for my part I thought Vice which fundamentally destroys all those things is here as well as in other theaters soe charmingly discover'd as to make men rather love than abhor it.[4]

Once inside the playhouse he showed himself a lively observer, though still inclined to moralize:

Having got my Ticket, I made a shift to crowd into the Pit where I made my Honors to Madam H—y . . . and to two or three other Ladies that I hapned to know. . . . I found . . . the Dublin Playhouse to be a place very contrary to its owners; for they on their out-sides make the best show: But this is very ordinary in its outward appearance, but looks much better on the inside, with its Stage, Pit, Boxes, two Galleries, Lettices, and Musick Loft. . . . There are some Actors here, particularly Mr. Ashbury, Mr. Husbands, Mr. Wilks, Mr. Hescot [Estcourt], Mr. Norris, Mr. Buckly, Mr. Longmore, Mrs. Smith, Mrs. School[d]ing, no way inferior to those in London; nor are the Spectators, by what I saw, one degree less in Vanity and Foppery, than those in another Place. . . . Yet the Diversion was not so great, but that the Crowd made me more

---

[1] Dunton, f. 27.   [2] Ibid.
[3] *The Dublin Scuffle*, p. 339.
[4] MS. Rawlinson D. 71, f. 25.

uneasie; . . . in a word, no Church I was in while at Dublin, cou'd I discern to be half so crowded as this Place.[1]

If this account can be taken as a fair representation of an ordinary afternoon's audience at Smock Alley, then the Theatre Royal was drawing well-dressed and well-filled houses in 1698. Dunton's reference to meeting several ladies of his acquaintance in the pit is of peculiar interest, because that section was looked upon in Dublin as a male preserve, occupied by beaux, collegians, well-to-do burghers, and gentlemen without escorts. Obviously some reputable females liked to sit there. Nevertheless, polite society rather frowned upon the practice until at least half-way through the eighteenth century. Unescorted ladies, especially the 'vizored masks', those city dames who were out for flirtation or for business, usually congregated in the middle gallery. In *St. Stephen's Green*, a Dublin comedy written a year or so after Dunton's visit, the affectedly modest Lady Volant condemns the imprudent attitudes of certain Dublin gentlewomen toward the playhouse proprieties:

And was not my Lady Blameless in a Mask in the Gallery? and was not Mrs. Wellbred heard most Impiously and Obscenely to wish it were the Custom in this Town for Women to sit in the Pit?[2]

The prologue to *St. Stephen's Green* emphasizes how the Dublin gallants

> Strut in the Pit, Survey the Gallery,
> In hopes to be lur'd up by some kind She.[3]

For the male majority the gallery witches added an indispensable charm to attendance at Smock Alley.

The 'ticket' which Dunton got at the playhouse entrance and delivered up to the pit doorkeeper was a round metal check. It corresponded in its markings to the one seventeenth-century Irish theatre 'ticket' now known. On one side, this specimen has stamped the British crown; underneath it, 'WM^{RR}' [William and Mary, Rex et Regina]; and then below this royal monogram, in three lines, 'The Upper/Gallery/

---

[1] *The Dublin Scuffle*, pp. 339–40.
[2] p. 49.   [3] ll. 15–16.

Theater Royall'. Stamped on the other side is Ireland's coat of arms encircled by laurel branches.[1] Dunton's check, however, must have read 'Pit' instead of 'Upper Gallery'. He presumably paid for it either half a crown or three British shillings. At this period admission to the upper gallery cost one British shilling; to the middle gallery, two shillings; to the lattices, probably three shillings; to the boxes, either four or five shillings.[2]

Upper Gallery check, Smock Alley Theatre, c. 1692–4.

The performance of *The Squire of Alsatia* which Dunton witnessed began somewhat later than the Smock Alley performances before the Williamite wars. If Dublin followed London's lead, as it almost surely did, then the curtain now rose at 4.00 or 4.30. After 1700 curtain time was advanced to 5.00, then in a few years to 5.30, and eventually to 6.00. The installation of city-wide street lighting by oil lamps in 1697 rendered the evening hours tolerable for those theatregoers who had to find their way home on foot.

In the latter part of July 1698 when 'his Grace ye Duke of Ormon[de] went to Kilkenny, the players with all their appurtenances strol[l]ed thither, to entertain ye Company there, as they gave out, tho everie one knows, where ye Carrion is, the Crows will follow, for Dublin was then without much of the people that are usually in it, many of them in the Summer

---

[1] See *Scribner's Magazine*, ix (May 1891), 635, and the reproduction herein.

[2] These figures are based upon the scale of prices in the theatres of Restoration London. The London and the Dublin scales must have nearly coincided, for Robert Ware in 1678 mentioned the cost for an upper gallery seat in Dublin as one shilling, the same price as in London. The theatrical advertisements in the Dublin newspapers from the 1730's onwards reflect in Irish currency what the earlier prices must have been.

retiring into ye Country'.[1] This rather caustic report by Dunton
does not paint a proper background for the Smock Alley
troupe's historic innovation. The present Duke of Ormonde,
the second of that title, had returned the year previous from
campaigning under King William in France and was now
acclaimed Ireland's most brilliant peer. Following in the steps
of his grandfather, the noted Lord-Lieutenant, he had set himself up as a warm patron of the Theatre Royal in Dublin and
had suggested, if not issued a definite invitation, that its company offer stage entertainment in his Kilkenny demesne. He
thereby inaugurated the first summer tour in the provinces by
an Irish troupe and created a precedent which took on far-
reaching importance in the next century.

The town of Kilkenny with a population of 7,000[2] and many
'fair' buildings,[3] including the distinguished 'College', possessed
unusual beauty, refinement, and wealth. The Ormonde family
dominated the community. Their castle was one of the show
places of Europe, 'rich on every side with marble, and ornamented with many things so curious, that those who have seen
it say that it surpasses many palaces of Italy'.[4] It contained
a 'Noble Gallery, which, for length, variety of gilded Chairs,
and the curious Pictures that adorn it, has no equal in the
Three Kingdoms, and perhaps not in Europe'.[5] The castle
grounds, 'finer than the Privy-Garden in Whitehall',[6] comprised 'Bowling green, Gardens, Walks, Orchards and a delightfull Waterhouse adjoining to the Bowling Green. . . . This
Waterhouse hath a pleasant summer banquetting room floor'd
and lin'd with white and black marble . . . with a painted skye
roof with Angells'.[7] In that idyllic setting the Smock Alley
players quite possibly entertained the Duke and his guests.

The Kilkenny performances were not confined, however, to
fashionable affairs at Ormonde Castle; at least some took place

---

[1] MS. Rawlinson D. 71, f. 25. Stockwell, p. 43, places the Kilkenny tour in
1699, but thereby contradicts herself, for on p. 41 she dates Dunton's Dublin
sojourn as 1698.

[2] MacLysaght, p. 194.

[3] Thomas Dineley (or Dingley), 'Observations in a Voyage through the Kingdom of Ireland', National Library of Ireland MS. 392, p. 202.

[4] Albert Jouvin de Rochefort, *Description of England and Ireland after the Restoration*,
as printed in Falkiner, p. 415.

[5] *The Dublin Scuffle*, p. 373.   [6] Ibid.   [7] Dineley, p. 202.

in the town before all sorts of persons, as an amusing incident related by Dunton proves:

'Twas reported in Dublin, that one Wilks, one of the best Actors, had play'd his last part, being kill'd in a Duel; this Report was so far believ'd, that an Ingenious Person writ an Elegy upon him, which was Printed and publickly Sold. This News of his Death was talk'd with such Assurance, that though Mr. Wilks soon after came to Dublin, and shew'd himself alive, they wou'd hardly believe him. The ground of this Report (as I was told) arose from this, That a *Countryman* seeing a Tragedy acted in Kilkenny, wherein Mr. Wilks acted the part of one that was to be kill'd, thought it was real, and so reported it.[1]

If during the next fifty years the Kilkenny citizens saw a Dublin company in another summer repertory, notice of the visit has been lost. It is difficult to understand why Ashbury never repeated the experiment.

While the Smock Alley players were sojourning at Kilkenny, Dunton took a sightseeing trip north of Dublin, staying among other places at the 'handsome, clean, Englishlike town'[2] of Drogheda, an old walled port of four to five thousand inhabitants. Here he happened upon an ambitious programme of private theatricals at the learned Mr. Walker's school. 'His Scholars were acting *Henry IV* and a Latin Play out of Terence; they were all Ingenious Lads, and performed their parts to a wonder; but one Ellwood (who acted Falstaffe) bore away the Bell from the whole School.'[3] This is the earliest instance of secular dramatics in an Irish school. Within the following half-century school plays of this kind came to be a frequent occurrence in some Irish towns and, eventually, helped to cultivate an audience for town theatres.

When the Smock Alley Theatre reopened in the fall of 1698, it exhibited a goodly number of accessions to its personnel. The most interesting female addition was twenty-one-year-old Miss Cross, whom London's Theatre Royal had been hailing as a second Nell Gwynn.[4] Apparently she had fallen suddenly into

---

[1] *The Dublin Scuffle*, pp. 341–2.
[2] MS. Rawlinson D. 71, f. 22.
[3] *The Dublin Scuffle*, p. 383.
[4] The Prologue to Thomas D'Urfey's *Don Quixote, Part III* (Drury Lane, 1695),

the snares of love, abandoned Drury Lane for a brief Continental elopement, and then, to avoid ridicule for her folly, taken herself to Ireland to enrol under Ashbury. In one of his racy epilogues 'Jo' Haynes in mourning attire lamented the flight of Drury Lane's incendiary hoyden:

Oh Collier! Collier! [the notorious stage reformer] Thou'st frighted
    away Miss Cross.
She to return our Foreigner's complizance
At Cupid's call, has made a Trip to France.
Love's Fire Arms here are since not worth a sous.
We've lost the only Touch-hole of our House.[1]

Known as 'Mrs.' Cross at Smock Alley she met so warm a response to her stage coquetry in Dublin that she did not return to Drury Lane until the winter of 1704–5.[2]

Among the male new-comers to Smock Alley there were two most promising novices: Thomas (later called 'Little') Griffith,[3] a Dubliner, aged eighteen; and Barton Booth, a Lancashireman, seventeen years old.[4] The latter made his début in *Oroonoko: or, The Royal Slave*, Southerne's tragedy of African slaves in Surinam on the South American coast. On his first and also second appearances Booth suffered odd accidents:

It being very warm Weather, in his last Scene of the Play, as he waited to go on, he inadvertently wip'd his Face, that when he

is spoken by Mr. Horden and Miss Cross. She boasts of the attention which the men pay to her:
            Some by Diversion of my Voice—and some
            In expectation of my Prime to come.
Horden then comments:
            Your interest with the Sparks is wondrous strong.
            Child, th' art three years too young.
Evidently Miss Cross at that time was eighteen, three years short of the accepted 'prime' or 'majority' age of twenty-one. In 1696 she played Miss Hoyden in Sir John Vanbrugh's new comedy, *The Relapse: or, Virtue in Danger*. Miss Cross is addressed as 'little Cherubim' in *The Female Wits: or, The Triumvirate of Poets at Rehearsal* (Drury Lane, 1697). See Genest, ii. 99, 103.
   [1] The Epilogue to George Farquhar's first comedy, *Love and a Bottle* (Drury Lane, *c.* Nov. or Dec. 1698).
   [2] The Drury Lane bill for 2 Jan. 1704/5, advertising Colley Cibber's *The Careless Husband* with songs and dances by 'Mrs.' Cross, stated that it was her first London appearance in five years. See Genest, ii. 318.
   [3] Chetwood, p. 164.   [4] Ibid., p. 91.

enter'd he had the Appearance of a Chimney-Sweeper (his own Words). At his Entrance, he was surpriz'd at the Variety of Noises he heard in the Audience (for he knew not what he had done) that a little confounded him, till he receiv'd an extraordinary Clap of Applause, which settl'd his Mind. The Play [*Oroonoko*] was desir'd for the next Night of Acting, when an Actress fitted a Crape to his Face with an Opening proper for the Mouth, and shap'd in form for the Nose; But in the first Scene, one Part of the Crape slip[p]'d off. And 'Zounds!' said he, (he was a little apt to swear) 'I look'd like a Magpie! When I came off they Lampblack'd me for the Rest of the Night, that I was flead [skinned] before it [the lampblack] could be got off again.'[1]

In addition to Booth and Griffith, Ashbury signed on two experienced and vigorous actors from London: William Bowen (b. 1666), a spirited Irishman 'easily drawn to mutiny',[2] and Joseph Trefusis, a Smock Alley figure before 1688, a fellow of shrewd humorous conceits with 'a long Chin, and a naturally most consummate foolish face'.[3] In order to procure from England performers of quality Ashbury seems to have revised about this time the organization of his company and, in accordance with London practice, instituted a shareholding corporation wherein a few leading players became 'sharers' in the annual profits.[4] One of the early shareholders later made the interesting assertion that 'most of the sharers at the time of the death of King William [in March 1702] had some profession besides Playing, or were known not to be in want of money'.[5]

For the season of 1698–9 the company numbered around thirty, the same number that played Scotland in 1681, but the present troupe represented a considerably finer array of acting talent—indeed, the finest since the beginning of the Theatre Royal in Dublin. The roster included the following:

Men	*Women*
Joseph Ashbury	Mrs. Ann Ashbury
Barton Booth	,, Elizabeth Buckley

[1] Chetwood, pp. 91–92. [2] Nicoll, p. 378; Genest, ii. 155.
[3] Chetwood, p. 169.
[4] 'The Case of John Thurmond' in Appendix B.
[5] See 'The Most Humble Answer of John Thurmond' in Appendix B.

PLATE V

BARTON BOOTH

MRS. CROSS

RICHARD LEVERIDGE

JAMES QUIN

William Bowen	Mrs. Cross
Richard Buckley	,, Elliott
Richard Estcourt	,, Harrison
— Elliott	,, Mary Hook
Thomas Griffith	,, Knightly
Benjamin Husband(s)	,, Martin
Theophilus Keen	,, Sarah Norris
— Longmore	,, Mary Norton
Henry Norris	,, Schoolding
Hugh Norton	,, Smith
— Schoolding	,, Elizabeth Wilks
Joseph Trefusis	
Robert Wilks	

With six natural comedians, Booth, Estcourt, Griffith, Norris, Trefusis, and Wilks, this was a company much more expert in the lighter dramatic vein. Hence Ashbury planned his repertoire accordingly and, during the single season of 1698–9, put on all three of Sir George Etherege's debonair satires of Restoration manners. Happily, Griffith preserved the casts:[1]

The Comical Revenge

Booth = Colonel Bruce	Mrs. Ashbury = Aurelia
Bowen = Dufoy	,, Harrison = Laetitia
Buckley = Lord Beaufort	,, Hook = Mrs. Rich
Estcourt = Wheedle	,, Knightly = Graciana
Keen = Louis	,, Martin = Mrs. Grace
Norris = Sir Nicholas Cully	,, Schoolding = Jenny
Schoolding = Lord Bevil	
Trefusis = Palmer	
Wilks = Sir Frederick Frolic	

She Would if She Could

Booth = Mr. Freeman	Mrs. Ashbury = Mrs. Sentry
Estcourt = Sir Joscelin Jolly	,, Harrison = Mrs. Gazet
Griffith = Mr. Rakehell	,, Hook = Gatty
Norris = Sir Oliver Cockwood	,, Martin = Mrs. Trinket
Trefusis = Thomas	,, Schoolding = Ariana
Wilks = Mr. Courtal	,, Smith = Lady Cockwood

[1] Chetwood, pp. 54–55.

The Man of Mode

Booth = Medley		Mrs. Ashbury = Harriet
Bowen = Shoemaker		,, Cross = Orange-Woman
Estcourt = Old Bellair		,, Elliott = Emilia
Elliott = Young Bellair		,, Harrison = Busy
Griffith = Sir Fopling		,, Hook = Pert
Norris = Handy		,, Knightly = Mrs. Loveit
Trefusis = Parson		,, Martin = Lady Woodvil
Wilks = Dorimant		,, Schoolding = Belinda
		,, Smith = Lady Townley

With so many skilled male performers of comedy Ashbury apparently elected for the time being to hold himself in reserve. His wife, after her irregular appearances some years back, was once again playing the leading young lady, while Mrs. Smith continued as the chief impersonator of dowagers or elderly women. Mrs. Ashbury 'had an amiable Person, a sweet, inno-cent, modest, winning Countenance', but in her acting never climbed 'to the Summit of Perfection'.[1] According to a close professional observer, she excelled as the supposedly naïve Mrs. Pinchwife in William Wycherley's comedy, *The Country Wife*.[2] Until long after 1700 the Dublin actresses as a group seem to have been much less impressive than the actors. This inferiority on the distaff side may, in large measure, be accounted for by the fact that a majority of the women gained admission to the company not because they had shown pronounced stage talents but because they were actors' wives.

The years 1699 and 1700 saw numerous changes in the Smock Alley personnel. John Evans, Philip Griffin, Richard Leveridge, and John Thurmond, all four with experience on the London stage, joined the company in the fall of 1699. Leveridge stayed but one season; Griffin two.[3] Leveridge, one of London's outstanding composers and bass singers, had sought temporary refuge in Ireland from a multitude of debtors. At Christmas 1699, that famous man of the theatre, Sir John Vanbrugh, lamented: 'Liveridge is in Ireland, he owes so much money he dare not come over, so for want of him we han't had one opera play'd this Winter.'[4] During his Irish exile Leveridge

---

[1] Chetwood, p. 86.   [2] Ibid.   [3] Genest, ii. 232.
[4] *The Complete Works of Sir John Vanbrugh* (ed. Bonamy Dobrée and Geoffrey Webb, London, 1927–8), iv. 4.

made himself very useful to Smock Alley by writing a number
of songs for Dublin plays, such as 'Marinda's Face like Cupid's
Bow is drawn to shoot at Hearts',[1] and the duet in *St. Stephen's
Green* with the refrain 'You, Bellamira, we admire'.[2] Evans,
rather indolent and 'inclineable to the Gross',[3] and Thurmond,[4]
merry but irresponsible, soon became sharers and remained in
Dublin for many years. Thurmond was on salary only for his
first season and got eighty pounds for his services.[5] But Ashbury's losses at this time more than offset the additions. Bowen,
Griffith, the Norrises, and the Wilkses left for London in 1699,[6]
and Booth and Husband(s) followed them in 1700.[7]

The departure of Wilks took on all the colourful point
counterpoint of a stage situation, if Wilks's first biographer may
be believed.[8] As the company's principal comedians Mrs.
Ashbury and Wilks were, of course, thrown much together.
Ashbury, aroused by town gossip about the two, began to sus-
pect Wilks of being 'amorously inclined', and finally became
convinced that the latter was having an affair with his wife.
He intimated as much to the young actor. 'If the Tittle-Tattle
of the Multitude shall be received as a Demonstration, or admitted as a sufficient Proof, whose Reputation is safe?' said
Wilks, and asserted not only his entire innocence but his wish
to restore the husband's 'former Tranquillity and Peace of
Mind'. To this Ashbury replied, 'The Arrow is lodged too deep
in my Breast to be drawn out with Safety.' 'Well,' said Wilks,
'in a very little Time I will put it out of the Power of Malice
to say that you shall disquiet yourself for the future on my
Account.' He then quietly proceeded to negotiate with Drury
Lane Theatre. At the same time Mrs. Ashbury tried to pacify
her husband by delivering a sworn statement of her innocence
to the rector of St. Michans before the Communion table. The
rector in turn brought the statement to Ashbury. The theatre
manager, twenty years older than his wife, still would not put
away all his irritation and suspicion. Mrs. Ashbury therefore

---

[1] 'A New Song set by Mr. Leveridge, Sung att the Theater in Dublin', *Mercurius Musicus* (London), Mar.–Apr. 1700.

[2] pp. 72–73.   [3] Chetwood, p. 143.
[4] Genest, ii. 172.   [5] See 'The Case of John Thurmond' in Appendix B.
[6] Genest, ii. 165, 168.   [7] Ibid., ii. 227, 240.
[8] O'Bryan, pp. 14–17.

begged to be permitted to give up acting, but her husband
refused the plea because he thought her too important an
actress to lose. At last Wilks broke the news to Ashbury that
he was leaving for Drury Lane. The jealous husband was now
transformed into the distraught manager. He used 'all his
Power and Rhetorick' to dissuade Wilks. The latter would not,
however, alter his decision. He soon went to England, never to
return to Dublin to act regularly.

Other than the Etherege comedies Smock Alley activities
about the turn of the century remain almost wholly unrecorded.[1] In 1699 or 1700 there was 'acted at the Theatre-Royal,
in Dublin' a newly-written comedy, *St. Stephen's Green: or, The
Generous Lovers*,[2] by William Philips, son of George Philips,
Governor of Londonderry from 1681 to 1684.[3] The play contains the usual romantic plot and repartee of the Restoration
'manners' genre, mixed with intrigue and characters typical of
the older comedy of humours. None the less, *St. Stephen's Green*
is a drama of importance because its presentation of Dublin
setting and talk makes it the first Smock Alley production to
depict local background and people. Philips began his dedica-
tion to the Earl of Inchiquin with the significant remark, 'My
Lord, This Play has a double Reson for seeking Shelter under
your Lordship; I Writ it, and for our Irish Stage, and you are

---

[1] Stockwell, pp. 43–44, accepts two unauthenticated facts about the 1700 and
1701 seasons from Thomas Wilkes. First, the latter claims that Farquhar's *The
Constant Couple* was performed in Dublin twenty-three nights at this time, but he
offers no authority and gives no details. (See *The Complete Works of George Farquhar*,
I. xvi.) Second, Wilkes gives a colourful account of the fall of the Smock Alley
galleries on 26 Dec. 1701. (*A General View of the Stage*, pp. 308–9.) Though he does
not so state, his source for this occurrence is *A Chronology of Some Memorable Accidents*
(Dublin, 1743), p. 89, which under 1701 reports: 'St. Stephen's Day the Play-
House in Smock-Ally fell, whereby several were kill'd, and Hurt.' The report is
obviously a careless misdating of the accident which occurred on St. Stephen's
Day, 1670. Wilkes has embellished the report with some details from the 1670
affair, and has changed the identity of the play to Shadwell's *The Libertine*. Then
he has added matter of his own about popular gossip at the time, that 'the candles
burnt blue and went out', and that a mysterious dancer with a cloven foot made
several appearances on the stage. It is significant that Chetwood, the earlier historian, makes no mention of any such event. Hitchcock, i. 33, follows Wilkes's lead.

[2] *St. Stephen's Green or The Generous Lovers. A Comedy, As it is Acted at the
Theatre-Royal, in Dublin. Written by Will. Philips, Esq; Dublin, Printed by
John Brocas in School-House-Lane; And are to be Sold by the Booksellers, 1700.

[3] See *D.N.B.*, xv 1068.

the chief Friend which either has.' Here is the earliest admission
by a native author of a concern for a self-contained and distinctive theatre in Ireland. Philips felt a deep attachment to
his Irish heritage and deplored his countrymen's habit of
depreciating their birthright. He neatly voiced his condemna-
tion through the English servant of Freelove, a gentleman
newly arrived in Dublin from London:

> I have observ'd that none Despise *Ireland* so much as those who
> thrive best in it. And none are so severe in their Reflections upon it,
> as those who owe their Birth and Fortune to it; I have known
> many of 'em, when they come first to London, think there is no way
> so ready to purchase the Title of a Wit, as to Ridicule their own
> Country.[1]

Hence it was in large measure Philips's patriotic feeling
which led him to be interested in the promotion of stage amusement at the Irish capital:

> I shou'd be extremely pleas'd, if my Success wou'd move any other
> who has a happier Genius, to divert this Town with some Perfor-
> mance of this kind.[2]

No doubt he was encouraged in his effort by the fact that an
ever-growing number of Dublin residents, even the more conservative and godly sort, viewed the Theatre Royal as a respect-
able and influential agency for public entertainment. In a
sermon preached before the Societies for the Reformation of
Manners in 1700, the Reverend Daniel Williams protested
against the increased patronage of the stage:

> I hear some Professors and Church Members are grown so loose
> as to frequent and plead for those nurseries and schools of wicked-
> ness, the Play houses, places the Devil claimeth as his own.[3]

Yet attacks, however vitriolic, by the rigidly pious could not
offset the trend in Ireland, as in England, for middle- and
lower-class citizens to indulge in theatregoing. By the time
King William III died on 8 March 1701/2, the Smock Alley
playhouse had ceased to be merely the plaything of the viceregal coterie and its fashionable hangers-on.

[1] p. 52.   [2] Epistle Dedicatory to *St. Stephen's Green*.
[3] Gilbert, ii. 70.

CHAPTER VI

The Smock Alley Theatre in the Reign of Queen Anne

THE succession of Princess Anne to the crown of the Three Kingdoms in 1702 produced no marked change in the progress of Dublin or of its Theatre Royal, usually designated the 'Queen's Theatre' during her reign. English restrictions on Irish industry and trade multiplied. The economy of Ireland as a whole deteriorated year by year, but her capital city went on prospering since it came more and more to be the constant resort of people from all parts of the island and of numerous overseas visitors on mercantile as well as governmental missions. Furthermore, an increasing number of the landed nobility and gentry were providing themselves with town houses for periodic occupancy, especially during the sessions of the Parliament. In the early years of the eighteenth century Dublin's population rose to seventy-five or eighty thousand,[1] while its limits steadily expanded, in particular to the east and west on the south side of the Liffey. The swampy lowlands in the direction of Ringsend were being filled and built upon. An extensive fashionable area was spreading toward the river in the neighbourhood of St. Stephen's Green, the gardens and the mall of which rivalled aristocratic St. James's Park, London.[2] To the north of the Green on Dawson Street the city in 1715 established an impressive official home for its lord mayor by purchasing the splendid mansion which gave name to the street. Another exclusive residential district was growing up on the south-west in the vicinity of historic Thomas Court and of the twentieth-century Guinness's brewery. As a principal attraction for this region, a large artificial basin of water laid out with

---

[1] An estimate based on MacLysaght, p. 187, and on *A Description of the City of Dublin in Ireland* (London, 1732), p. 4.
[2] *A Description*, pp. 24–25.

fountains and surrounded by green walks was constructed south of James's Street.[1] Phoenix Park on the far western outskirts was also becoming a rendezvous for 'the quality'.[2] In the midst of its 'delightful wood' there now existed, as in London's Hyde Park, a coaching ring encircled by a wall, 'where the beaux and belles resorted in fair weather'.[3] Thus the gaiety and splendour of the capital kept mounting in contrast to the steady impoverishment of the Irish nation.

King William's death closed Smock Alley for the period of official mourning through March and April 1702. Knowing that this long cessation of performance would cause financial hardship to many of the company, several kind-hearted ladies of the city's high society arranged a plan of weekly subscription for the support of the actors. That plausible rascal of the playhouse, John Thurmond, heard of the scheme, 'obliged Bowman, the then Boxkeeper, to shew him where those Ladys lived, and received the subscription, applying it to his own Use, tho' the Boxkeeper did believe he shared it with the Company'.[4] Thurmond's conduct appeared the more reprehensible because several of his fellows 'were at that time in very great Extremity'.[5] This proved to be only the first of a series of colourful incidents which demonstrated in the next half-dozen years that 'Mr. Thurmond did in all things during his being a Sharer pursue his own private Ends to the mighty prejudice of the Company'.[6]

Performers on the Dublin stage continued in Queen Anne's reign to shuttle back and forth between England and Ireland as much as ever. With the beginning of the 1702–3 season Smock Alley lost to London Mrs. Hook and Mrs. Martin,[7] two of the most able Dublin actresses of the period. A year later, however, the company received from London Mrs. Martin again,[8] Mrs. Wilkins of Drury Lane,[9] and two superior actors, William Bowen[10] and Thomas Griffith,[11] both of them already

---

[1] Ibid.   [2] Ibid.
[3] Falkiner, 'The Phoenix Park: Its Origin and Early History', *Proceedings of the Royal Irish Academy*, 3rd series, vi, no. 3, p. 481.
[4] See 'The Sharers' Reply' in Appendix B.
[5] See 'The Case of the Patentee and Sharers' in Appendix B.
[6] Ibid.   [7] Genest, ii. 255.
[8] Ibid., p. 293.   [9] Ibid., p. 276.
[10] Ibid., p. 269.   [11] Ibid., p. 263.

familiar to Dublin audiences. In the summer of 1704 Richard Estcourt left Ireland permanently to join the Drury Lane troupe.[1] For a decade he had shone as one of Smock Alley's leading comedians and had attained such public esteem that he was chosen to deliver the poem of public welcome to James, the second Duke of Ormonde, when as the new Lord-Lieutenant he was given a great civic reception in June 1703.[2] Another Dublin veteran, Theophilus Keen, followed Estcourt within a few months.[3] In January 1704/5 the restive and fiery Mr. Bowen 'left off playing on account of some Disgust'[4] and soon turned up in London on the Haymarket stage.[5] Before long he vented his spleen against Ashbury by petitioning the queen that, since Ashbury was 'very ancient' and Ashbury's son Charles was dead, the Irish theatre patent granted to them in 1683 should be bestowed upon the petitioner, Bowen, at Ashbury's death.[6] This brash appeal came to nothing.

Sometime in 1704 George Farquhar, now a successful London playwright, journeyed to Dublin to visit his friends and 'lodged at his brother's, who kept a bookseller's shop in Castle-street; he proposed publishing his works by subscription; but not meeting with encouragement according to his expectations, he was advised to have a Benefit Play, and to perform a character in it'.[7] The actor-playwright therefore decided to appear as Sir Harry Wildair in his own comedy, *The Constant Couple*. Fortunately the present Lord-Lieutenant, Ormonde, was a devoted supporter of Dublin theatricals. His Grace 'honoured the performance with his presence'[8] and occasioned a crowded house. Farquhar netted from the benefit one hundred pounds instead of the usual fifty,[9] but 'he executed the role so lamely,

[1] Genest, ii. 311.

[2] See 'A Speech delivered to the Duke of Ormond on his Entertainment in Dublin by the Citizens, written and spoken by the late R. Estcourt' in Matthew Concanen, *Miscellaneous Poems by Several Hands* (London, 1724), p. 268. Ormonde was sworn in at Dublin on 4 June 1703.

[3] Genest, ii. 320.

[4] *Impartial Occurrences, Foreign and Domestic* (Dublin), 23 Jan. 1704/5.

[5] Genest, ii. 330.

[6] *Hist. MSS. Commission: Report on the Manuscripts of his Grace the Duke of Portland* (London, 1907), viii. 358. The report gives the probable date of the petition as between 1704 and 1708.

[7] Farquhar, *Works* (Dublin, 1775), i. ix.

[8] Ibid.   [9] Wilkes, p. 312.

as an actor, that his Friends were ashamed for him'.[1] Without any more fanfare he took his final exit from his native land.

About a year subsequent to the Farquhar performance the Duke of Ormonde once more displayed his devotion to the Dublin theatre on the eve of his departure for a long stay abroad. Realizing that his absence might have an adverse effect on its fortunes, he publicly appealed to the Lords Justices and the nobility of the Irish kingdom to undertake a subscription for the support of the Smock Alley Players.[2] Strangely enough, the company chose the unreliable Mr. Thurmond to wait upon the prominent subscribers and receive their contributions. On this occasion, however, he brought in his collection of some sixty pounds and divided honestly with his fellow actors.[3]

Thurmond, to be sure, possessed a most ingratiating manner which made him a favourite with the gentlemen who frequented the playhouse. It was a custom of the period for officials of distinction to give to an admired actor the new clothes which they had worn at their birthday celebrations. Between 1703 and 1708 Thurmond skilfully managed to be presented with at least three 'birthday suits': the first by the Duke of Ormonde; the second by John, Lord Cutts, Commander-in-Chief of the Army in Ireland, 1705–7; the third by General Richard Ingoldsby, Commander-in-Chief, 1707–12.[4] Unfortunately the birthday suits and other articles of stage finery which Thurmond got into his hands excited his propensity for financial chicanery. In 1705 or 1706 Smock Alley was preparing a production of the still popular Restoration opera, *The Island Princess: or, The Generous Portuguese,* by Pierre Motteux. Thurmond and his wife, Winifred, were allowed twelve pounds 'for making and Embellishing some Spanish Shapes' for the opera. Yet neither of the Thurmonds 'would deliver up the Dresses the day that the Play was to be Acted, unless the Sharers would oblige themselves to pay the sum of fifty-two Pounds for the same, tho' barely worth the sum agreed for'.[5] Outraged by this demand,

---

[1] Chetwood, p. 154 n. [2] See 'The Sharers' Reply'.
[3] See 'The Most Humble Answer of John Thurmond' in Appendix B.
[4] See 'The Sharers' Reply' and Chetwood, p. 224.
[5] See 'The Sharers' Reply'.

the company called upon their most influential patron, Lord Cutts, to intervene. His Excellency at once commanded Thurmond 'to deliver the Shapes, and severely chid him for Endeavouring at so great an Imposition'.[1]

Next, the spendthrift actor turned to pawning his birthday suits plus several costumes belonging to the company, namely, 'a Roman Shape, two Spanish Shapes, and a Modern Coat trim[m]'d with Silver'.[2] This method of raising funds nearly led to his complete disgrace in the eyes of his aristocratic benefactors. During the season of 1707–8 he 'put in Buckle [a cant word for Forty in the Hundred Interest]'[3] the rich suit with which General Ingoldsby had recently honoured him:

One night notice was given that the General would be present with the Government at the play, and all the performers on the stage were preparing to dress out in the suits presented. The spouse of Johnny (as he was commonly called) try'd all her arts to persuade Mr. Holdfast, the pawnbroker (as it fell out, his real name) to let go the Cloaths for that evening, to be returned when the play was over; but all arguments were fruitless; nothing but the ready, or a pledge of full equal value. . . . Well! what must be done? The whole Family in confusion, and all at their wits end; Disgrace, with her glaring eyes, and extended mouth, ready to devour. . . . At last Winny, the wife, . . . put on a compos'd countenance . . .; stepp'd to a neighbouring tavern, and bespoke a very hot negus [wine with nutmeg, lemon, and sugar], to comfort Johnny in the great part he was to perform that night, begging to have the silver tankard with the lid, because, as she said, a covering, and the vehicle silver, would retain heat longer than any other metal. The request was comply'd with, the negus carry'd to the playhouse, piping hot—popp'd into a vile earthern mug—the Tankard *L'argent* travelled incog. under her apron (like the Persian ladies veil'd), popp'd into the pawnbroker's hands in exchange for the suit—the latter put on, and play'd its part, with the rest of the wardrobe; when its duty was over, carried back to remain in its old depository—the tankard return'd the right road; and, when the tide flowed with its lunar influence, the stranded suit was wafted into safe harbour again, after paying a little for dry docking, which was all the damage receiv'd.[4]

[1] See 'The Sharers' Reply'.   [2] Ibid.
[3] Chetwood, p. 224.   [4] Ibid., pp. 224–5.

Early in 1708 Thurmond's finances had reached so desperate a condition that his army friends, the officers of two regiments stationed at Dublin, subscribed a day's pay to enable him 'to continue in the Kingdom'.[1] Their generosity did not long avail. McKensie, a tailor, had Thurmond arrested for a debt of fourteen pounds. Ashbury, on the actor's promise to repay him by an agreed date, settled the debt and procured Thurmond's release. In a little while Ashbury heard that Thurmond, who had failed to reimburse him as promised, designed 'quitting the Kingdome, under the pretence of going into the Country'.[2] Hence the theatre manager brought action to recover his loan. The bailiffs accordingly seized Thurmond 'with his Bootes on'.[3] Ashbury, however, soon had his irresponsible colleague released at the intercession of Evans and Griffith, who guaranteed payment. Then Thurmond persuaded the company to allow him a benefit play before any of the others in the customary spring schedule. Finally, to cap the climax of his misbehaviour, he proceeded, without paying any part of his debt from the proceeds of his benefit and without acting in any of the other benefits, to desert in May to Drury Lane.[4] Not only did he 'unhandsomely' break his articles and bonds as a sharer, but he also left the Smock Alley Company 'involv'd in many grievous Debts . . . and disjoynted their whole Stock of Plays for want of his parts'.[5]

A little previous to Thurmond's desertion the Dublin troupe suffered another mishap. John Verbruggen for twenty years had been a leading London actor, noted especially for such tragic roles as Bajazet in Nicholas Rowe's *Tamerlane* and Alexander in Nathaniel Lee's *The Rival Queens*. Tall, well-built, in-kneed, shambling in gait, 'he was an Original and had a Roughness in his Manner, and a negligent Wildness in his Action and his Mien, which became him well'.[6] In the fall of 1707, when the London theatres were heavily beset by financial troubles and their reorganization imminent, Verbruggen, now a widower, evidently found his situation unsatisfactory and crossed to Ireland

---

[1] See 'The Sharers' Reply'. [2] Ibid.
[3] Ibid. [4] Ibid.; Genest, ii. 403.
[5] See 'The Case of the Patentee and Sharers'.
[6] *The Laureate: Or, The Right Side of Colley Cibber, Esq.* (London, 1740), p. 58.

to act.[1] His coming promised to add considerable strength to the Dublin company. Unfortunately his Irish career turned out to be brief. The only known detail of his Smock Alley tenure is that he was cast as the Governor of Barcelona in *The Spanish Wives*, a popular Restoration farce by Mrs. Mary Griffith Pix; but, according to the still existent prompt-book, he was withdrawn from the part before the performance,[2] presumably on account of illness. By April 1708 he had died,[3] probably at Dublin, since no London notice of his decease ever appeared.

The Smock Alley prompt copy of *The Spanish Wives* indicates that the playhouse was still employing much the same collection of scenery as it had in stock a quarter-century earlier. Though only two sets are specifically recorded, the 'Chamber'[4] and the '[Garde]n Scene [wi]th Wall',[5] both of these recall similar sets described in the Smock Alley Shakespeare folio, especially the 'Garden' in *Macbeth*, Acts I and IV.

With the assistance of this same prompt-book[6] the major

[1] Verbruggen's last London appearance was at the Haymarket Theatre in Aug. 1707 (Genest, ii. 375).

[2] The Smock Alley prompt copy of *The Spanish Wives* (London, 1696, quarto), now reposing in the Harvard Theatre Collection, was called to my attention by Dr. William Van Lennep, who had identified it and completed those marginal prompt notes that had been cut into by a later binder. The volume bears the signature of its one-time owner, Adam Hallam, a member of the original cast. John Verbruggen's name, spelled 'Verbracken', appears only on the page of 'The Actors Names', written opposite the part of the Governor of Barcelona. The Governor's speeches on pp. 6, 24, 36, 44, 47 of the text bear in the margin manuscript annotations identifying 'Mr Goddard' as the actual performer.

[3] The approximate date of Verbruggen's death is determined by the fact that Drury Lane Theatre gave a benefit on 26 Apr. 1708 'for a young orphan child of the late Mr. and Mrs. Verbruggen' (Genest, ii. 401). Mrs. Verbruggen died in 1703.

[4] p. 1.   [5] p. 22.

[6] The Smock Alley cast is written in alongside the printed 'Actors Names', as follows:

Mr Verbracken = Governor of Barcelona
    Longmore = Marquis of Moncada
[Mrs.] Fitzgerald = Camillus
    Thurmond = Colonel Peregrine
    Evans = Friar Andrew
    Hallam = Hidewell
    (blank) = Diego

Mrs Thurmond = The Governor's Lady
Wilkins = Elenora, Moncada's wife
(blank) = Spywell, woman to the Governor's Lady
(blank) = Orada, woman to Elenora

In addition, prompt notes within the play's text indicate Bowman as Servant to

portion of the Smock Alley personnel for the season of 1707–8 can be enumerated:

Men	Women
Joseph Ashbury	Mrs. Ann Ashbury
John Bowman	,, Elizabeth Buckley
Richard Buckley	,, Fitzgerald
George Daugherty	,, Martin
John Evans	,, Schoolding
— Goddard	,, Winifred Thurmond
Thomas Griffith	,, Wilkins
Adam Hallam	,, Wolf
— Kendall	
— Longmore	
— Schoolding	
John Thurmond	
John Thurmond, Jr.	
Joseph Trefusis	
John Verbruggen	

Ashbury, Evans, Griffith, Thurmond, and possibly the veterans Buckley and Trefusis, composed the group of sharers.[1] Trefusis was now Dublin's leading comedian and a great favourite because of his inimitable clownish antics. On one occasion he danced the awkward Country Clown so well that General Ingoldsby, always a most enthusiastic and generous patron of the actors, in delight sent Trefusis

Five Guineas from the Box where he sat. Jo dressed himself next Day, and went to the Castle to return Thanks. The General was hard to be persuaded it was the same Person; but Jo soon convinc'd him, by saying, *Ise the very Mon, an't please your Ex-cell-en-cey*; and, at the same time, twirling his Hat, as he did in the Dance, with his consummate foolish Face and Scrape. *Nay, now I am convinced*, reply'd the General (laughing), *and thou shalt not show such a Face for nothing here*—So gave Jo Five Guineas more.[2]

Colonel Peregrine, Daugherty as Diego, Kendall as Servant to Camillus, Mrs. Martin as Orada, and Mrs. Wolf as Spywell. The repeated annotations on pp. 3, 25, 45 prove beyond question that Mrs. Fitzgerald took the role of the Roman count, Camillus. She still 'generally play'd the Part of a young Man' in 1714–15, according to Chetwood, p. 58 n.

[1] See 'The Case of the Patentee and Sharers'.
[2] Chetwood, p. 170.

John Bowman had come with Verbruggen from Haymarket Theatre in the fall of 1707, but he stayed at Smock Alley only two seasons.[1] Goddard and Mrs. Wolf soon disappeared from the Dublin stage; Kendall and Mrs. Fitzgerald continued for about a decade in minor parts. Daugherty and Hallam had but recently commenced at Smock Alley their theatrical careers; both achieved considerable prominence there in the course of many years' service. Hallam became the father of a more celebrated actor, Lewis Hallam, who in 1752 took a company of players from England to Williamsburg, Virginia, the first wholly professional troupe to perform on the North American continent. The men of the Smock Alley organization, though not the equal of the male group a decade earlier, still far surpassed the women in talent. No one of the latter could be acclaimed an actress of genuine distinction. The Dublin theatre did not yet offer to young females sufficient financial or social emoluments to encourage the development of feminine stars.

After Thurmond's desertion in May 1708 Ashbury, as patentee, and the remaining sharers 'did mutually enter into articles and Bonds to continue in the Kingdom for the Diversion of the Nobility and Gentry'.[2] In December they were cheered by the news of the appointment of Thomas, Earl of Wharton, as Lord-Lieutenant. A profligate and witty man of literary inclinations, he enjoyed patronizing the arts. His coming to Ireland presaged an upturn of business at the Smock Alley playhouse. One of Lord Wharton's London entourage informed a Dublin official in February 1708/9 that the new Irish viceroy 'had got a set of Players to go over into Ireland in May next, so what with Parliament att Chichester House, Balls in the Castle, and Comedys att the Theatre, I hope we shall pass our time well this summer in Dublin'.[3] When Lord Wharton finally assumed office in April, he brought over with him, as his state secretary, the essayist Joseph Addison, and, as director of court diversions, the musical composer Thomas Clayton. During the Lord-Lieu-

[1] Genest, ii. 373, 443.
[2] See 'The Case of the Patentee and Sharers'.
[3] Letter of 22 Feb. 1708/9 by Charles Dering to Joshua Dawson (British Departmental Papers, no. 1031, Public Record Office, Dublin). Destroyed by fire in 1922, but previously copied by W. J. Lawrence and now in his Irish theatre collection, University of Cincinnati.

tenant's residence at Dublin from April to September Clayton put on at the Castle numerous entertainments, including perhaps his two operas: *Arsinoe, Queen of Cyprus*; and *Rosamund* with libretto by Addison.[1] The only players recorded as visiting Ireland in consequence of Lord Wharton's invitation were the renowned London comedian, Anthony Aston, and his wife. Aston 'strain'd forth a Comedy, call'd *Love in a Hurry*, which was acted on the Theatre at Smock-alley, but with no success'.[2] Then, with more happy results, he introduced a pastoral of his own composition, *The Coy Shepherdess*, which featured a good deal of singing. The Astons, of course, took the chief parts of Melanctio and Pastora. Smock Alley's new luminary, John Leigh, a handsome twenty-year-old Irishman with a fine voice, played Meliboeus, and another young member of the local troupe, Mrs. Dumeney, a promising singer, filled the role of Flora.[3] With these Dublin appearances of 1709 the Astons inaugurated the custom of having London stage celebrities perform as guest stars with an Irish company. They thereby set a precedent which, after the middle of the eighteenth century, exerted a profound effect upon the policies of theatre managers in Ireland.

In November 1709 John Evans, one of the Smock Alley sharers, must have received a London offer which he and his Dublin friends considered too handsome to be refused. The earliest theatrical advertisements to be discovered in an Irish newspaper announced, under the dates of both 22 and 29 November, that on Monday, 2 December, *The Pilgrim*, a very popular comedy written originally by John Fletcher and revised by Sir John Vanbrugh, would be performed 'by Their Excellencies the Lords Justices Special Command for the Benefit of Mr. Evans, All the Parts Acted to the Best Advantage, with the Celebrated Masque of Acis, Galatea, and Polyphemus, with several other Entertainments which are mentioned in the Bills'.[4] These announcements of Evans's benefit night provide the first specific evidence that the Dublin theatre, in line with the

---

[1] *Journal of the Royal Society of Antiquaries of Ireland*, 5th series, xviii (1908), 237.
[2] Chetwood, p. 87.
[3] The cast is printed under the dramatis personae in '*The Coy Shepherdess*. A Pastoral. As it was Acted at The Theatre Royal. By Antho: Aston, Comedian. Dublin: Printed by Cornelius Carter, for the Author. Anno. Dom. 1709'.
[4] *Dickson's Dublin Intelligencer*, 22 and 29 Nov. 1709.

London playhouses, was attempting to swell its audiences by bait-
ing them with longer bills at no increase in admission prices. It
had now become the custom for the dramatic *pièce de résistance* to
be followed by a number of brief miscellaneous features, such as
song and dance acts, as well as by a light afterpiece of some kind
—in this case, Pierre Motteux's musical masque or interlude of
Acis and Galatea, which contained an unusually appealing comic
underplot (or 'antimasque') about two country lovers, Roger
and Joan. The resulting programme afforded four hours or more
of amusement, certainly a generous money's worth. Evans, after
his December benefit, went to England and finished out the
season at the Haymarket Theatre.[1] He rejoined the Smock Alley
troupe in the fall of 1710, however, and resumed his former
status of sharer.

By 1711[2] the Dublin playhouse began to feel the effects of the
virulent political feuding between the Whigs and the Tories.
The installation of a Tory ministry in 1710 gave the Whigs profound concern, for they feared as a consequence an early peace
with Louis XIV of France, who favoured the Catholic Stuart
succession to the British throne. They quickly seized upon the
coincident anniversaries of the late King William III's birthday,
marriage, and landing in Ireland on 4 November as the most
appropriate occasion for arousing Protestant fervour to prosecute the war against France and Spain. They then went on to
establish as a leading feature of these anniversary celebrations
the performance of Nicholas Rowe's political tragedy *Tamerlane*,
which depicted in the title role (William III) an heroic figure of
virtue, and in Tamerlane's enemy, Bajazet (Louis XIV), a
monster of villainy.

One of the most active and zealous Whigs in London, Dr.
Samuel Garth, a fashionable author of occasional verse, proceeded to write what he and his party considered a patriotic

[1] Genest, ii. 450.
[2] W. H. Grattan Flood, *A History of Irish Music* (Dublin, 1913), p. 266, reports
without citing any authentic evidence that Nicolo Grimaldi brought his Haymarket opera company to the Smock Alley Theatre in the early spring of 1711
for a series of operatic performances. Equally unreliable is the statement of Thomas
Wilkes in *A General View of the Stage*, p. 311, that Robert Wilks in the summer of
1711 sojourned three months at Dublin and 'performed the character of Sir Harry
Wildair for nineteen nights running at Smock-alley'.

'Prologue for the 4th of November, 1711. Being the anniversary of or the birth-day of the late King William',[1] to be delivered before the acting of *Tamerlane*. This prologue promptly made its way to Dublin and the Smock Alley Theatre. Manager Ashbury, desirous of avoiding offence to the Tory sentiments of the present heads of the Irish government, the Lords Justices, applied to them for leave to present the prologue at the anniversary performance to be held on Monday night the fifth since 4 November fell on Sunday that year. The Lords Justices in turn refused permission.[2]

Of course the suppression of the Garth prologue much enhanced its popular appeal in Dublin. A Tory comment had to be forthcoming, and it took the form of a broadside entitled 'The Shortest Way to Peace; or An Answer to a Prologue that was to be spoke at the Queen's Theatre in Dublin on the 5th of November, 1711.'[3] This rejoinder only served to incite the determination of the Whigs that by hook or crook the Garth prologue should be spoken on the occasion for which it was intended. As the next anniversary approached, they put pressure on Ashbury. He with understandable caution again sought the approval of the Lords Justices to introduce 'a prologue for the 4 November 1712, being the anniversary for the birth, landing, and marriage of William III, written by Dr. Garth'.[4] Once more the Lords Justices, led by the Lord High Chancellor, Sir Constantin Phipps, a rabid Tory, prohibited its delivery.[5] Their prohibition brought about the first of the many riots which have since made the Irish stage notorious.

Partisan tension electrified the Smock Alley atmosphere on Tuesday night, the 4th of November. The Tory ladies in the galleries wore red roses 'in Honour to the English Nation', while the Whig ladies in the boxes wore orange decorations.[6] At curtain time a call went up for the forbidden prologue, but it met

---

[1] British Museum no. 1163, bb. 28.

[2] See the reference to 'a Prologue which has been forbid by the Government two years successively' in *Sir Constantin Phipps's Address at Dublin Castle to the Mayor, Aldermen and Magistrates of the City of Dublin, on January 16, 1712/13*, a Dublin broadside.

[3] Henry Bradshaw Irish Collection (Cambridge University Library), no. 4133.

[4] *Hist. MSS. Commission: Eighth Report* (London, 1881), appendix, pt. i, 16a.

[5] Ibid.   [6] *Lloyd's Newsletter*, 8 Nov. 1712.

with no response from backstage. Finally Dudley Moore, a Whig leader who was sitting in the pit, clambered up on the stage and, amid violent hissing, recited the incendiary eulogy of the late King William:

Today, a mighty Hero comes to warm
Your curdl'd blood and bids you Britons arm.
To Valour much he owes, to Virtue more;
He fights to save and conquers to restore.
He strains no texts, nor makes Dragoons persuade,
He likes Religion but he hates the trade.
Born for mankind, they by his labours live,
Their property is his prerogative.
His sword destroys less than his mercy saves,
And none except his passions are his slaves.
With how much haste his Mercy meets his Foes!
And how unbounded his Forgiveness shows!
What Trophies o'er our captur'd Hearts he rears,
By MODERATION greater than by Wars!
His generous Soul for *Freedom* was Design'd,
To pull down Tyrants, and unslave mankind;
He broke the Chains of Europe; and when we
Were doom'd *for Slaves*, he came and *set us free*;
Shew'd us how Grace made Majesty rever'd,
And that the Prince BELOV'D was truly fear'd.
Such Britons is the Prince that you possess
In council greatest, and in camps no less:
Brave but not cruel, wise without deceit,
Born for an age curs'd with a Bajazet.
But you, disdaining to be too secure,
Ask his protection, but yet grudge his Pow'r.
With you a Monarch's right is in dispute,
Who gave Supplies are only absolute.
Britons for shame, your factious feuds decline;
Too long you've laboured for the Bourbon line.
Assert lost rights, an Austrian Prince alone
Is born to nod upon a Spanish throne.
A cause no less could on great Eugene call,
Steep alpine rocks require a Hannibal.
He shews you your lost honour to retrieve,
Our troops will fight when once the Senate give.
Quit your cabals & factions, and in spight
Of Whig and Tory in this cause unite.

One voice will then send Anjou back to France,
There let the meteor end his airy dance,
Else to the Mantuan soil he may repair.
Ev'n abdicated Gods were Latium's care.
At worst he'll find some Cornish boroughs there.[1]

When Moore finished speaking this prologue, scuffling broke
out all over the theatre. Six grenadiers posted on the stage as
guards moved down into the audience and at last quelled the
disturbance.[2]

An amusing, though malicious, ballad on the riot shortly
appeared in the Tory *Lloyd's Newsletter*:[3]

*A New Song on the Whiggs Behaviour at the Play House on the 4th of this
Instant, November 1712, at a Play call'd TAMERLAIN.*

To the Tune of ye Commons and Peers:

You Whiggs of Renown
Both of Country & Town,
Who of late in our Play-House were seen;
And mounted the Stage
With Fury and Rage,
As if each a Great Hero had been:
How comes it about,
You now grow so stout!
Thus quite to run out of your sphere;
We think it were fit,
You should stay in the Pit,
Unless each has a mind to turn Play'r.
Think not to invade
Our Privilege and Trade,
As you would the Prerogative Royal;
At this rate to be sure,
We must soon shut our door,
If we strive to be Honest or Loyal.
From the Tholsel and Rose
Came many a red Nose,

---

[1] There are variant texts of the Garth prologue. The one inserted here comes
from a broadside, entitled 'The Prologue that was spoken At the Queen's Theatre
in Dublin, on Tuesday the 4th November, 1712', and printed by E. Waters, the
New Post Office Printing House in Essex Street, Dublin, 1712.

[2] *Lloyd's Newsletter*, 8 Nov. 1712.

[3] Ibid., 11 Nov. 1712.

Where they went with their paunches to fill 'em;
And did merrily cry,
We'll an Ocean drink dry
For thy memory, O! glorious William!
Thus at their Bachanals,
And drunken Cabals,
They with nonsense & fury attack us;
Like so many Swine
They were drunk at his Shrine,
Who was rather a Mars than a Bacchus.
Their Speaker so fine,
Full of madness & wine,
Read over a Prologue most witty;
They huzza'd! & they huff'd,
They hector'd and snuff'd,
Being back'd by some Whiggs of the City.
They were hiss'd at by some,
Who were challeng'd to come,
And encounter with them on the Stage:
No Courage they lack't for a Tragical Act,
When they found none but Women t'engage.
At some ladies they bawl'd
Flux'd Whores they were call'd,
With a deal of Such Bear Garden cant;
But each She-Whigg whose breast
With an Orange was drest,
Most certainly past for a Saint.
Their Speaker so bold
Who of late I am told
Is chosen the mouth of the Faction,
Now cares not a fig
To own he's a Whigg,
Which was prov'd in a very late Action.
To shew he was rank
He openly drank
Her *Grandfather's fate* to our Q[uee]n,
If she follow'd his ways
They would shorten her Days,
Thus he vented his Treason and Spleen. . . .

The authorities placed Mr. Moore along with other Whig
'sparks' under arrest, and charged them with 'Riotous and

Seditious Practices'.[1] Ashbury and John Leigh, representing the playhouse, testified against the accused rioters at the inquiry held by the grand jury toward the latter part of November. On the twenty-eighth the jury, a majority of whom were Whigs, voted to throw out the bill of indictment, but the foreman, Ralph Gore, the Lord Mayor, by mistake wrote on the bill that the indictment was confirmed, and sent it to the court thus incorrectly attested.[2] His egregious blunder naturally caused deep chagrin to both the jurymen and the presiding magistrate. The latter ruled, however, that the indictment had been upheld, and that Moore with his associates must stand trial.

On 16 January 1712/13 the Lord High Chancellor attempted to influence the attitude of public officials toward the trial by calling together at Dublin Castle the mayor, aldermen, and magistrates, and haranguing them. In the course of his speech he referred to 'the great riot committed at the Playhouse' and to the necessity that government officers should 'exert themselves in defence of Her Majesty's authority'.[3] He concluded with the heated accusation that the prologue which was spoken in defiance of the government's edict 'sounds an alarm and invites Her Majesty's subjects to make war against those [i.e. the French] with whom Her Majesty thinks fit to make peace'. Despite the Lord Chancellor's vehement stand, the court quashed the indictment against the rioters and dismissed the case when it came to trial on 5 February 1712/13.[4] Consequently, the commotion which might have involved the Dublin Theatre Royal in a *cause célèbre* was quickly forgotten.

During these same years in which the Smock Alley Company had to cope with political tensions, it had to adjust itself to frequent and important shifts in personnel. In the early spring of 1712 Thomas Griffith, deciding to follow the precedent set by his fellow-sharer, Evans, two years before, journeyed to London to spend the balance of the theatrical season on the Drury Lane stage.[5] Back again at Smock Alley in the fall, he enjoyed a special benefit on Monday, 26 January 1712/13, 'by Their

<hr />

[1] *Lloyd's Newsletter*, 18 Nov. 1712.   [2] Ibid., 29 Nov. 1712; 3 Jan. 1712/13.
[3] See *Sir Constantin Phipps's Address*.
[4] *Dickson's Dublin Intelligencer*, 10 Feb. 1712/13.   [5] Genest, ii. 497.

Excellencies the Lords Justices Command'.[1] The evening's entertainment, specially advertised in the newspapers, consisted of Thomas Shadwell's 'diverting' Restoration comedy, *The Woman Captain*; Colley Cibber's recent two-act farce of *The Rival Queans; or, Alexander the Great*; and a choice programme of singing and dancing 'as is express'd in the small and large Bills'.[2] This last statement is the earliest specific revelation that the Dublin management put forth regularly two kinds of playbills: (1) small dodgers or fliers, which were distributed around the coffee-house and tavern tables, in the rooms of the Exchange, at the bookshops and the doors of the principal residences; (2) large posters, which were affixed to the walls of buildings or to the pillars at the Tholsel and the Cornmarket.

It was very likely Griffith who persuaded Thomas Elrington, a most promising young actor, to return with him to Dublin for the 1712–13 season.[3] Elrington, born in 1688 at Golden Square, London, had started life as an upholsterer's apprentice.[4] Then in 1709 he began to act at Drury Lane and at once made an impression with his tall well-proportioned figure and strong, sweet voice.[5] Within his first year at Smock Alley he married Ashbury's daughter, Frances,[6] and was chosen one of the four theatre directors, the others being Ashbury, Evans, and Griffith.[7] John Thurmond, Jr., son of the former Smock Alley sharer, also came over from Drury Lane in the autumn of 1712,[8] accompanied by his wife (*née* Lewis), a sterling actress as well as a vocalist of no mean ability.[9] In November John Leigh threatened to sever his Smock Alley connexions. The company then made overtures through young Thurmond to his father at London, but after the terms of the contract had been supposedly agreed upon, the mercurial Mr. Thurmond declined to go through with it. The company therefore had to come to terms at Christmastime with Leigh and to raise his salary to sixty pounds per annum in order to retain him.[10]

---

[1] *Lloyd's Newsletter*, 24 Jan. 1712/13.　　[2] Ibid.　　[3] Genest, ii. 498.
[4] Chetwood, p. 132.　　[5] Ibid., p. 135.　　[6] Ibid., pp. 83, 84, 134.
[7] See the lease of Mar. 1713 for playhouse property at Cork. This document was signed by the four men who were obviously the Smock Alley sharers.
[8] See Genest, ii. 499, and 'The Sharers' Reply to John Thurmond'.
[9] Chetwood, p. 226.
[10] See 'The Sharers' Reply'; also 'The Case of the Patentee and Sharers'.

The elder Thurmond was, however, far from done with the Dublin stage. In the spring of 1713 he decided that, after all, the future looked more golden at Smock Alley than at Drury Lane. Knowing that he stood in no one's good graces in Ireland, he shrewdly obtained from the Duke of Ormonde, who was again titular Lord-Lieutenant of Ireland though in residence at London, a letter recommending to Ashbury that the erstwhile Dublin performer be offered all possible consideration. When Thurmond arrived at Smock Alley in April he brought forth Ormonde's letter and, at the same time, the brazen demand that he be readmitted to the company in his old status of sharer.[1] Upon Ashbury's refusal Thurmond aired his grievance in a formal petition to the Lord Chancellor that the latter should compel the company to take him back into the fold as a sharer.[2]

Hence, absurd as it now seems, this petty dispute between Thurmond and the Smock Alley Theatre required the attention of the Lords Justices, to whom in due course Ashbury and his fellow sharers submitted a counter plea. In it they asserted that 'thro' the slender Encouragement and the constant heavy Charges of the Theatre the Sharers lye under many Debts and Difficulties, which yet they don't doubt to surmount by . . . the Prospect of Happiness from this Glorious Peace [the Peace of Utrecht just concluded with France on 11 April], the prospect of which furnish'd them with Resolution to persevere in the Business in the worst of Times'.[3] They emphatically denied that Thurmond 'who has been absent Six years . . . has an equall pretence to the Profits of the Theatre with the Sharers who have continued in the Kingdom and have greatly impair'd their little Fortunes by endeavouring to support the Company'.[4] Nevertheless, in obedience to the Lord-Lieutenant's recommendation, they were willing to give Thurmond 'all the Encouragement they possibly can', namely, to take him back on salary at sixty pounds per year.[5] After another exchange of arguments between the two parties to the case had advanced it no further, the Lords Justices turned to the Lord-Lieutenant at London for a decision. To them the Duke of Ormonde's secretary sent on 28 May this properly disdainful answer: 'My Lord Duke will

[1] Ibid. [2] See 'The Case of John Thurmond'.
[3] See 'The Case of the Patentee and Sharers'. [4] Ibid. [5] Ibid.

not trouble himself with the arguments pro and con about Mr. Thurmond, but seems inclined to favour Mr. Ashbury, and that Mr. Thurmond be content with a Salary.'[1] The Lord-Lieutenant's judgement so deflated Thurmond that he quickly gave up his pretensions and joined the Dublin troupe on a salaried basis.

The 1712–13 season at Smock Alley included a number of anniversary or special performances subsequent to the one for King William's birthday that provoked the historic riot. The appearances of the 'Government' at playhouse celebrations were decidedly on the increase. Ashbury encouraged the custom of 'government nights' because they resulted in crowded houses and stimulated theatre business in general. On Friday, 6 February 1712/13, Her Majesty's Birthday 'was observ'd with greater Respect than has been for several years past'.[2] The Lords Justices, 'attended by most of the Nobility and Gentry', went to the Castle at noon for a concert of music, a song, bell-ringing, and gun-firing. After a sumptuous dinner there in the banqueting house, 'at Night they adjourn'd to the Play, and afterwards to the Fireworks'. Her Majesty's 'happy Accession to the Throne' was celebrated on the night of Monday, 9 March, by a formal assemblage of the officers of state for 'a Consort of Musick at the Playhouse'.[3] When the Peace of Utrecht was officially proclaimed on Saturday, 16 May, 'the Day's rejoycing ended with a Play, Ringing of Bells, Bonfires, Illuminations and other Demonstrations of Joy'.[4]

On Friday, 5 June, by reason of the sitting of the higher courts, 'the Play-House was very full, His Excellency my Lord Chancellor, and most of the Nobility, Judges, Lawyers, and Gentlemen in Town being Present'.[5] That favourite tragedy, *Cato*, with John Evans in the title role of the great Roman patriot 'who so bravely opposed Julius Caesar from being perpetual Dictator', provided the main attraction of the evening. Addison's drama, according to *Lloyd's Newsletter*, 'was well

---

[1] Letter of 28 May 1713 by Edward Southwell (British Departmental Papers, carton 6, no. 1928, Public Record Office, Dublin). Destroyed by fire in 1922, but previously copied by W. J. Lawrence and now in his Irish theatre collection, University of Cincinnati.

[2] *Lloyd's Newsletter*, 7 Feb. 1712/13.   [3] Ibid., 10 Mar. 1712/13.

[4] Ibid., 19 May 1713.   [5] Ibid., 6 June 1713.

Played, considering the Discouragement the Players here lie under'.[1] The queen appointed Monday, 15 June, as a day of thanksgiving for the Peace of Utrecht. 'In the Evening their Excellencies the Lords Justices, attended by the Lords of the Council, the Judges, and the rest of the Nobility and Gentry of the Kingdom, went to the Theatre Royal, where there was a Musical Interlude perform'd, call'd *Peace Triumphant*; with a Loyal Prologue Writ and Spoke . . . by Mr. Griffith, Sworn Servant to Her Majesty, and an Epilogue by Mr. Leigh.'[2] As early as this year of 1713 the Theatre Royal may have begun to receive from the government a fixed subsidy for the performing of plays and other entertainment on official days of festivity, though no authentic record of such payments before the 1720's has come to light.[3] The subsidy arrangement provided for the admission of 'the Ladies' to the boxes gratis on 'government nights', a proviso which in time the fair sex of Dublin badly abused.

Whatever the 'discouragement' *Lloyd's Newsletter* might have considered the Smock Alley players to 'lie under' in June 1713, it was not serious enough to prevent them from carrying out an epoch-making enlargement of their theatre enterprise. Early in the spring the directors, Ashbury, Elrington, Evans, and Griffith, had taken steps to extend stage activities to Cork, the fastest-growing city of Ireland. An ambitious but still ugly metropolis of twenty-five to thirty thousand inhabitants,[4] situated 160 miles by road south-west of Dublin, Cork was thriving beyond all other Irish ports on account of its immense export of provisions (such as pork, butter, tallow, hides, wool, and yarn) to the American colonies, the West Indies, Spain, and France.[5] Built on an island made by the river Lee, the city was intersected, like so many Dutch communities, by canals. Through

[1] Ibid.

[2] Ibid., 16 June 1713. The musical interlude or masque of *Peace Triumphant* is not recordedi n Allardyce Nicoll's *A History of English Drama, 1660–1900*: vol. ii, *Early Eighteenth Century Drama* (3rd edition, Cambridge, 1952). It quite probably was an original Dublin entertainment.

[3] Stockwell, p. 183, prints the earliest known official records, dated 2 Nov. 1722 and 11 June 1723. Hitchcock, i. 84, is clearly incorrect in asserting that these government nights with the freedom of the boxes for the ladies were established 'on the first rise of the stage in Ireland'.

[4] MacLysaght, p. 195.   [5] Ibid., p. 226.

these waterways small ships and lighters penetrated near the heart of the town to the quays, along which lay numerous warehouses.[1] The Exchange, erected in 1709, was a magnificent structure of hewn stone with a front of five arches and a handsome cupola.[2] It stood mid-way between the North and South Gates on High (later Main) Street, where most of the buildings were designed in the Spanish style with balcony windows, and were faced with brick.[3] The second story of the Exchange contained assembly rooms, the gathering place of 'the quality'. Rich merchants, many of them either English Quakers or French Huguenot emigrés,[4] formed the backbone of Cork society, a society which as a result of its mercantile contacts had tended to develop Continental manners of elegance and cultivation. 'The people follow pretty much the French air in conversation [i.e. mode of living], bringing up their children to dance, play on the fiddle, and fence, if they can give them nothing else'—so one local trader commented.[5] It was this widespread combination of wealth and refinement which to the Dublin Theatre Royal made Cork a tempting site for a branch playhouse.

In March 1713 the Smock Alley directors leased from John King, a Cork joiner or builder, his 'great cellar or malt house together with the upper part of the said John King's Dwelling house as it now stands'.[6] By tearing out floorings and partitions they refashioned the building into a small and unpretentious theatre with its pit presumably in the 'great cellar'. The site may have been in Dingle Lane off North High (Main) Street.[7] The unexpectedly heavy costs of remodelling led the Dublin promoters to issue through *Lloyd's Newsletter* a public appeal for funds:

Whereas Her Majesty's Company of Comedians have undertaken the fitting up of a Theatre at Cork; and find the said Place much

---

[1] Charles Smith, *The Ancient and Present State of the County and City of Cork* (Dublin, 1774), i. 402.

[2] Ibid., pp. 395–6.   [3] Ibid., p. 401.

[4] MacLysaght, p. 235.   [5] Ibid., p. 227.

[6] MS. 79/98/54780, Office of the Registry of Deeds, Dublin, as quoted in Stockwell, pp. 358–9, n. 8.

[7] See J. W. Flynn, *Random Recollections of an Old Playgoer* (Cork, 1890), p. 7, for reference to an ancient Cork playhouse on this site.

more Expensive than it was at first conceiv'd: Therefore 'tis humbly hop'd, that the Nobility and Gentry, in and about the said City of Cork, will contribute to the said Undertaking. And all such as are Generously Inclin'd to Encourage that polite Entertainment, are desir'd to Subscribe (towards the defraying the said Charges) at the Turk's Head Coffee-House, opposite to the Exchange in the said City; where there will be a Book for the Purpose, and constant Attendance given.[1]

The financing went forward successfully, and the theatre opened in July or August for a month to six weeks of acting by the Smock Alley troupe.[2]

This summer season at the Cork playhouse in 1713 marked the true beginning of the provincial theatre in Ireland. The Dublin company, however, behaved in the same unenterprising fashion as it had after its Kilkenny tour of 1698, and apparently did not repeat its Cork venture for twenty years. Nevertheless, the Smock Alley directors had initiated the pattern for future professional stage undertakings in the Irish towns. After 1730 they moved out in several directions from Dublin to raise up playhouses where the parent organization could send a troupe for seasonal performances. Meanwhile the little malt house theatre at Cork had been relegated to less glamorous uses.

For John Evans, the leading Smock Alley tragedian, the Cork sojourn occasioned some exciting by-play. On a certain evening after the theatre performance the officers of a regiment stationed in the city invited him to a tavern for drinks.[3] When it came his turn to propose a toast, he proposed the health of Queen Anne. One of the officers, infuriated by Evans's toasting of Her Majesty, left the room and sent back a drawer with a challenge. The actor then descended below stairs and proceeded to disarm the regiment's 'doughty hero'. A short while afterwards the discomfited officer came up to Dublin and told of the affair in such a way that 'the whole Body of Military' felt themselves to have been affronted by Evans. They therefore turned out in large numbers for a Smock Alley production of *The Rival Queens* in which he

---

[1] *Lloyd's Newsletter*, 14 Mar. 1712/13, and occasional issues thereafter. Stockwell, p. 358, n. 8, reprints this notice with a few inaccuracies.

[2] Chetwood, p. 144, states: 'In the last Year of the Reign of Queen Anne the Company of Dublin went down, in the Summer Season, to play at Corke.'

[3] Ibid., pp. 144–5.

was advertised to play Alexander the Great, and raised such a clamour that the management threatened to dismiss the house. Yet the hecklers among the military present would not allow the performance to go ahead until Evans had begged for pardon from the stage. At last he consented to do so, but when he appeared before the curtain, a certain officer in the pit shouted, 'Kneel, you rascal!' Evans with composure replied in the same peremptory tone, 'No, you rascal! I'll kneel to no one but God, and my Queen'. His bold retort helped to reverse the tide of feeling. The few 'worthy Gentlemen of the Army who knew the whole Affair' now intervened and silenced their taunting comrades. Evans then proceeded to impersonate the world-famous military leader to the satisfaction of his recent soldier opponents, the perfect ironic conclusion for this little Irish melodrama.

Ashbury as well as Evans was having trouble in the fall of 1713. The seventy-four-year-old patentee, who had been Master of the Revels in Ireland for three decades, heard that a report of his death had circulated around London and that, in consequence, 'some needy courtier' was doing all in his power to be appointed to the Revels office.[1] Much disturbed, Ashbury hastened to embark for London as soon as he had seen the Dublin theatre well started on the new season. When he reached England, he had his fears quickly set at rest by influential friends. He so informed his wife in a letter of such homely charm that it still deserves the full reproduction which the first Irish stage historian gave it two centuries ago:

Chester, October 13, 1713

My Dear,

This is only to let you know that I am safely arrived at Chester, where I had the good Fortune to meet with Sir John Stanley, who was well pleas'd to see me. After I had told him the Cause of my Journey, relating to my Patent, he bid me be assured, he would render me all the good Offices in his Power, and was of the Opinion, it lay in the Will of the Duke of Shrewsbury our good Lord Lieutenant, without giving our gracious Queen the least Trouble concerning it. This Morning I had the Honour of a Visit from Mr. Kightly and Sir Richard Levinze who are of the same Opinion with Sir John, and have both promised me their utmost Assistance. Good

---

[1] Chetwood, p. 84.

Mr. Kightly tells me, he will put her Majesty in mind of her old Master, as he was pleas'd to call me. I am so well satisfy'd in the Affair, that I would return to thee on the first Opportunity, if I had not resolv'd to see my Sister, and my Son Tom Elrington's Father and Mother. Thou knowest it is Troublesome to me to write, but to satisfie thee in thy longing Desire to hear from me, I take the Trouble with Pleasure. I remain thine for ever,

Joseph Ashbury

My Blessing to all my dear Children.[1]

The suit of the 'needy courtier', whoever he may have been, caused no further trouble to the man who had taught the art of acting to the sovereign in her teens.

Consequently Ashbury made of his last visit to London a pleasure trip. He did not even undertake any recruiting for his company. Hence, during the 1713–14 season, the Dublin theatre had to rely for fresh talent upon a group of rising young players who had started their stage careers at Smock Alley:[2] John Hall, later a corpulent, thick-speaking comedian at London; James Quin (b. 1694), a versatile, flashy actor of high repute in England within a few years; John Watson (b. 1689), a solid performer of sober supporting roles; and Miss Schoolding, an attractive vivacious comedienne, whose parents had played with the troupe since before the turn of the century.

The queen's 'old Master' arrived home in time to participate on Saturday, 6 February 1713/14, in Dublin's celebration of Her Majesty's birthday, her final anniversary as it proved. The usual day's programme of morning parade, noon music, and afternoon banquet at the Castle concluded in the evening with 'the Play' at the Theatre Royal, followed by 'very fine' fireworks.[3] Anne's death on the first of August must have given Ashbury more than a melancholy pang. He had always cherished the memory of his close association with her in one of the outstanding events of his long theatrical experience, even though later, as queen, she never bestowed any favours upon him. Yet he had had no need for Anne's personal interest, because during

---

[1] Ibid.

[2] The roles which these four young players acted in the plays of the 1714–15 season evidence that they all had undergone at least one year's previous training at Smock Alley.

[3] *Lloyd's Newsletter*, 9 Feb. 1713/14.

her reign the most significant feature of his playhouse's development had been the tightening of its connexions with the Government of Ireland. The Smock Alley Theatre had moved well beyond the position of being a viceregal apanage; it had attained the status of a governmental institution with a regular part to play in the official observances and rituals of the Anglo-Irish Ascendancy.

CHAPTER VII

The Dublin Stage in the Last Years of Ashbury's Management: 1714 to 1720

THE commencement of the Georgian era found Dublin, now a city with close to 100,000 inhabitants, more affluent, more spacious, and more urbane than ever in spite of persistent English legislation to repress Ireland's prosperity. The capital's elegance in manners and taste steadily advanced because of the growing number of titled residents—particularly country gentry who, like Sir Jowler Kennel in *Irish Hospitality* (1717), came up to town at the Michaelmas and Easter terms—and of wealthy merchant families who, like the Sevilles in *The Sham Prince* (1719), aped the aristocracy. The patterns of fashionable activity were not changed but intensified. Public entertainments became more frequent and lavish: the all-day anniversary festivals, the state concerts at the Castle, the Lord Mayor's 'feasts' at the Tholsel, the municipal processions known as 'the riding of the franchises'. Of this last ceremony Lady Homebred in a contemporary play speaks with especial pleasure: 'When the Corporations ride the Fringes, I carry [my Girls] to a Relations of mine in Castle-Street, where they take their Bellies full of the Show.'[1] As for private diversions,

> Visiting and Ombre so intoxes,
> The Ladies quite forget to fill our Boxes,

lamented a Dublin prologue speaker in 1716.[2] Servants and coaches multiplied. Parading in stylish finery increased at the seaside to the north of the Liffey's mouth and at the circular drive in Phoenix Park. One pert young lady of the smart set quipped on the local stage:

> To flaunt it on the Strand, or in the Ring,
> Oh! Equipage is a delightful thing.[3]

[1] *The Sham Prince*, Act I, in Charles Shadwell's *Five New Plays* (London, 1720), p. 127. [2] Shadwell's Prologue to *The Hasty Wedding*, ll. 29–30. [3] *The Hasty Wedding*, Act III, in *Five New Plays*, p. 67.

The world of fashion most abundantly exhibited itself out-
doors at St. Stephen's Green, the heart of the rising exclusive
district. In fair weather, coaches, with their occupants ogling
one another through the glass windows, streamed around the
mile-long circuit of the park. Many beaux and belles preferred,
however, to walk the Stephen's mall and garden paths, while
their coaches waited by Dawson Street or some other thoroughfare adjoining the Green.[1] Sir Bullet Airy, the fat spark in a
Dublin comedy of the day, follows the prevailing mode when
in mid-morning he calls by coach on Mr. Trueman, a young
citizen of fortune, and urges him, before dinner at a tavern,
to take the air: 'But come, are you for Stephen's-Green, 'tis
a fine Morning, and there will be a great deal of Company.'[2]

For this polite society the playhouse in Smock Alley, though
decidedly inelegant, still served as the indoor equivalent of St.
Stephen's Green. At the playhouse, however, 'the quality' increasingly had to rub shoulders with the general populace. In
the pit city baronets, squires, army officers, and 'wits' sat alongside of bucks, law clerks, collegians, and 'extravagant male
citizens', as one prim reporter termed those bourgeois bachelors
who were enjoying a merry evening at the theatre.[3] In the box
circle behind the pit *nouveaux riches* social climbers infiltrated
among the people of rank and distinction. Such 'impudence'
on the part of the female sex was encouraged by the now well-
established custom of 'government nights'. On these occasions
the boxes were thrown open to all ladies who dressed in full
regalia. The official invitations to a free performance met with
enthusiastic feminine response, well illustrated by Lady Homebred, the genteel matron in *The Sham Prince*. She 'hate[s] all
publick Places, and all publick Diversions', and keeps her two
daughters as well as herself pretty much at home, but she takes
care that 'when the Government invites, they always see the
Play'.[4]

In Smock Alley's middle gallery the masked coquettes and
ladies of pleasure mingled with business and professional men,

[1] See *The Sham Prince*, Act I, in *Five New Plays*, p. 128.
[2] Ibid., p. 125.
[3] See *The Tricks of the Town laid open, or A Companion for Country Gentlemen*
(Dublin, n.d.), p. 37.
[4] *Five New Plays*, p. 127.

their wives and daughters. Numerous beaux also invaded this precinct to carry on heavy flirtations. ' "Nymph" is never said to anything but a Vizard in the Middle Gallery', observes a wise young belle to an over-zealous admirer in *The Sham Prince*.[1] More ardent love-making occurred in the 'lattices', the two boxes in line with the middle gallery on either side of the stage above the doors. The greater privacy of the lattices made them the favourite resort of the courtesans and the rakehells. 'My Lord talk'd a great deal to me in the Lattice last Play Night; I know he likes my Colour, and he prais'd my Hand and Neck'— so runs a strumpet's letter in *The Hasty Wedding* (1716).[2]

The more foppish gallants, taking their cue from London, were beginning the practice of locating themselves upon Smock Alley's stage and of strutting about there like peacocks during the programme intervals. A Dublin epilogue of the time refers disparagingly to

> One of these Fops who crowd behind our Scenes,
> To shew their ill-shap'd Legs, and awkward Meins;
> Their want of Sense to the whole Pit expose,
> To charm the Boxes with embroider'd Cloaths.[3]

In the upper gallery the plebeians held complete sway. Here soldiers, apprentices, journeymen, lackeys, housemaids, and yokels of all sorts formed the most rowdy, but also the most enraptured, group in the entire theatre.

Thus the Smock Alley audience, though it continued to be dominated by the titled and fashionable coterie to an extent no longer true in London, was slowly taking on a metropolitan character. To cater to its more varied attitudes and interests proved difficult for the entertainers, as one epilogue of the period plaintively demonstrates:

> Now, 'tis observ'd, our Friends two Story high
> Do always Laugh, when other People Cry,
> And murdering Scenes to them are Comedy.
> The middle Region seldom mind the Plot,
> But with a Vizard chat of *You know what*,
> And are not better'd by the Play one Jot.

---

[1] Ibid., p. 130.   [2] Ibid., p. 56.
[3] Epilogue to *The Amorous Widow*, ll. 28–31, in Concanen's *Poems upon Several Occasions* (Dublin, 1722), p. 27, and also in his *Miscellaneous Poems*, p. 69.

> But you great Judges of the Pit, who come,
> In order to be sent with Pleasure Home,
> Are like the Waterman, that looks Two Ways,
> You first observe the Ladies, then our Plays.[1]

Another epilogue points out in even sharper detail the disturbing range of taste:

> Ladies will smile, if Scenes are modest writ,
> Whilst your *double Entendres* please the Pit.
> There's not a Vizard sweating in the Gallery,
> But likes a smart Intrigue, a Rake, and Raillery.
> And were we to consult our Friends above,
> A pert and witty Footman 'tis they love;
> And now and then such Language as their own,
> As, *Damn the Dog*, *You lie*, and *Knock him down*.
> Consider, then, how hard it is to show
> Things that will do Above, and please Below.[2]

Despite the increasingly mixed patronage the approbation of the ladies of high station, 'the bright Nymphs, who in the Circle sit, / And with a Look can govern all the Pit',[3] still possessed a far larger importance to the stage in the Irish capital than in the English. Charles Shadwell, Dublin's leading playwright of the moment, recognized their decisive influence in local theatrical matters by dedicating in 1720 his collected plays to the Right Honourable Lady Newton and asserting that 'the Countenance You have shewn, and the Persons of Quality You have brought with You [to the Theatre], are convincing Demonstrations how much the Spirit and Gaiety of Dublin center in Your Ladyship'.[4]

The spirit and gaiety to which Shadwell paid homage failed to bring about at the Theatre Royal any marked changes or renovations in celebration of the beginning of George I's reign. As for some years past, the doors opened between four and five o'clock so that the ladies and, much more rarely, the gentlemen could send their servants early to keep good seats in the boxes. Performances in general started at six o'clock and took place

---

[1] Shadwell's Epilogue to *Rotherick O'Connor*, ll. 16–25, in *Five New Plays*, pp. [214–15].

[2] Shadwell's Epilogue to *Irish Hospitality*, ll. 8–17, in *Five New Plays*, p. [321].

[3] Epilogue to *Rotherick O'Connor*, ll. 29–30.

[4] *The Works of Mr. Charles Shadwell* (Dublin, 1720), I. iv.

twice a week, usually Monday and Thursday.[1] The curtain hour may have shifted a little with the time of year, as in London. The weekly schedule varied, of course, whenever a special occasion demanded a production on other than the conventional days. A new play, if warmly applauded at its première, was repeated again and again so long as the first enthusiasm lasted. The playwright did not look upon his work as a success until it had reached at least the third night of performance, the night set aside for the author's 'benefit'. Only then, remarked Shadwell to his Smock Alley audience in the prologue to *The Hasty Wedding*, could he feel assured that his creation had achieved a kind of permanency in the current stage repertory:

> For if two Nights we can your Persons see,
> 'Tis well: a Play becomes a Wife in Three.[2]

The Theatre Royal's supply of costumes and scenery remained very limited and tawdry. Additions to the threadbare wardrobe still chiefly depended upon the generosity of the Dublin playgoers, and fresh donations often incited a public acknowledgement from the stage. A prologue of 1717 was expressly designed to permit a young actress to exhibit 'a new Suit of Cloaths' which a group of solicitous ladies had bestowed upon her.[3] The charming Mary Lyddal enters all decked out and is pursued by Thomas Griffith, Smock Alley's star comedian. To his exclamation, 'You'r[e] finely drest to Day, and why all this?', she makes the perfect retort: 'Your Play-House Cloaths gains no Lovers.' Then Griffith proceeds to tease her about her present splendour:

> Full oft, I've seen You act in Tragick Love,
> With a bedraggled Tail, and dirty Glove,
> Representing then, some beauteous Goddess,
> With a poor wretched Head, and ill Shap'd Boddice.
> But so Transformed, you will surprize the Town,
> I fear some cully, child, has lay'd thee down—
> That Head, that Hoop, that Petticoat, that Gown!

With surprising frankness this little skit thus ridicules the mean

---

[1] The conclusion of Hercules Davis's Epilogue to *Rotherick O'Connor* in *Five New Plays*, p. [217], refers specifically to Monday as a performance night. The newspaper advertisements of Dublin productions, 1720–4, offer overwhelming evidence that Monday and Thursday were the customary days of acting.

[2] Prologue to *The Hasty Wedding*, ll. 23–24.

[3] Shadwell's Prologue to *The Drummer* in *The Works*, ii. 339.

appearance of the customary stage dress at Smock Alley in early Georgian times.

The condition of the scenery was little better. Current stock sets, such as 'The Field',[1] 'A Parlour',[2] 'A Prison',[3] 'The Street',[4] had been used repeatedly and were refurbished only when worn out. Stock pieces were put together now and again in various combinations with the hope that the reshuffling of parts would give some freshness to a too familiar stage background. For example, the 'Windmill Scene', a back flat, was framed by a pair of wing flats from the scene of 'the Wood' to depict a rural landscape in *Irish Hospitality*.[5] Strictly localized sets which were not often employed had lasted for decades. The set of 'St. Stephen's Green' probably saw its first use in 1699 and then reappeared twenty years later in *The Sham Prince*.[6] Infrequently a new scene had to be built to fit a peculiar and specific setting. 'Dermott's Cabbin' in *Irish Hospitality*[7] may well have required 'getting up', since the representation of anything other than an Irish tenant cottage would surely have seemed absurd to the Smock Alley spectators.

The ageing Theatre Royal might have undergone to its considerable advantage a few renovations in observance of its fiftieth season and its first under the new monarch. Its ageing manager, Joseph Ashbury, who had just completed forty years in that post, stood in no such need. At seventy-six he still presided over the playhouse affairs with vigour and still performed regularly. By now he had moved across the river at some distance from Smock Alley and lived in the attractive Bowling Green House, Oxmantown, a place with which he had enjoyed almost half a century of association. On its grounds he had played bowls with the fashionable in the days of Charles II. A young Englishman, William Rufus Chetwood, who assisted Ashbury around the theatre in 1714–15, long afterwards recalled the manager's Oxmantown residence as 'the finest spot of its

---

[1] *Irish Hospitality*, Act V, sc. 2; *Rotherick O'Connor*, Act II, sc. 3.

[2] *The Sham Prince*, Act II, sc. 2; *Irish Hospitality*, Act III, sc. 2.

[3] *Rotherick O'Connor*, Act II, sc. 2; Act IV, sc. 1.

[4] *The Hasty Wedding*, Act II, sc. 3; Act III, sc. 2.   [5] Act III, sc. 1.

[6] William Philips's *St. Stephen's Green: or, The Generous Lovers*; *The Sham Prince*, Act I, sc. 2.

[7] Act IV, sc. 2.

Kind in the whole Universe'.[1] Chetwood also preserved a lively impression of the distinguished Smock Alley leader:

His Person was of an advantageous Height, well-proportioned and manly; and, notwithstanding his great Age, erect; a Countenance that demanded a reverential Awe, a full and meaning Eye, piercing, tho' not in its full Lustre; . . . a sweet-sounding manly Voice, without any Symptoms of his Age in his Speech.[2]

Ashbury's pre-eminence as a teacher of acting continued to draw aspirants from Britain. In the early fall of 1714 Thomas Elrington's younger brother Francis arrived from London to serve his apprenticeship at Smock Alley. At the same time a twenty-one-year-old Englishwoman, Mrs. Eliza Fowler Haywood, who later became a well-known dramatist and novelist of London, put herself under Ashbury's tutelage. Recently abandoned by her husband, she had decided to try the stage as a means of livelihood. In December 1714 Robert Wilks, now an outstanding figure on the current London stage and an Ashbury product, sent his nephew William over to Dublin for training with the declaration that 'no one . . . is able to give him so just a Notion of the Business as Mr. Ashbury'.[3]

In addition to these three novices two former Smock Alley actors, John Bowman and Benjamin Husband(s), crossed from England in the early fall of 1714 to rejoin their old troupe. At the start of the season the known acting personnel of the Theatre Royal comprised twenty-one men and eleven women:[4]

Men	Women
Joseph Ashbury	Mrs. Ann Ashbury
John Bowman	,, Dumeney
Richard Buckley	,, Fitzgerald
George Daugherty	,, Hallam
Francis Elrington	,, Eliza Haywood
Thomas Elrington	,, Martin
John Evans	,, Schoolding
Thomas Griffith	Miss Schoolding
John Hall	Mrs. Thurmond, Jr.
Adam Hallam	,, Wilkins

[1] Chetwood, p. 81 n.   [2] Ibid., p. 85.   [3] Ibid., p. 82.
[4] This list is compiled from the casts of the four productions given in the fall of 1714.

Men	*Women*
Benjamin Husband(s)	Miss Wilson
— Kendall	
John Leigh	
— Minns	
— Oates	
James Quin	
— Schoolding	
John Thurmond	
John Thurmond, Jr.	
Joseph Trefusis	
John Watson	

This roster of thirty-two differs little in size from those of 1681 and 1698, the years of the Edinburgh and Kilkenny tours respectively. It would seem that throughout his managership Ashbury maintained the Smock Alley organization at an almost uniform level. Nine of the 1714 group—Ashbury, Buckley, Griffith, Husband(s), Schoolding, Trefusis, Mrs. Ashbury, Mrs. Martin, and Mrs. Schoolding—belonged to the company of 1698; only two, Ashbury and Trefusis, dated back to 1681. The male actors did not equal in overall excellence those of fifteen years before. The chief tragedians, Elrington and Evans, could not match their predecessors, Booth and Wilks. Of the brilliant 1698 sextet of comedians the company included Griffith and Trefusis but contained no really promising men, except young Quin, to balance the earlier comic talent. The Smock Alley women of 1714, however, surpassed all previous feminine contingents there; indeed they probably constituted the finest body of actresses who ever played at any one time under Ashbury. Yet no one of them finally ranked as an eminent performer at either Dublin or London, though several later enjoyed creditable seasons in the English theatres.

Within the first month or six weeks of the 1714–15 season Ashbury produced Shakespeare's *Timon of Athens* and two popular Restoration comedies, Sir Robert Howard's *The Committee* and Thomas D'Urfey's *The Comical History of Don Quixote*. There is no previous record of this Shakespearian tragedy on the Dublin stage, although the London theatres had produced it occasionally for a good many years. Of the two comedies,

The Committee had long been in the Smock Alley repertoire. It contains one of the earliest stage Irishmen, Teague, a servant whose brogue and humorous antics Thomas Griffith could carry off with fine comic effect. Ashbury's casting of these three productions throws very full light on the standing and capabilities of practically the entire troupe at the Theatre Royal:[1]

The Committee

Ashbury = Colonel Careless	Mrs. Ashbury = Arabella
T. Elrington = Colonel Blunt	„ Martin = Mrs. Day
Evans = Lieutenant Story	„ Thurmond, Jr. = Ruth
F. Elrington = Mr. Day	Miss Schoolding = Mrs. Chat
Quin = Abel	
Trefusis = Obadiah	
Griffith = Teague	
Hall = 1st Committeeman	
Minns = 2nd Committeeman	
Bowman = 3rd Committeeman	
Hallam = Bookseller	
Kendall = Bailiff	

Don Quixote

PART I

Quin = Don Quixote	Mrs. Dumeney = Luscinda
Griffith = Sancho Pancha	„ Martin = Teresa Pancha
Evans = Don Fernando	„ Schoolding = Dorothea
Leigh = Cardenio	„ Thurmond, Jr. = Manella
Thurmond = Ambrosio	Miss Schoolding = Mary the
Schoolding = Percy	Buxom[2]
Hall = Vincent	
Hallam = Nicholas	
Watson = Gines de Passeronte	

PART II

Quin = Don Quixote	Mrs. Dumeney = Luscinda
Griffith = Sancho Pancha	„ Martin = Teresa Pancha
Evans = Duke Ricardo	„ Schoolding = Duchess
Leigh = Cardenio	„ Hallam = Dulcina del
Thurmond = Ambrosio	Pobosa

[1] The casts of *The Committee* and *Timon of Athens* were printed in Chetwood, pp. 56 and 58; that of *Don Quixote*, in a Dublin edition of 1727. Stockwell, p. 321, misreads 'Bowen' for 'Bowman' as the Jeweller in *Timon*.

[2] The 1727 edition names Miss Schoolding as Mary the Buxom in Part II but in Part I lists her by her married name, Mrs. Moreau.

Schoolding = Pedro Rezio   Miss Schoolding = Mary the
Buckley = Bernardo   Buxom
Husband(s) = Manuel

Timon of Athens

Ashbury = Apemantus   Mrs. Thurmond, Jr. = Evandra
T. Elrington = Timon   ,,   Wilkins = Melissa
Evans = Alcibiades   ,,   Haywood = Chloe
F. Elrington = Nicias   Miss Schoolding = Phrinia
Quin = Cleon   ,,   Wilson = Thais
Trefusis = Aelius
Thurmond = Phaeax
Leigh = Demetrius
Hall = Isidore
Daugherty = Thrasillus
Griffith = Poet
Bowman = Jeweller
Hallam = Musician
Oates = Painter

One of these plays may have been the entertainment that
the Theatre Royal provided on the coronation day of George I,
Wednesday, 20 October 1714. Dublin observed the event with
a most elaborate programme of communal festivity. The Lords
Justices and the Lord Mayor opened the celebration by attend-
ing a morning service at Christ Church. About eleven o'clock
'a very great number of the Nobility, Clergy, Judges and
Gentry, and a great many Ladies in very fine Cloathes, went
to the Castle'.[1] There at about twelve 'a Coronation Song in
honour of his Majesty was performed by the best Masters'.[2]
When the music ended, the great guns of the Castle fired three
times, and were answered by three volleys of small arms from
the regiments drawn up in College Green. Then the Lord
Mayor spread a banquet at the Tholsel.[3] 'In the Evening there
was a Play, and at Night Their Excellencies went to a fine set
of Fireworks burnt on the Custom House Quay and on the
Water, and the Night concluded with Ringing of Bells, Bonfires,
Illuminations [of the houses by candles], and all other Demonstrations of Joy',[4] including a ball at the Castle.

Two weeks later the city indulged in another magnificent

[1] *Dublin Gazette*, 19–23 Oct. 1714.   [2] Ibid.
[3] *Whalley's Newsletter*, 26 Oct. 1714.   [4] *Dublin Gazette*, loc. cit.

round of festivity to mark the birthday anniversary of the late
King William III, the great hero of 'Glorious and Immortal
Memory' to the Whig party. The overthrow of the Tory ministry
in England at Queen Anne's death three months previous had
led to a similar change in the Government of Ireland. For the
first time in five years, therefore, the strong Whig majority in
Dublin could celebrate without any official restraints, and their
jubilation ran high. On Thursday, 4 November, 'about four
hundred Gentlemen, with the Lord Mayor and twenty honest
Aldermen, . . . met in their Coaches at St. Stephen's Green,
marched thence in order to College Green, and made a Stop
to see the Truncheon put into the hand of the Statue of his . . .
late Majesty'.[1] The truncheon had been spirited away on the
night of Sunday, 10 October, presumably as a political gesture
by Jacobite Tory sympathizers. After the ceremony of restoration the large and genteel assemblage proceeded to the Tholsel
for a 'very splendid' dinner.[2] When they had finished the repast,
they attended a performance of the usual anniversary play,
Tamerlane, at the Theatre Royal. There Whig partisans absolutely dominated the audience. Sir Samuel Garth's prologue,
which had been forbidden by the Tory Lords Justices in the
three preceding years, and which had given rise to a playhouse
riot in 1712, was at last delivered 'without interruption'[3] and
'to the great Satisfaction of all the Company'.[4] Happily the
Smock Alley manager's new assistant, Chetwood, went to the
pains of recording the assignment of parts for this 1714 revival:[5]

Ashbury = Tamerlane	Mrs. Thurmond = Arpasia
T. Elrington = Bajazet	Miss Wilson = Selima
Evans = Moneses	Mrs. Fitzgerald = Haly
Leigh = Axalla	
Quin = Prince of Tanais	
Hall = Omar	
F. Elrington = Dervise	
Bowman = Zama	
Minns = Mirvan	
Oates = Stratocles	

---

[1] *Dickson's Dublin Intelligencer*, 9 Nov. 1714.   [2] Ibid.
[3] *Whalley's Newsletter*, 6 Nov. 1714.   [4] *Dickson's Dublin Intelligencer*, loc. cit.
[5] Chetwood, pp. 57–58.

It is of particular interest that Mrs. Fitzgerald, whose acting in masculine attire had appealed to the Dublin theatre-goers for almost a decade, filled the role of a male court attendant.

The omission of Trefusis, a leading member of the company, from the *Tamerlane* cast suggests that at the moment he may have been absent on the amusing excursion in which he suddenly got involved during either October or November.[1] 'Honest Jo', an experienced angler, was fishing on the bank of the Liffey when several acquaintances of his passed by in a boat to embark on the packet for England. Jo 'called to them to take him in, that he might see them safe on board. He gave his Fishing-Rod to a Friend on Shore to take care of till his Return; but Jo, it seems, was prevailed upon by his Companions to make the Journey to London with them, with his Fishing-cloaths upon his Back, not a second Shirt, and but seven Shillings in his Pocket'.[2] At London he parted from his companions without securing any assistance for the return journey. By chance his old Smock Alley colleague, Robert Wilks, found him absent-mindedly gazing at the large sundial in Covent Garden Square. At first Wilks did not know Trefusis in his shabby fishing attire, but soon recognized his peculiar gait, 'which was beyond Imitation'. The London actor then asked the Irishman how he came to be in London and in such a state of apparel. 'Hum! ha! why, faith, Bobby', replied Jo, 'I only came from Dublin to see what it was o'Clock at Covent Garden.' Wilks then took his droll friend in hand, supplied fresh clothing as well as money, and sent him on his way back to Ireland.

The defection of Trefusis from the Theatre Royal was, of course, unpremeditated and brief, but very shortly the theatre began to suffer many withdrawals which proved to be either permanent or of considerable duration. The changes of management at both Drury Lane and Lincoln's Inn Fields during the fall of 1714 led to the direct recruiting of certain players from Dublin. They in turn inspired other Smock Alley actors to seek out employment in London because of the improved theatrical

---

[1] The remarks of Robert Wilks in his letter to Ashbury on 6 Dec. 1714 indicate that Trefusis had departed from London at least some weeks before the letter's date. See Chetwood, pp. 82–83.

[2] Chetwood, pp. 82 n.–83 n., recounts the circumstances of the journey.

conditions there. Griffith led off the series of migrations by departing for Drury Lane in November.[1] Within a month afterwards Bowman, Hall, Husband(s), Leigh, Schoolding, Mrs. Schoolding, and Miss Schoolding left for Lincoln's Inn Fields.[2] Elrington, Evans, and Quin crossed to Drury Lane in January 1715.[3] Three months later Thurmond, Sr., along with Mr. and Mrs. Thurmond, Jr., set out for Lincoln's Inn Fields.[4] By late spring the Dublin company had been thoroughly decimated. It had lost the cream of its male talent, eleven men in all, and three of its best actresses. Ashbury, Mrs. Ashbury, Mrs. Martin, and Trefusis remained as the only players of much consequence. The veteran manager must have experienced the most upsetting season of his long career. About May, however, his situation brightened when his fellow sharers, Elrington, Evans, and Griffith, returned from Drury Lane to settle down again at their own playhouse.[5]

The first weeks of summer in 1715 saw Smock Alley performances twice disturbed by those turbulent outbursts of personal as well as party feeling which then characterized the behaviour of both Dublin and London audiences. On Monday, 30 May, a certain Alexander Hall, not liking the political implications that he found in the evening's prologue, hissed it; whereupon a Major Dunbar and other nearby spectators who resented the hissing 'drew their Swords, and made Mr. Hall Prisoner, and committed him to the Guard all Night'.[6] Thus Irishmen of 'the quality' thought no more of composing their differences by force inside the playhouse than out. On Monday evening, 20 June, that famous Dean of St. Patrick's Cathedral, Jonathan Swift, witnessed two 'gentlemen' get into a dispute about seat reservations in a box. Next day the inveterate satirist reported with affected casualness that 'a gentleman was run through in

[1] Genest, ii. 548.   [2] Ibid., pp. 566–8.
[3] Ibid., p. 548.   [4] Ibid., pp. 568, 570.
[5] Elrington and Evans had benefits at Drury Lane in late March 1715 (Genest, ii. 552–3). No record of Griffith's benefit survives. All three may safely be presumed back in Ireland by May. Wilkes, p. 311, states that Nicholas Rowe's *Lady Jane Grey* which opened at Drury Lane on 20 Apr. 1715 was performed this same year in Dublin 'seventeen nights successively'. The statement, like others by Wilkes, seems without any foundation in fact. The play's original run in London lasted only ten nights, and they were not in succession.
[6] *Dickson's Dublin Intelligencer*, 2 June 1715.

the playhouse last night upon a squabble of their footmen's taking places for some ladies'.[1] After violent incidents of this sort the actions on stage, even in tragedy, could not have seemed unduly exciting to the Smock Alley onlookers.

In September, before the opening of the regular season at the Theatre Royal, the renowned strolling comedian, 'Tony' Aston, turned up at Dublin. Six years earlier he had visited the city with his wife and had joined forces with the Theatre Royal company. Now in 1715 he went his own way and asked the permission of the Lord Mayor to offer public entertainment with a troupe consisting of himself, his wife and son, and several musical accompanists. The Lord Mayor complied with the following authorization:

I do hereby give Liberty and Licence to Antony Aston, gentleman, with his wife and son, and musick to exhibit and represent, within this City and the Liberties thereoff, such lawfull Diversions as may tend to the innocent Recreation of all those who are willing to see the same, they behaving themselves faithfully and honestly, as becomes His Majesty's Subjects. In testimony whereoff I have hereunto subscribed my name, and affixed the Seal of Mayorality, this 10th day of September 1715.

James Barlow[2]

Barlow, though not specifying dramatic representations in his licence, certainly intended it to cover any such exhibitions. He therefore was encroaching upon the authority of the Master of the Revels in Ireland, who under royal grant possessed the sole power to issue licences for all kinds of staged spectacles. His action was the earliest formal abrogation of the monopoly which Ashbury, and Ogilby before him, had exercised for fifty-five years in Dublin. Evidently Mayor Barlow subscribed to the dubious claim later set forth by the city corporation to the Parliament that 'the Chief Magistrate of Dublin has been for Ages the Civil and Military Governor of this Metropolis and as such has Lycenced all Plays Interludes and pastimes within his Liberty for the Entertainment of the Publick, where the

[1] *The Correspondence of Jonathan Swift, D.D.* (ed. F. Elrington Ball, London, 1911), ii. 283.
[2] Dibdin, p. 40.

proper officers of the said city by his Directions and under his Authority constantly attend to preserve the Peace of the said City and to prevent Tumults and Riotts'.[1] Once armed with the chief magistrate's blessing, the resourceful Mr. Aston worried not at all about its legality and proceeded in hall, tavern, or street to put on 'his Medley, as he call'd it, which consisted of some capital Scenes of Humour out of the most celebrated Plays . . .; between every Scene, a Song or Dialogue of his own Composition fill'd up the Chinks of the Slender Meal'.[2] Aston's shows, conducted as they were with the express approval and sanction of Barlow, brought the Lord Mayor's office for the first time into active connexion with the city's theatrical affairs. Seemingly of little consequence at the time, this incident led to the decisive intervention of the Lord Mayor in Dublin stage matters from 1730 onwards.

Sometime during the 1715–16 season a new resident writer, Charles Shadwell, appeared on the Smock Alley bills with a now lost work, bearing perhaps the title of *The Crafty Executors*.[3] The younger son of Thomas Shadwell, Restoration dramatist and Poet Laureate, he had gained a modest reputation in London as the author of three comedies, *The Fair Quaker of Deal* (1710), *The Humours of the Army* (January 1713), and *The Merry Wives of Broad Street* (June 1713). During the latter part of 1713 he had settled himself at Dublin near the Castle on William Street, where, according to his newspaper advertisement, he 'kept the only Office of Assurance for the support of

---

[1] 'The Humble Petition of the Lord Mayor, Sheriffs, Commons, and Citizens of the City of Dublin', dated 24 Feb. 1780, and preserved among the Irish Parliamentary Papers in the Public Record Office, Dublin, until the fire of 1922. A full transcript, made in 1909 by W. J. Lawrence, is contained in his Irish theatre collection, University of Cincinnati.

[2] Chetwood, p. 88.

[3] The Prologue to *The Hasty Wedding*, which was first published at Dublin in 1717, opens with these lines:

> Encourag'd by your last Year's kind Applause,
> Our Poet once again submits his Cause.

Obviously a Shadwell play had been acted in the season preceding the performance of *The Hasty Wedding*. This now lost work, Shadwell's first Dublin effort, may well be, however, the play a prologue to which was printed in the *Dublin Weekly Journal*, 20 Aug. 1726. In that issue of the newspaper a notice of Shadwell's death on 12 Aug. concluded with 'the Prologue written by an unknown hand to his Play call'd *The Crafty Executors*'.

Widdows and Orphans (by raising Sums of Money upon Mar-
riages, Births, and Deaths, for the Payment either of Three
Pounds or Six Pounds and Ten Shillings a year) erected by her
Majesty's Authority and manag'd by persons of the highest
Quality and Station, both in Church and State'.[1] After two
years in the insurance business he had resumed his old avocation
of playwriting 'in order to help out a small Income towards the
support of [his] family'.[2]

From 1715 to 1720 Shadwell composed at least one play a
season for the Smock Alley boards and established himself as
the first dramatist since the Caroline poet, James Shirley, to
form any extended affiliation with the Dublin stage. Far more
than Shirley, however, Shadwell made use of the Irish environment as dramatic background and sought to be a spokesman
for Irish attitudes and loyalties. Three of his Smock Alley
comedies are laid in Dublin, and the fourth, *Irish Hospitality*,
on a country estate in Fingall, the northern part of County
Dublin. They contain numerous allusions to local places and
activities, such as 'Change-Time', the opening of the day's
trading at the Tholsel Exchange;[3] public hangings on St.
Stephen's Green;[4] rowboats for the English packet at Aston's
Key;[5] harlots' lodgings on the Blind Key near the playhouse;[6]
potato wenches on Ormonde's Key across the river;[7] merchants'
daughters who 'make all their own linen' as well as 'work an
Elbow Chair and Two Stools in Irish Stitch'.[8]

Now and again Shadwell introduced a character with definite
touches of native colour. *Irish Hospitality* exhibits the first of the
hearty fox-hunting baronets in Anglo-Irish literature, Sir Jowler
Kennel, who boasts of the best pack of hounds in Ireland.
Devoted to his dogs and horses, he goes about roaring as if at
the hunt and takes his leave with the field cry of 'So ho! ho!'[9]

---

[1] *The Dublin Intelligence*, 19 Dec. 1713. Stockwell, p. 321, misdates the advertisement as of 19 July 1712.
[2] *The Works of Mr. Charles Shadwell*, i. v.
[3] *The Hasty Wedding*, Act I, in *Five New Plays*, p. 14.
[4] *The Hasty Wedding*, Act V, p. 106; *The Plotting Lovers*, p. 313.
[5] *The Sham Prince*, Act V, p. 203.
[6] *The Sham Prince*, Act IV, p. 185.
[7] *Irish Hospitality*, Act I, p. 330.
[8] *The Sham Prince*, Act I, p. 128.
[9] Act I, pp. 328, 336, 337; Act III, p. 372.

In contrast to his frivolity stands the wife of the tenant overseer, Shela Dermott, hard-working and faithful to the interests of her landlord, Sir Patrick Worthy. She apologizes to him that her daughter 'has three pounds of the last Parcel of Wool to spin off still'.[1] She complains to the girl about 'playing at Gentlefolks' and asks her querulously: 'Who must go to Oven this Evening, and get the Plowmen their Suppers?'[2] Another Irishwoman of more distinctly peasant type, bred in 'the North-Country', enters for one very brief scene in *The Plotting Lovers*. Pretending to have been abandoned by a stupid squire, she upbraids him in heated and outlandish language:

Wellaneerin, I'se lick to Swoon—Ah! thou reefy Dog, thou's gar me ho of monny a weabit; have I foond thee, I'se do thee reeght, I'se do thee reeght; Byrlady, I'se have thee hong'd, thoort my Hoseband, and Deel gang away with thee, I'se have thee hong'd.[3]

Shadwell's gentle ridicule of Irish manners, whether urban or rural, was mixed with an interpretation of Irish patriotism surprisingly sympathetic for an Englishman who had been domiciled only a very few years in the land. *The Sham Prince* sincerely represents the views of loyal and substantial Irishmen that 'your fine, gay, sprightly Irish women' cannot be equalled abroad,[4] and that the supposed ambassador to a small German kingdom should conduct himself with proud assurance in the Irish nation: 'For the Honour of our Country, appear as grand as you can, and let those Germans see, that we of Ireland are no despicable People.'[5] The most significant patriotic sentiment is voiced in *The Hasty Wedding* by the brisk young Squire Daudle, who roundly condemns the maidservant Lettice for infidelity to her Irish heritage:

Here's a Jade now; it is not above Two Years ago, since she was taken out of an Irish Cabbin, with her Brogues on, and yet begins to despise her own Country, and is fond of every thing that's English; . . . I think we have Enemies enough abroad, without encouraging those within our selves— . . . I have no Mind to make my self known to this Hussey, for she that would betray her own Country, would, no doubt, betray me.[6]

---

[1] Act IV, p. 389.   [2] Ibid., p. 388.   [3] p. 311.
[4] Act IV, p. 184.   [5] Act II, p. 145.   [6] Act III, p. 52.

This severe declaration upon the theme of disloyalty much exceeds the character's grounds for irritation. It therefore seems certain that Shadwell was seizing the opportunity to express his own indictment of the current state of mind in Ireland. Citizens of every class and sect were growing more and more inclined to adjudge all things Irish as inferior. Contrariwise, a frenzy of admiration for English ways and goods had pretty well infected the whole country. For at least a century this curious bias had been building up pressure to drive budding talent abroad and to depreciate any genius hardy enough to produce at home. A few thoughtful critics like 'Hibernicus' in *The Dublin Weekly Journal* were beginning to deplore publicly both the destructive and the absurd consequences for the domestic literary market:

Wanting suitable Encouragement at home, Men of Genius and Education, born in this Kingdom, are forced out of it to a more kindly Soil, for making a Fortune by their Abilities. . . . We bestow the Ornaments of our own Nation to our Neighbors, and then pay them a dear Rate for the Use of them at second hand. . . . If a good Piece happens at any time to be wrote among ourselves, there is scarce one in ten will vouchsafe it a reading, unless it be made authentick by being printed at London.[1]

Hence Shadwell, as an English man-of-letters who had transplanted himself and had decided to cast his lot with Ireland, was speaking out in enlightened self-interest against that cultural treason which so widely prevailed in the land of his adoption. He had fast become aware that the Dublin-based playwright must contend with a public whose habitual indifference to or even derogation of native authorship rendered success a grave question.

Shadwell's earliest surviving Irish play, *The Hasty Wedding: or, The Intrigueing Squire*, got its initial production at the Theatre Royal during the 1716–17 season, probably in the spring of 1717 after Mrs. Haywood had severed her Smock Alley connexion and gone to London.[2] The author intended this comedy to depict 'the reigning Follies of this spacious Town',[3] namely,

---

[1] *Dublin Weekly Journal*, 3 Apr. 1725.
[2] Genest, ii. 611.   [3] Epilogue, l. 14.

Dublin, but he permitted his scheme of amorous intrigues to predominate so completely that the scenes lack for the most part the localized affectations and the wit commonly associated with the comedy of manners. Shadwell's contrivances of action reveal some of the interesting stage procedures then in vogue at Smock Alley. Both doors at each side of the proscenium continued to be used, sometimes simultaneously. In *The Hasty Wedding* Townley emerges from Mrs. Friendless's house (that is, he enters from one of the doors) and starts to cross the stage as if he were walking down the street.[1] A moment after his entrance Sir Ambrose Wealthy comes out of the adjoining door, spies Townley as just having left Mrs. Friendless's house, and turns back through the door by which he entered so that Townley never observes him.

The proscenium curtain was still employed as scantily at Smock Alley as at the London theatres. Shadwell made no reference to it in any of his Dublin compositions. Instead, like his London contemporaries, he inserted, after the seventeenth-century fashion, riming tags at the close of the acts, even at the end of the play, to enable the characters to make their exit with proper effect. At the conclusion of *The Hasty Wedding*, Sir Ambrose Wealthy herds the celebrants of his daughter's wedding off the stage to the accompaniment of this lengthy tag:

> In vain We Parents lay down Schemes for Life;
> I wisely chose Her husband and my Wife,
> Which might have caus'd a plaguy deal of Strife.
> Fortune will o'er our Actions still preside;
> 'Twas Fortune made my Girl a happy Bride:
> And Fortune, to her Honour be it spoke,
> Eas'd my poor Shoulder of the Marriage-Yoke.

In place of the drawing of the proscenium curtain the device of scene-drawing was developed. Hence the instances of an opening or a shutting of the flats for the introduction or withdrawal of characters noticeably increased. *The Hasty Wedding* at one point offers a striking combination of scene-shifting for the purpose of swift dramatic movement.[2] Aurelia, left alone on stage in 'Sir Ambrose's Hall', starts to cross the apron towards

---

[1] Act II in *Five New Plays*, p. 35.   [2] Act III, p. 62.

the door of Mrs. Friendless's house at the same time that 'the Scene draws to the Street'. She is therefore now in the street. Sir Ambrose enters through one of the doors on the far side from Aurelia, catches sight of her about to go into Mrs. Friendless's house, and follows at a distance. As he disappears through the same door where Aurelia made her exit, the 'Scene draws, and discovers Widow Friendless, Herriot, and Aurelia' in the Widow's house. Shadwell's next play, *Irish Hospitality*, exhibits a similar application of scene-drawing.[1] Sir Jowler Kennel and Lucy meet in the 'dark Parlour' of Sir Patrick Worthy's house. Sir Jowler goes out by a stage door to find the chaplain at the same time that 'the Scene shuts Lucy in'. The stage now represents another room, into which Sir Jowler and Trusty the pretended chaplain enter from different doors. As they leave the stage after a brief conference, 'the Scene draws to the dark Room, where is Lucy in a Corner'.

The cast which originally presented *The Hasty Wedding* affords evidence aplenty that by the 1716–17 season Ashbury had considerably reinforced his depleted company:[2]

Dumott = Sir John Dareall	Mrs. Lyddal = Lady Daudle
Giffard = Jack Townley	Miss Mary (Molly) Lyddal =
Griffith = Squire Daudle	Aurelia
Hallam = Sir Jeremy Daudle	,, Nancy Lyddal = Herriot
Trefusis = Timothy Cash	Mrs. Martin = Lettice
Vanderbank = Sir Ambrose	,, Vanderbank=Mrs. Friend-
Wealthy	less
Watson = Monsieur Decuir	

With the exception of Squire Daudle, done by Griffith, the more prominent characters were impersonated by seven new performers—Dumott, Henry Giffard, James Vanderbank and his wife, Mrs. Lyddal and her two daughters. Almost all must have made their professional débuts under Ashbury, and within a year or two. Certainly no one of them had had a previous record on the London stage. Ashbury much needed these reinforcements, because Buckley, Kendall, Mrs. Dumeney, Mrs. Fitzgerald, and Mrs. Wilkins seem to have permanently retired about 1716, and Thomas Elrington spent the whole season of

---

[1] Act III, pp. 372–4.   [2] Dramatis Personae, pp. [7–8].

1716–17 acting in London.[1] Griffith did not follow his fellow sharer abroad; he stayed at Smock Alley and took his end-of-the-season benefit in May or June 1717 with a performance of Joseph Addison's *The Drummer*, a sentimental comedy first seen in London the year before. For this benefit Charles Shadwell wrote the unusual vaudeville-like prologue to which reference has already been made.[2] After three minutes of repartee between Griffith and Mary Lyddal, the star *ingénue*, over her fine new costume, Griffith brought the fooling to a gracious end by an expression of gratitude to the ladies in the box circle:

> To thank 'em, we have both a Just Pretence,
> You for your Suit of Cloaths, I for the Pence.

At the commencement of its 1717–18 season the Theatre Royal greeted the new Lord-Lieutenant, Charles Paulet, Duke of Bolton, and his wife with a fresh Dublin-born play by Shadwell, fortuitously entitled *Irish Hospitality: or, Virtue Rewarded*. The prologue, spoken by Thomas Elrington, hailed the Duke, who had assumed office in August, as the long-awaited Maecenas of a national theatre:

> Hibernia, then, from Wars and Tumult free,
> Bless'd with a Bolton, Happy Days shall see,
> And long indulge in Peace and Poetry.[3]

Irish Hospitality, like *The Hasty Wedding*, is a comedy of conventional amorous intrigue with 'humours' characters, but it contains much more moral sentiment as well as somewhat more wit than its predecessor. The varied and numerous dramatis personae attached to its Irish country locale called for most of the experienced Smock Alley personnel:[4]

Daugherty = Sir Wou'd-Be-Generous	Mrs. Lyddal { = Lady Peevish / = Shela Dermott
Dumott = Goodlove	Miss Mary Lyddal = Winifred
Ralph Elrington = Jacob Trusty	Mrs. Martin = Lucy
Thomas Elrington = Charles Worthy	,, Vanderbank = Penelope
Evans = Sir Patrick Worthy	Miss Wilson = Myra

---

[1] Genest, ii. 604, 611. [2] See p. 147.
[3] Lines 16–18. [4] Dramatis Personae in *Five New Plays*, pp. [322–4].

Griffith = Sir Jowler Kennel
Hallam = Clumsey
Thomas = Ned Generous
Trefusis = A Poor Man
Vanderbank = Morose

This cast includes the names of two new-comers, Ralph Elrington and a Mr. Thomas. The latter left no other trace of his presence in Dublin; the former was a younger brother of Thomas and Francis Elrington, and had just launched himself on a stage career. All three Elringtons participated in the managemént of the Smock Alley Theatre at different times in the next twenty years. Mary Lyddal, who also delivered the epilogue to *Irish Hospitality* at its première, married Henry Giffard within the following eighteen months, and, as Mrs. Giffard, made herself the leading young actress of the company for the next few years.[1] Mr. and Mrs. Ashbury did not appear in either *Irish Hospitality* or *The Hasty Wedding*, or in Shadwell's subsequent plays. Obviously they were avoiding new roles in order to reduce their burden of acting, an understandable desire after almost thirty-five years of joint performance.

About 1716 or 1717 a taste for the theatre began to be skilfully inculcated in the younger generation by one of Dublin's leading educators, the Reverend Thomas Sheridan, D.D., grandfather of Richard Brinsley Sheridan the dramatist. Dr. Sheridan had recently established a boys' school at 27 Capel Street, a short distance beyond the north end of Essex Bridge, and had instituted as a feature of his curriculum periodical representations

[1] That the Mr. Giffard of the Smock Alley Theatre was Henry Giffard, born at London in 1699, is clearly attested by Chetwood, pp. 166–7, though the latter gives a confused account of Giffard's early career. Stockwell, p. 321, mistakenly lists the Smock Alley actor as Thomas Giffard. Henry Giffard may have crossed from Dublin to London for the season of 1717–18 and may be the Mr. Giffard mentioned in the Lincoln's Inn Fields Theatre notices for that one season only (Genest, ii. 627, 631). This London actor, however, could have been the William Giffard who joined Henry at the Goodman's Fields Theatre in 1729 (op. cit., iii. 274). The Mrs. Giffard who opened her stage career at Lincoln's Inn Fields in November 1717 (op. cit., ii. 625) was certainly *not* the former Mary Lyddal from Dublin. This London comedienne, perhaps a sister of Henry Giffard, played steadily at Lincoln's Inn Fields, married in 1721 a fellow actor Egleton, and, as Mrs. Egleton, continued on the London stage until 1733 (op. cit., iii. 83, 395–7). Mrs. Henry Giffard played the heroine in *The Sham Prince* (1719), *Rotherick O'Connor* (1719–20), *The Fatal Extravagance* (1720–1), and other later Dublin plays.

of classical or Shakespearian plays. To these dramatic exhibitions he invited such high city notables as the Archbishop of Dublin and the Lord-Lieutenant.[1] In 1718 the Sheridan schoolboys acted *Julius Caesar*. The epilogue was delivered by Lord Mountcashel,[2] one of the many students who kept up their interest in the stage and later encouraged the Smock Alley players with various benefactions, especially gifts to the wardrobe. In 1720 Dr. Sheridan chose for performance Euripides' *Hippolytus* in the Greek, and for the occasion his good friend Dean Swift composed a prologue and epilogue.[3] The epilogue warmly defended 'this new method' of theatrical pedagogy, 'to act plays first and understand them after'. By 1723 the Sheridan school dramatics attracted so large a following that the master moved the production of that year, Sophocles' *Oedipus Rex*, to the more commodious hall of the King's Inns,[4] where private theatricals had been held in the early seventeenth century.[5]

In the fall of 1718 two of Smock Alley's chief performers, Thomas Elrington and John Evans, accepted London engagements for the ensuing season,[6] a loss somewhat mitigated by the re-engagement of Benjamin Husband(s), who had been playing at Lincoln's Inn Fields.[7] Evans fell ill in November and died at Chester *en route* back to Ireland.[8] Without him and Elrington Ashbury had no first-rate tragedian, for Husband(s), though a veteran of some versatility, did not qualify as an impressive 'lead' in tragedy. Ashbury, like the managers in London, had been forced by local taste some ten years ago to subordinate tragedy to comedy in the Smock Alley repertoire, but now he was compelled to turn more than ever to the lighter

[1] Alicia Lefanu, *Memoirs of the Life and Writings of Mrs. Frances Sheridan* (London, 1824), p. 12.

[2] The Lanesborough MSS., iii. 273.

[3] *The Correspondence of Jonathan Swift*, iii. 125 n.; *The Poems of Jonathan Swift, D.D.* (ed. William E. Browning, London, 1910), ii. 355.

[4] The performance of *Oedipus Rex* in Greek took place on 10 Dec. 1723 according to a note in the W. J. Lawrence Irish theatre collection, University of Cincinnati.

[5] See Chapter I, p. 20.

[6] Genest, ii. 635, 647. For a digest of Elrington's stage career see op. cit., x. 293-4.

[7] Genest, ii. 633; x. 297-8. Chetwood, p. 180, misdates Husband(s)'s return to Ireland as 1713.

[8] Genest, ii. 649; Chetwood, p. 145. The latter misdates the year of Evans's death as 1716.

species of drama. Two humorous plays, recently successful in England, appeared at the Theatre Royal in Dublin for the first time during the winter of 1718–19: *Woman is a Riddle*,[1] a comedy of intrigue by Christopher Bullock, and *A Bold Stroke for a Wife*,[2] a comedy of intrigue and manners by Mrs. Susannah Centlivre. Toward the end of the 1718–19 season Ashbury produced two more new comic pieces: in May or June, *The Sham Prince: or, News from Passau*, a Dublin satire by Charles Shadwell; and on Monday, 20 July, Charles Johnson's mixture of intrigue, manners, and sentiment, *The Masquerade*,[3] which had delighted London just a few months earlier.

Shadwell got his inspiration for *The Sham Prince* from a remarkable Dublin swindle brought to light in the spring of 1719. One of the victims colourfully described the trickery in a rare and curious pamphlet entitled: *Passaw or the German Prince Being a Genuine Relation of the late Transactions of Sir William Newsted alias Prince of Passaw, wherein that Notable Piece of Knight Errantry is trac'd from its first Original to its final Exit. Together with a List of the Officers Civil and Military, under the Establishment of his Lunary Highness, and true Copies of the Letters, Schemes and Articles of Alliance, by means of which the Cheat was so long supported. Now made publick from the Original Papers.*[4] In 1718 William Newsted, the twenty-year-old son of a County Westmeath gentleman who had moved to Dublin to keep a lodging-house, forged a number of letters and other documents to show that he had been created Prince of Passau by His Imperial Majesty the King of this small German state in Lower Bavaria. On the strength of his spurious papers Newsted borrowed considerable sums of money from relatives and acquaintances in order to maintain his princely station until official funds should arrive. The fraud was uncovered when Newsted, anticipating exposure, fled to England in April 1719.

Shadwell adapted Newsted's imposture to a dramatic plot which linked the deception of Dublin tradesmen by the sham

[1] *Dickson's Dublin Intelligencer*, 10 Jan. 1718/19.
[2] *Dublin Courant*, 11 Mar. 1718/19.
[3] *Harding's Dublin Newsletter*, 18 July 1719.
[4] The pamphlet bears at the bottom of the title-page: 'Dublin: Printed for John Crawford, at the Exchange on Cork-Hill. 1719.' See Tract 3, Box 163, in the Holiday Collection of the Royal Irish Academy.

prince with the romantic intrigues of city-bred young ladies and gentlemen of fortune. The kind-hearted or, maybe, politic playwright felt, however, that 'there were too many People of good Sense and Reputation concern'd, to be expos'd'[1] by an unvarnished representation. Hence, in his depiction of the swindling, he 'took Care to do it so, that even the People, from whom I stole my Characters, could not take it ill, and came to see themselves represented'.[2] In fact, he dealt so mildly with the folly of the duped tradesmen that his comedy lacks the vigour and bite of true Jonsonian satire. Nevertheless, the gentleness of Shadwell's ridicule paid off excellently, for he later boasted of 'how well the Town receiv'd it' and of the fact that he 'was the only Man in Dublin that got Money by [the sham prince's] going off'.[3]

The Sham Prince, according to its author, 'was written in Five Days, and by the Actors got up in Ten more'.[4] The première took place either in late May or at the beginning of June 1719. Mrs. Giffard spoke the prologue; Griffith, the epilogue; and the cast was as follows:[5]

Daugherty = Mr. Kersey, a Draper
Dumott = Trip, Welldone's Footman
Giffard = Welldone
Griffith = Mr. Shred, a Tailor
Hallam = Mr. Seville, a Merchant
Lyddal = Sir William Cheatly, the Sham Prince
Rogers = Cheatly, Sr.
Trefusis = Shoulder-Dab, a Bailiff
Vanderbank = Sir Bullet Airy
Watson = Trueman

Mrs. Giffard = Araminta
 „ Lyddal = Lady Homebred
 „ Martin = Mrs. Twist
 „ Vanderbank = Mrs. Seville
Miss Nancy Lyddal = Miss Nancy Homebred
 „ Schoolding = Miss Molly Homebred

This cast included two important additions to the Smock Alley Company within the 1718–19 season, both of them from Lincoln's Inn Fields: Mr. Rogers, the husband of a well-known London actress recently deceased, and Miss Schoolding, a

---

[1] The Preface to *The Sham Prince*.   [2] Ibid.   [3] Ibid.
[4] Ibid.   [5] Dramatis Personae in *Five New Plays*, p. [116].

former Smock Alley comedienne.[1] 'Jo' Trefusis cannot be traced subsequent to *The Sham Prince* and must be thought to have retired by 1720. His acting career extended over approximately forty-five years, thirty-five of them in Dublin. Barring Ashbury, Trefusis was the only important Smock Alley graduate who settled down at his stage *alma mater* and remained content with the applause of Irishmen rather than Londoners.

Ashbury celebrated his eightieth birthday late in 1718 and a few months afterwards discovered that his advanced age had once again attracted the attention of English place-hunters to the post which he held under the Crown. During the winter of 1718–19 he lost the privilege of arranging the succession to the office of Master of the Revels in Ireland. A 'gentleman' named Anthony Twyman took it into his head that the office might prove a desirable sinecure, though it then carried no salary. Under date of 31 January 1718/19 Twyman obtained at St. James's Palace a royal warrant which granted him, and his assigns during his life, the reversion of the Irish Revels office on the death, surrender, or forfeiture of Joseph Ashbury, the co-patentees 'William Morgan and Charles Ashbury being now dead and only Joseph Ashbury surviving'.[2] The warrant further stated that all persons were forbidden to erect any theatre or stages in Ireland without Twyman's licence, and that no person deserting from Twyman's company was to be entertained by any other company without Twyman's consent, given under his hand and seal. These provisions copied similar articles in the existing patent. The king's warrant was duly forwarded to Dublin, and the chancery there issued on 9 April 1719 a new patent to the office of Master of the Revels in Ireland, granting

---

[1] Genest, ii. 648, 655–8, evidences that Mrs. Rogers's career came to an end at L.I.F. in Nov. 1718. Miss Schoolding's London career is shrouded in much uncertainty. She may well be the 'Mrs. Schoolding' listed in the L.I.F. notices of the 1716–17 season (Genest, ii. 609, 611). For the 1717–18 season there are no surviving references to a 'Mrs.' or a 'Miss' Schoolding on the London stage. Some time before the 1718–19 season Miss Schoolding may have married (Chetwood, p. 51 n., gives no date or place for her marriage to the dancer Anthony Moreau), and, if she did so, she may be identified with the 'Mrs. Moreau' whom L.I.F. notices mentioned from Oct. 1718 to Feb. 1719, and never thereafter (Genest, ii. 648–52).

[2] Mason, 'Collection for a History of the City of Dublin', Egerton MS. 1773, f. 25, and *Liber Munerum Publicarum Hiberniae*, vol. i, pt. ii, p. 93, give the dates of the royal warrant and of the patent at Dublin, but no further details.

Twyman the reversion of the office after Ashbury.[1] In addition
to recapitulating the items in the warrant, Twyman's patent
imitated the preceding one of 1684 by forbidding all obscene
plays and all acting of men garbed as women, and by ordering
all mayors, sheriffs, bailiffs, constables, and other officers to aid
Twyman in suppressing unlicensed plays and players. This
patent of 1719 significantly departed from the past, however,
in that the office was bestowed upon a man connected in no
way with the theatre business of either Dublin or London and
not intending to engage in such business. Thus Twyman's appointment initiated the transformation of the office of Master
of the Revels in Ireland into a purely nominal position which
from 1722 onwards remunerated the holder at the rate of £300
per year.[2] The office continued as an absurd charge on the Irish
Establishment until 1817.[3]

Twyman's patent could not and did not affect Ashbury's
conduct of the Theatre Royal. For the 1719–20 season Ashbury
augmented his company with Lewis Layfield, who for fifteen
years past had been dancer, musician, and player of minor
roles on various English stages.[4] Ashbury's son-in-law, Thomas
Elrington, rejoined the troupe after a season's absence at Drury
Lane and provided much-needed strength on the side of tragedy.[5]
During the succeeding decade both Layfield and Elrington
engaged conspicuously in Dublin theatrical affairs as directors
of the Smock Alley playhouse.

Charles Shadwell continued to furnish original entertainment
for what he conceived as Ireland's national theatre. From the
English adaptation of Molière's *Monsieur de Pourceaugnac*, which
William Congreve and Sir John Vanbrugh had brought forth

[1] W. J. Lawrence made notes (now in his Irish theatre collection, University
of Cincinnati) of the main provisions in the royal warrant and in the patent from
the original documents originally preserved at the Public Record Office, Dublin,
but destroyed by fire in 1922.

[2] The Right Honorable Edward Hopkins, Secretary to the Lord-Lieutenant,
succeeded to the Revels office on the death of Twyman and was awarded by his
patent of 11 Oct. 1722 this fee of £300. See Mason's 'Collection', loc. cit., and
Liber Munerum, loc. cit.

[3] The Revels office was abolished on the death of the ninth holder, William
Meeke, in 1817.

[4] Layfield made his stage début as a dancer at Lincoln's Inn Fields on 10 July
1704.

[5] Genest, ii. 642.

in 1704 under the title of *Squire Trelooby*, Shadwell fashioned an abbreviated version of his own, in which he transplanted the Cornish squire Trelooby to Dublin surroundings for a projected marriage to a merchant's daughter. This hour-long farce, called *The Plotting Lovers: or, The Dismal Squire*, was intended to serve as an after-piece on the long evening programmes at Smock Alley. Its première occurred during the 1719–20 season with the following cast:[1]

Daugherty { = Countryman
     = Pretended Wife
       to Trelooby
	Miss Wolfe = Celia, Tradewell's
	   daughter

Dumott = Physician	Mrs. Martin = Sentry, Celia's maid
Giffard = Lovewell, a Gentle- man	Miss Waters = Countrywoman
Griffith = Squire Trelooby	
Hallam = Tradewell, a Merchant	
Vanderbank = Witwou'd, Lovewell's servant	

Watson { = Physician
     = Constable
     = Pretended Wife to Trelooby	

Watson, Jr. = Apothecary	

This is the first and only surviving notice of the three young actors, Mr. Watson, Jr., Miss Waters, and Miss Wolfe. Their appearance in *The Plotting Lovers* may indicate that Ashbury advanced the training of his novices by giving them their first speaking parts in the after-pieces.

In the course of the same season Shadwell's most ambitious composition, 'his first Essay in Tragick Strains',[2] was also presented to the Dublin public. Very appropriately he drew from Irish history his basic materials of tragic struggle—the twelfth-century feud between Rotherick O'Connor, King of Connaught, last of the High Kings of Ireland, and Dermond MacMurrough, King of Leinster. *Rotherick O'Connor: or, The Distressed Princess* is constructed after the manner of the earlier seventeenth-century romantic tragedy rather than of the more recent 'heroic' or 'pathetic' species. It telescopes historical incidents, mingles fact with fiction, and aims to create tragic effect mainly by

---

[1] Dramatis Personae in *Five New Plays*, p. [292].
[2] Epilogue 'written by Mr. Shadwell', l. 8.

recurrences of physical violence. The plot grows out of the invasion of Ireland by the English earl, Richard Strongbow, as ally of Dermond. The subsequent fighting between the forces of Rotherick and of Strongbow produces numerous captures, imprisonments, duels, suicides, and killings.

To these actions of war Shadwell attached the requisite love interest in the shape of two fictitious romances which involve Rotherick's daughter, Avelina, and Dermond's daughter, Eva. Avelina, in love with Cothurnus the son of her father's Irish foe, commits suicide in the fourth act after her father has murdered her lover. Eva's destiny is less readily solved. She is in love with Maurice Regan, her father's confidant, and he with her, but Dermond has betrothed her to Strongbow. Soon Rotherick grows infatuated with her; eventually, however, he is stabbed to death by Strongbow. Regan's unauthorized murder by Strongbow's guards cools Eva's feelings towards the victorious English earl. Thus, out of ten major participants, Eva and Strongbow are the only characters to escape alive from the turmoil. The play disposes of them in a sentimental finale typical of the prevailing stage taste. As Strongbow leads the sadly bereaved Eva off towards an abbey to meditate upon his proffer of marriage, he utters this curtain prayer:

> With Love, ye Gods, possess the charming Fair,
> That she may raise her Lover from Despair.

Ashbury allocated Strongbow to Smock Alley's newest experienced recruit, Lewis Layfield. Mrs. Giffard assumed the female 'lead' as Eva. The only other feminine part, that of Avelina, was filled by Mrs. Moreau, formerly Miss Schoolding, who had married Anthony Moreau, a stage dancer, in 1718 or 1719,[1] and, with her husband, was to occupy an increasingly prominent position in the Smock Alley repertory of the 1720's. Shadwell listed the complete cast thus:[2]

Daugherty $\begin{cases} = \text{Mortagh, Eva's guardian} \\ = \text{First Guard} \end{cases}$ Mrs. Giffard = Eva
Mrs. Moreau = Avelina
Dumott = Dermond MacMurrough
Ralph Elrington = Third Guard
Giffard = Maurice Regan

[1] See p. 168, n. 1.   [2] Dramatis Personae in *Five New Plays*, p. [218].

Rogers = Rotherick O'Connor
Vanderbank = Catholicus, Archbishop of Tuam
Watson $\begin{cases} = \text{Auliffe O'Kinaude, Dermond's friend} \\ = \text{Second Guard} \end{cases}$

Rotherick O'Connor, though an ill-designed and uninspired drama that did not long hold the stage, merits attention as a significant theatrical document. Its interpretation of the twelfth-century warring between English and Irish connected that era with the conflict of political feelings in eighteenth-century Ireland. The prologue brings to view Ireland as Shadwell imagined it to have been five to six hundred years before, divided and oppressed by its own rulers:

> Heroes nurs'd up in Slaughter, Blood, and Woe:
> And Kings that Rul'd by Arbitrary Sway
> Their slavish Subjects, born but to Obey. . . .
> When Church and Clergy were the Monarch's Tools,
> And who oppos'd their King were reckon'd Fools.[1]

To this torn and suffering land comes the English conqueror, Strongbow, to bestow law and order and prosperity:

> I come not to destroy, but give you Liberty,
> And bring this barbarous Nation to such Laws
> As will draw Peace and Plenty to your Country.[2]

The Church in the person of Catholicus, Archbishop of Tuam, plays a crafty and servile game of allying itself with the winning temporal ruler of the moment. When Strongbow emerges the ultimate victor and announces that he 'would not prosecute the Church', Catholicus promises him:

> The Clergy in their Pulpits shall declare
> That you have all the Right you would have,
> We'll found it on what Principle you please.[3]

Strongbow replies:

> The Right of Conquest is the Right I own.

[1] Prologue 'written by Mr. Shadwell', ll. 12–14, 19–20.
[2] Act V, p. 279.
[3] Ibid.

Catholicus without hesitation counters:

> Then they shall preach up that, and in such Terms,
> That, were you beaten, they should say you conquer'd;
> 'Tis good to have the Roman Churchmen on your Side,
> We can preach up Peace, or raise Rebellion.
> Observe that Prince sits easiest on his Throne,
> Who strives to make the Clergy all his own.

In contrast to the clerical attitude of expediency Eva, the daughter of Dermond, embodies a consistent and zealous adherence to the cause of Ireland's independence. Up to the final curtain she cannot be moved beyond a grudging respect for the agent of foreign intervention, Strongbow. In her presence Regan eulogizes the enlightened state of the English:

> Their Country seems more civiliz'd than ours;
> With Arts and Sciences they pollish all
> The rude, the wild ungovernable Crew. . . .
> One mighty Monarch Governs thro' the Land;
> He takes Advice, indeed, of all those Men,
> Who are, by long Experience, made most wise:[1]

But Eva rebukes him for his blindness to the virtues of the Irish:

> You have forgot you were in Ireland born,
> Where pure Religion, by St. Patrick taught,
> Is still kept up with a becoming Zeal:
> Here we are govern'd by Nature's Dictates,
> Not by dissembling Art, which teaches Men
> To act quite opposite to what they think:
> Wisdom makes Hypocrites, Nature makes none.[2]

She deplores her father's stratagem of calling on the English for help:

> I have a Soul, that would not sell
> The barren Part of all my Land, to be
> Reveng'd of Millions of my Enemies:
> Bring in Strangers to cut the Throats of those
> Who are my Friends, my Children, and my Subjects.[3]

[1] Act I, p. 223.
[2] Ibid.
[3] Act III, p. 255.

Later still, when Regan indulges in lavish praise of Strongbow,
Eva cuts him off with the prophetic comment:

> But I shall curse the Day he landed here,
> And you your self, ere long, will wish him dead.[1]

Shadwell, it seems likely, intended these lines as a meaningful
observation on the embitterment of the native Irish in consequence of repeated 'liberations' by forces from England.

Thus *Rotherick O'Connor* through its warm characterization
of Eva turns a sympathetic spotlight upon that devoted and
honourable Irish patriotism which persistently refused to accept
with complacence the English Ascendancy. This play quite
evidently was for Shadwell the climax of his endeavour to relate
the Dublin drama and theatre to the nationalistic sentiments
then gathering force among Protestant as well as Catholic Irish.

Shadwell wrote no more for any stage, and early in 1720 set
about the printing of his dramatic works by subscription. Of
the Smock Alley actors, Ashbury, Thomas Elrington, and Benjamin Husband(s) responded favourably to his soliciting and
had their names listed as subscribers. The elderly manager did
not live, however, to see published *The Works of Mr. Charles
Shadwell* in two volumes.[2] 'Retaining his Judgment to the last
Moment of his Life',[3] Ashbury died on Wednesday, 24 July
1720, in his eighty-second year.[4] He was buried near his Oxmantown residence in the yard of St. Michan's,[5] the church at
which he and his second wife, Ann, had been married thirty-five
years before.

The death of Joseph Ashbury ended a career of historic importance to the English-speaking theatre. Fifty-eight years an
actor, forty-five years a manager, Master of the Revels in
Ireland under the five monarchs from Charles II to George I,
Ashbury developed the Theatre Royal at Dublin into the fore-

---

[1] Act IV, p. 270.

[2] *The Works*, bearing the imprint of 1720, were published in October or November. On the one hand Shadwell in his preface writes of Elrington and Griffith as
now in charge of the Smock Alley Company, and, on the other hand, Swift in
A Letter of Advice to a Young Poet, 1 Dec. 1720, refers to 'plays, especially the new,
and above all, those of our own growth, printed by subscription', an obvious
indication that Shadwell's two volumes of plays had already made their appearance.

[3] Chetwood, p. 86.   [4] Ibid.   [5] Ibid., p. 136 n.

most stage nursery of the British Isles, a position which it maintained for well over a century. At least a dozen of his young actors achieved top ratings in London: Francis Baker, Barton Booth, Thomas Doggett, Thomas Elrington, Richard Estcourt, Thomas Griffith, Theophilus Keen, John Leigh, Henry Norris, William Pinkethman, James Quin, and Robert Wilks. Furthermore, he transformed the Irish stage from a Dublin Castle recreation to a popular enterprise of nationwide interest patronized by but not dependent upon the Government of Ireland, an enterprise centred in the capital but already extending its activity into outlying towns.

The success of Ashbury's leadership sprang in particular from two qualities, diplomacy and prudence, as his one-time assistant Chetwood confirmed in these elegiac lines:

> By Judgment's Compass ev'ry Course he steer'd,
> And watch'd the Signals ere the Storm appear'd.
> His Prudence o'er the Surges did prevail,
> With Ballast still proportion'd to his Sail— . . .
> By Grace instructed, and by Nature mild;
> Nor relish'd Life, but when he reconcil'd.[1]

Ashbury's policies, however, demonstrated also the defect of his virtues by proving notably sound but wholly orthodox. The English-born manager, conservative in both temperament and training, showed himself a firm supporter of the English Ascendancy from the time when he first set foot on Irish soil. He always held to the traditional view that the Dublin Theatre Royal was an outpost of the London stage and, as such, should be guided by London modes and repertory. In consequence he never felt an ambition to rear up a truly indigenous theatre. He never went out of his way to encourage playwriting in Ireland for domestic consumption. He did accept and produce the infrequent contributions of home talent which came to hand, but, when he did so, he was not motivated by any deep-seated concern for the promotion of an Irish literary movement. His behaviour for the greater part reflected the cautious Englishman of business. It was not an easy task to wrest a comfortable living and social position out of managing the playhouse in

[1] Ibid., p. 87.

Dublin. Ashbury persistently avoided jeopardizing his invest-
ment by unrequired expenditures. During his lengthy régime
Smock Alley underwent no major alterations or refurbishings.
Indeed the building was quietly allowed by its proprietor to
age into perhaps the most unprepossessing public edifice of the
Irish capital.

Nevertheless, these shortcomings in Ashbury's policies were
those which in all probability any man on the English stage
during the seventeenth and early eighteenth centuries would
have displayed if he had moved to what was then commonly
regarded as the hinterland and there had had to earn his
fortune in management. On the other hand, no one of Ashbury's
contemporaries in England, not even the distinguished Thomas
Betterton, equalled the former's acumen and perseverance as
a director. It was an exceptional achievement to have nurtured
the Dublin theatre through an adolescence plagued with political unrest to a secure maturity by 1720.

A few months after Ashbury's death the city's most forthright
critic, Dean Swift, in *A Letter of Advice to a Young Poet*, published
some bantering remarks about the state of the arts and letters
in 'this our large and polite city'. The raillery which Swift
directed towards the Smock Alley playhouse served to emphasize
that it had attained the status of an indispensable civic institution:

> We have here a Court, a College, a Playhouse. . . . That
> Simple House is the Fountain of all our Love, Wit,
> Dress, and Gallantry.[1]

Plainly the Theatre Royal had come of age; it was now recognized to be one of the foci of the nation's culture.

The housing of the Theatre Royal, however, corresponded
in no respect to its eminence as an institution. All parts of the
sixty-year-old fabric had fallen into a decay so serious that
repairs would only alleviate for a brief space the unpleasant and
perhaps dangerous condition. Ashbury's decease made oppor-
tune a building campaign. The new proprietors issued their
first challenge to the pride and beneficence of their compatriots

---

[1] *Satires and Personal Writings by Jonathan Swift* (ed. William A. Eddy, London
and New York, 1932), pp. 52, 55.

in an epilogue spoken by Thomas Griffith before the Lord
Deputy, Charles Fitzroy, Duke of Grafton, and his Duchess:

Illustratious Pair, the Blessing of this Isle
Who, Gracious, on our humble Labours smile:
To You, thus Low, your Servants bow;—to You
Their only Hope, they for Protection sue,
And beg your Aid against the Assaults of Time.
We suffer by that old Offenders Crime:
The Ladies trembled at a loud Applause,
When in soft Scenes we exercis'd our Calling,
We mov'd their Terror, lest the Roof was falling.
Scarce durst we represent a Tragick Battle,
And, strook with Dread, they heard our Thunder rattle. . .
This Pile, the Temple of Apollo rose,
When Charles return'd, to give his Realm repose: . . .
This House we hope is not of long Duration,
The Hint suffices to a gallant Nation:
Let not the Ladies Fears their Joys restrain,
Nor with their Pleasures mix perpetual Pain.
With a new Theatre oblige the Fair,
Who, else, will all to London Plays repair;
With one Consent, like Swallows, bad adieu t'ye,
And leave poor Dublin destitute of Beauty.
The greatest Patriots have in every Age,
Made it their Glory, to support the Stage:
Your Ancestors to raise this Stage combin'd,
Improv'd our Pleasures, and our Taste refin'd:
May you, like them, the Arts of Peace maintain,
Since George, like Charles, renews a Peaceful Reign.[1]

This public appeal for the erection of a more noble 'Temple of
Apollo' at Dublin illustrated how deeply in the life of Ireland
the drama had taken root. Though its literary materials still
expressed a feeble and tentative Irishism, so far furnished to
a great extent by men of English birth, the inhabitants of the
island were enlisting more and more heavily in the theatrical

---

[1] 'An Epilogue Spoke by Mr. Griffith, to their Graces, the Duke and Duchess
of Grafton, at the Theatre Royal in Dublin. Written by Ambrose Phillips, Esq.',
Dublin Courant, 4 Oct. 1721. Phillips (?1675–1749), a London poet of moderate
reputation, was apparently sojourning at Dublin in the fall of 1721 (a fact un-
mentioned by all his biographers). After a return to England, he in 1726 assumed
the office of Purse Bearer in the Irish Government.

profession and were soon to become a major source of supply to the English-speaking world. From the early days of the Dublin pageants and the Kilkenny religious plays the native tradition had grown and clarified. Now the vision of a 'national' stage was emerging. At last the great theatrical genius of the Irish had begun its long journey toward full self-realization.

APPENDIX A

Documents Relating to the Office of Master of the Revels in Ireland, 1660–1684

1. Warrant, dated 26 September 1660, to the Lords Justices of Ireland to issue to Sir William Davenant a patent for the Office. (S.P. 63, State Papers, Ireland, vol. 304, no. 171, Public Record Office, London.)

Charles R.

Right trusty and right well beloued Councello[rs] We greet you well. Wheras We have thought fitt and convenient to allow in Our Citty of London such Publique Presentations of Tragedies and Comedies as have been formerly pmitted by Our Royall Predeceso[rs] for y[e] harmelesse Recreation & divertisem[t] of such of Our owne Subjects or fforregners as shall be disposed to resort to them wth a strick Injunction that all such Tragedies & Comedies as have been formerly or shall be hereafter psented shall be purged and freed from all obsenenesse and pfaness & soe become instructive to Morality in Our people. And Wheras S[r] William Dauenant Kn[t] hath had a Pattent under y[e] broad Seale of England from our Royall ffather of blessed memory to erect a Theater in Our Citty of London and hath been lately authorized by Us to exercise the said priviledge Therefore Our will and pleasure is (being willing to allow y[e] same harmelesse recreations to Our Subjects in Ireland) that you forthw[th] cause a Pattent to be drawne & passed wherby the said Sr William Dauenant may be authorised to erect or pvide a Theater in Our Citty of Dublyn, confirming ye said priviledge to him ~~for his life~~[1] and his heyres.

And wheras We have lately authorised Two Howses or Theaters and noe more to be erected in Our Citty of London, soe in consideracõn of the expences necessary to that work We doe enjoyne that noe more Theaters or Play Houses be pmitted in Our Citty of

---

[1] These three words have been struck out in the original manuscript.

Dublyn then that One Theater or Play house to be erected or prouided by the said Sr William Dauenant. And Our further Will and pleasure is That by the said Pattent the said Sr William Dauenant shall enjoy the authority and office of Master of Revells of Ireland during his life wth such priviledges annext unto it as you shall thinke fitt; for wch this shall be your Warrant. Given at Our Court at Whitehall this 26th day of November in the Twelfe yeere of Our Reigne.

By his Maties Comand
Edw. Nicholas

Sr Wm Dauenant M^r of ye Revills in Irel^d.

2. Petition (undated) of John Ogilby for grant of the Office. (S.P. 63, State Papers, Ireland, vol. 345, no. 50, Public Record Office, London.)

To the kinges most Excellent Maiestie./
The humble peticõn of John Ogilby./
Sheweth

That yor peticõner had a graunt from the Right Hono^ble Thomas Earle of Strafford then Lieutenant of Ireland for the enjoying and executing the place and office of the Master of the Revells of that kingdome which after his great preparacõns and disbursements in building a new Theatre stocking and bringing over a Company of Actors and Musitians and setling them in Dublin fell to utter rueine by the Calamities of those times to the utter undoeing (by the Damage of Two Thousand pounds att least) of yor peticõner./

Hee humbly requests notwithstanding Sr William Davenets [sic] pretences that yor Maiestie would bee graciously pleased, (that yor peticõner may have some reparacõn of his great losses) to conferr the said office on him./

And yor pet^r shall ever pray &c

3. Warrant (undated) for the issue to John Ogilby of a patent to the Office. (Signet Docquet Books, Index, 6813, March 1660/1, p. 4, Public Record Office, London.)

The Office of M^ar of the Revells in Ireland (now erected) graunted to John Ogilby dureing his Life wth all Fees &c thereunto belonging in as ample manner as ye M^ar of ye Revells enjoyed his place in England[,] And a License to him to build upon such grounds by him to be purchased in Fee in Dublin or elsewhere in Ireland such Theatre or Theatres as to him shall seeme most fitt, To hold to him

& his heires for ever[,] And therein to represent Comedyes Tragedyes and Operas and other Enterludes decent & not obnoxious wth a prohibition to all persons to performe ye same wthout License first obteyned from him[,] And a Revocacõn of all Graunts made to other under ye Signett or Signe Manuall for representing any thing of ye same or like nature. Subtt^d by Mr Solicit^r. By war^t Under S. Manuall Pow^r by Mr Secrty Nicholas.

4. Patent, dated 8 May 1661, creating the Office and granting it to John Ogilby. (C. 66/2995 Patent Roll, 13 Charles II, Part 40, no. 37, Public Record Office, London.)

Charles the second by the grace of God King of England Scotland and Ireland defender of the Faith &c To all to whome these psents shall come greeting Whereas John Ogilby gentleman was heretofore by Instrumente of the hand and seale of Thomas late Earle of Strafford then deputie of our said Kingdome of Ireland bearing date at Dublin the Eight and twentieth day of February in the yeare of our Lord one thousand sixe hundred thirtie and seaven nominated and appointed Master of the Revells in and through our said Kingdome of Ireland and in pursuance thereof he did at his owne greate cost and charges as wee are informed erect a publick Theater in our Cittie of Dublin and did effectually reduce the publick presentations of tragedies and comedies to the pper and harmeles use whereby those recreacõns formerly obnoxious were made inoffensive to such of our subjects and other strangers voluntarily resorting thereunto which theater for some yeares now last past hath beene wholly neglected and gone to ruine and decay And whereas wee have thought fitt that our subjects of our said Kingdome of Ireland should enjoy the like priviledges in that kind as our subjects here in our Kingdome of England and that all maskes operas enterludes tragedies and comedies and other things of that nature there to be represented should be represented as innocently and inoffensively as may be Know yee therefore that wee doe hereby for us our heires and Successors declare our will and pleasure to bee that from henceforth there shall be an office of Master of our Revells and Masques in our said Kingdome of Ireland And reposing especiall trust and confidence in the loyaltie integritie and abilitie of the said John Ogilby hath ordained named constituted and appointed and by these presents for us our heires and Successors doe ordeine name make constitute and appoint the said John Ogilby Master of all and every our Playes Revells Masques and enterludes within our said Kingdome of Ireland To have hold exercise and enjoy the said

office of Master of all Playes Revells Masques and enterludes in our
said Kingdome of Ireland unto him the said John Ogilby by himselfe or his sufficient Deputie or Deputies for and during his naturall
life with all Fees proffitts priviledges advantages and emolum^{ts}
whatsoever in as ample manner and forme as the nowe Master of
our Revells in our Kingdome of England or any other pson or psons
formerly enjoying the said Office have lawfully received taken enjoyed or ought to have received taken and enjoyed And further
knowe yee that wee of our more abundant grace certaine Knowledge
and meere mocõn have given and granted and by these presents for
us our heires and Successors doe give and grant unto the said John
Ogilby his heires and Assignes full and sole power licence and
authoritie to erect and build one or more Theatre or Theatres in
what place or places to him shall seeme most fitt and convenient
either in our Cittie of Dublin or elsewhere in our said Kingdome of
Ireland on such ground as the said John Ogilby his heyres or
Assignes shall purchase to himselfe or themselves in Fee And in such
Theatre or Theatres soe built and erected as aforesaid at all lawfull
times publickly to present and act or chuse to be psented and acted
all Comedies tragedies Operas and other enterludes of what kind
soever decent and becoming and not prophane and obnoxious To
have hold and enjoy the said Theatres and Theatre soe to be erected
and built as aforesaid unto him the said John Ogilby his heires and
Assignes for ever And further wee doe hereby for us our heires and
Successors streightly charge and comand inhibite and forbid all pson
and psons whatsoever that they nor any of them psume to erect or
build any Theatre or Theatres stage or stages wheresoever And
therein to present or act any Comedies tragedies Operas or other
Enterludes whatsoever without licence from the said Ogilby or his
Assignes in writing under his or their hands and seales or hand and
seale first had and obteyned And we doe hereby streightly charge
and comand all Maiors Sheriffs Bayliffs Constables Headborroughes
and all other our Officers and Ministers within our said Kingdome
of Ireland that they cause all stage Playes and enterludes which shall
at any time be presented or acted by any pson or psons contrary to
the meaning of these presents to be suppssed from time to time and
they be from tyme to tyme ayding helping and assisting unto the
said John Ogilby his heyres and Assignes in the suppressing thereof
and apprehending of all such comon players as shall presume to
act any stage playes or enterludes without licence as aforesaid as
they and every of them shall answer the contrary at their prlle And
our further will and pleasure is and we doe hereby declare our will

and pleasure to be that all former grant or grants obteyned by any pson or psons from us under our signett or signe manuall for touching or concning the premisses or any part or parcel thereof shall be from henceforth voyd and of none effect And the same and every of them we doe revoake detmine annihilate and make voyde by these presents And lastly our will and pleasure is and wee doe by these presents declare that these our Letters Patents or the Inrollment or Exemplificatione thereof shall be in all things firme good and effectuall in the lawe according to the true intent and meaning of the same any lawe statute act ordinance proclamation pvision or restricõn or any other matter cause or thing whatsoever to the contrary thereof in any wise notwithstanding Although expresse mencõn &c In witnesse &c Witnesse the King at Westm^{r} the eigth day of May. ₵x^{iii}.

5. Petition (undated) of John Ogilby for a revision of his patent to include a co-patentee. (S.P. 63, State Papers, Ireland, vol. 276, no. 62, Public Record Office, London.)

To the kinges most Excellent Maiestie

The humble peticõn of John Ogilby.

Most humbly sheweth

That yor Maiestie out of your Princely Grace and favour hath bin Graciously pleased by Letters Pattents under your Great Seale of England to constitute and appoint yor peticõner to bee Master of the Revells in yor Maiesties kingdome of Ireland, as alsoe by other Letters Pattents to bee Master of yor Maiesties Royall Imprimerie,/

Yo^{r} pet^{r} most humbly prayeth yor Maiestie would bee pleased to accept the Surrender of the former of the said Letters Pattents, and graunt the said office of Master of the Revells in your Maiesties said kingdome of Ireland unto your peticõner and some such other person whom hee shall choose for his Assistant, whereby hee may the more freely attend the service of your Maiesties Royall Imprimerie./

And yor pet^{r} shall pray &c

6. Draft of a warrant (undated) for a patent granting the Office to John Ogilby and Thomas Stanley, Jr., jointly. (S.P. 63, State Papers, Ireland, vol. 345, no. 51, Public Record Office, London.)

Whereas Wee did by Lett^{rs} Pattents under O^{r} Gr Seale of Engl^{d} beareing date of ye 8th day of May last, constitute & appoint O^{r}

trusty & wellb^d Jo. Ogilby Gen^t to be O^r Master of Y^e Revells & Masques in O^r Kingdome of Ireland, Our Will & Pleasure is That upon surrend^r of ye s^d Lett^rs Patents by ye s^d John Ogilby, you forthw^th prepare a Bill to pass O^r Gr Seale of England containing a Grant of ye s^d Place & Office of M^r of Y^e Revells unto ye s^d Jo. Ogilby & Th. Stanley Gent jointly to be by them held & enjoyed for & during their n[atu]rall lives & ye life of ye longer live^r of them, together wth all & every ye Powers, priviledges &c in ye said Lett^rs Patents of ye 8th of May menc̃oned & contained. For w^ch &c.

7. Warrant, dated 7 September 1661, to the Solicitor-General to draw up a patent to the Office for John Ogilby and Thomas Stanley, Jr., jointly. (S.P. 63, State Papers, Ireland, vol. 307, no. 201, Public Record Office, London.)

Charles R

Whereas Wee did by Our Letters Patents under Our Great Seale of England bearing date ye 8th of May last constitute & appoint Our trusty & well-beloved John Ogilby Gent to be Our Master of Our Revells & Maskes in Our Kingdome of Ireland, Our Will & Pleasure is that upon surrender of ye said Letters Patents made by ye said John Ogilby you forthwith prepare a Bill for Our Royall Signature to passe Our Greate Seale of England, containing a Grant of the said Place & Office of Master of Our Revells & Maskes of that Our Kingdome of Ireland, unto ye said John Ogilby & Thomas Stanley Gent jointly, to be by them held & enjoyed for & dureing their naturall lives, & ye life of ye longer liver of them, together with all & every ye powers & priviledges in ye said Letters Patents of ye 8th of May menc̃oned & contained. For Which this shall be yor Warrant. Given at Our Court at Whitehall ye 7th day of Sept. 1661.

By his Ma^tys Command
Edw Nicholas

To Our trusty & well beloved
Sr Heneage Finch Kn^t & Bar^tt
Our Solicit^r Gr̃all
Renewing of ye Grant of M^r of ye Revells in Ireland to Mr Ogilby & Mr Stanley.

8. Warrant, dated 23 January 1661/2, to the Lords Justices of Ireland to issue a patent for the Office to John Ogilby and Thomas Stanley, Jr., jointly. (Signet Office Records, Irish Letter Books, vol. 5, p. 108, Public Record Office, London.)

Charles R.

To the Ld^s Justices
on ye behalfe of
Mr Ogilby: Ma^r
of the Revells

Right trusty and right welbeloved Cozen, and right trusty and right welbeloved Cousin and Councello^r: Wee greete yo^u well.

Whereas wee did by o^r Letters patents under our Great Seal of England beareing date the 8th of May in the 13th yeare of o^r reigne Constitute & appoint o^r trusty & Welbeloved John Ogilby Gent to bee our Master of our Revells & Masks in that our Kingdome of Ireland[.] Our Will & pleasure is, That upon surrender of the said Letters patents yo^u forthwith cause other Letters patents to passe under the Great Seale of that o^r Kingdome of Ireland, conteineing a Grant of the said Place & Office of Ma^r of o^r Revells and Maskes of that o^r Kingdome unto the said John Ogilby To hold & enjoy to him the said John Ogilby his exct^rs & assignes for by and dureing the n[atu]rall Life of him the said John Ogilby & of Thomas Stanley Junr sonne & Heire of Thomas Stanley of Camberloe in the County of Hertford Esqre & the Life of the Longer liver of them together wth all the powers priviledges in the said Letters patents of the 8th of May men-cõned & conteined. For wch this shalbee yor Warr^t. Given at o^r Court at Whitehall the 23th day of January in the thirteenth yeare of o^r reigne: 166½.

By his Ma^ts Comannd
Edw Nicholas

9. Warrant, dated 13 July 1662, to the Lord-Lieutenant of Ireland to issue a patent for the Office to John Ogilby and Thomas Stanley, Jr., jointly. (S.P. 44, Domestic Entry Book, vol. 3, pp. 67-68, Public Record Office, London.)

Right trusty &c Whereas wee did by O^r Letters Patentes under Our Great Seale of England bearg date ye 8th of May in ye 13th yeare of Our Reigne constitute & appoint Our trusty & welbeloved John Ogilby Gent to be Our Master of Our Revells and Masks in y^t Our Kingdom of Ireland, Our will & pleasure That upon surrender of ye said Letters Patents you forthwith cause other Letters Patents to

passe under ye great Seale of that Our Kingdom contayning a grant
of the s^d place and office of M^r of Our Revells and Masks of that
Our Kingdome unto ye said John Ogilby to hold & enjoy to him
ye s^d John Ogilby his Executours & Assignes for[,] by[,] and dureing
ye naturall life of him the s^d John Ogilby, & of Thomas Stanley Junr
Sonne and heire of Thomas Stanley of Cumberloe in Our County
of Hertford within this Our Kingdome Esquire and ye life of y^e
Longer liver of them together wth the profitts to arise & come by the
acting of plays or operas in any Theater or Theaters within that
Our Kingdome and all other Powers, Priviledges, advantages, &
emolum^ts in Our said Letters Patents of ye 8th of May menc̃oned
and conteyned. For which &c[.] Given at Our Court at Whitehall
ye 13th day of [July] in ye 14th yeare of Our Reigne.

10. Patent, issued by the Lord-Lieutenant of Ireland, and dated
    at Dublin, 5 April 1663, granting the Office to John Ogilby
    and Thomas Stanley, Jr., jointly. (Formerly preserved in
    the Irish Chancery Rolls, Public Record Office, Dublin,
    and copied in full by W. J. Lawrence before destruction
    by fire in 1922.)

CHARLES the second by the grace of God King of England,
Scotland and Ireland, defender of the faith &c To all to whom
these psents shall come greeting. Whereas wee having thought fit
that all masques, operas, interludes, tragedies and comedies and
other things of that nature to be represented in our kingdom of
Ireland should be represented as innocently and inoffensivily as
might be, and that our Subjects of our said Kingdome of Ireland
should enjoy the like privileges in that kind as our subjects in our
kingdome of England, by our letters pattents under our Great Seale
of England bearing date the eight day of May in the thirteene yeare
of our Reigne did declare our will and pleasure to be that from
thenceforth there should be the office of master of Revells and
masques in our said kingdome of Ireland and thereby for us our
heires and successors did erect and establish the said office to be for
ever called and knowne by the said name of master of our Revells
and Masques in our said kingdome of Ireland. And wee, reposeing
especiall trust and confidence in the loyalty, integrity and ability
of our wellbeloved subject John Ogilby, gent, by our said lres
patents did constitute and appoint the said John Ogilby to be master
of all and every our playes, Revells, Masques and Interludes in our
said kingdome of Ireland during his naturall life as by the said letters

patents doth more at large appeare. And whereas the said John Ogilby hath voluntarily surrendered unto us the aforesaid lres patents and the said office thereby granted unto him, KNOW yee therefore that wee still reposeing the like speciall trust and confidence in the loyalty, integrity and ability of the said John Ogilby of our especiall grace, certaine knowledge and meere motion by and with the advice and consent of our right trusty and right intirely-beloved Cousin and Counsellor, James, Duke of Ormond, our lieutenant-generall and Governor generall of our said kingdome of Ireland and according to the tenor and effect of our lres under our privy Signett bearing date at our Court att Whitehall the twenty third day of January in the thirteenth yeare of our Reigne and now inrolled in the Rolls of our Chancery of Ireland have given and granted and by these psents for us our heires and successors do give & grant unto the said John Ogilby the said Office of Master of our Revells and Masques in our said Kingdome of Ireland. TO have, hould, exercise and enjoy the said office of master of our Revells and masques in our said kingdome of Ireland unto him the said John Ogilby his execu-tors and assignes for and during the naturall life of him the said John Ogilby and of Thomas Stanley Junior sonne and heire of Thomas Stanley of Cumberloe in the County of Hertford in our kingdome of England Esquire, and the life of the longer liver of them, together with all fees, profitts, privileges, advantages and emoluments whatsoever in a ample manner and forme as the now Master of our Revells in our kingdome of England or any other pson or psons formerly enjoying the said office have received, taken and enjoyed, or ought to have taken and enjoyed, the said office to be executed by the said John Ogilby his executors and assignes or his or their sufficient Deputy or Deputys during the lives of the said John Ogilby and Thomas Stanley aforesaid. AND further know yee that wee of our more abundant grace, certain knowledge and mere motion have given and granted and by these psents for us our heires and successors do give & grant unto the said John Ogilby his Executors and Assignes full and sole power, license and authority to erect and build one or more theatre or theatres in whatsoever places to him shall seeme most fit and convenient either in our Citty of Dublin or elsewhere in our said kingdome of Ireland on such ground as the said John Ogilby his heires or Assignes shall purchase to himself or themselves in fee and in such Theatre or Theatres so built and erected as aforesaid at all lawfull times publiquely to psent, Act or cause to be psented and acted all comedies, tragedies, operas or other enterludes of what kind soever decent and becoming and not pfane and obnoxious. TO have, hould and enjoy the said Theatre or Theatres so to be erected and built as aforesaid unto him the said John Ogilby his heires and Assignes for ever. AND further wee doe hereby for us our heires and successors streightly charge and comand, inhibite and forbid all pson and psons whatsoever that they nor any of them psume to erect or build any theatre or theatres, stage or stages whatsoever and therin to psent or act any comedies, tragedies, operas or other enterludes whatsoever without license from the said John Ogilby his Executors or Assignes in writing under his or their hands or seales or hand and seale first had and obteined. AND wee doe hereby streightly charge and command all mayors, sheriffes, bailiffes, constables, head bur-roughs and all others our officers and ministers within our said kingdome of Ireland that they cause all stage playes and enterludes which shall at anytime be psented or acted by any pson or psons contrary to the meaneing of these psents to be suppressed from time to time, and that they be from time to time aiding, helping and assisting unto the said John Ogilby his Executors and Assignes in the suppressing thereof and apprehending of all such common players as shall psume to act any stage playes or enterludes without license as aforesaid as they and every of them will answeare the contrary att their prlle. AND our further will and pleasure is and wee doe hereby declare our will and pleasure to be that all former grant or grants obteined by any pson or psons from us under our Signett or Signemannuall for, touching or concerning the premisses or any pt. or parcell thereof shalbe from henceforth void and of none effect and the same and every of them we do revoke, determine, annihilate and make void by these psents. AND lastly our will and pleasure is and wee doe by these psents declare that these our letters patents or the Inrollment thereof shalbe in all things firme, good and effectuall in the law according to the true intent and meaning of the same any law, statute, act, ordinance, proclamation or pvision or any other matter, cause or thing whatsoever to the contrary kind in any wise notwithstanding, although expresse mention of the true yearly value or certainty of the pmisses or any part thereof or of any gifts or grants by us or any of our pgenitors to the said John Ogilby heretofore made in these presents is not made. Any statute, act, ordinance or pvision or any other thing, cause, or matter whatsoever to the contrary or in any wise notwithstanding. IN witness whereof we have caused these our letters to be made patents, witness our aforesaid lew^t generall and Governor Generall of our said kingdome of Ireland at Dublin the fifth day of Aprill in the fifteenth yeare of our Reigne.

11. Petition (undated) of William Morgan for grant of the Office. (S.P. 63, State Papers, Ireland, vol. 343, no. 77 B, Public Record Office, London.)

To the Kings most Excellent Matie
The Humble Petition of William Morgan Master of yor Maties Revells
in yor Kingdome of Ireland
Humbly Sheweth

That yor most Gratious Matie Having Granted unto yor Petition^rs Unkle, John Ogilby Esqr the office of Master of yor Maties Revells in yor Maties Kingdome of Ireland, to Him His Executo^rs and Assignes, during the Natural Life of Him the said John Ogilby and one Thomas Stanley.

And whereas yor Petition^r togeather with His said Unkle was at great Charge in building a Theatre, Raising and Setling a Company of Acto^rs at Dublin and that yor Petition^r hath been sworn yor Maties Servt as Deputy of ye Revells and Executed the said office, during the life of His said Unkle, by Assignment And hath been at very great Charge to maintain and uphold a Company of good acto^rs who still continue at the Theatre in Dublin, being alsoe left very much in Debt by the said Mr Ogilby.

Yo^r Petition^r Humbly prayes, yor Matie would be pleased to give Him leave, to pass the Pattent in His own name, in the stead of Mr Thomas Stanley's Name.

And yor petition^r shall
ever pray & c—

12. Warrant, dated 28 November 1683, to the Lords Justices of Ireland to issue to William Morgan a patent for the Office. (Signet Office Records, Irish Letter Books, vol. 11, pp. 234–6, Public Record Office, London.)

Charles R.

Right and Right Welbeloved Cousin and Councillo^r: Wee greet you well.—Whereas William Morgan Gent and Our Cosmographer hath by his humble petition informed Us, That Wee were graciously pleased by Our Lett^rs patents bearing date at Dublin the 21th day Aprill in the fiveteenth year of Our Reigne to Constitute his Uncle John Ogilby Esqr his Exct^rs and Assignes Master of the Revells in that Our Kingdome of Ireland with all the power priviledge and advantage of right belonging to the Master of Our Revells in

England. Also Granting to the said John Ogilby his heires and Assignes the sole power and priviledge of building One or more Theatre or Theatres in Dublin or any other places in Our said Kingdome of Ireland for the Acting and Representing of all Comedies Tragedies Operas Interludes, &c: to remain with the Governm^t of the Company to him his heires and Assignes for ever. That pursuant to Our said Lett^rs patents with the great favour and Encouragem^t of Our Right Trusty and Right Entirely Beloved Cousin and Councillo^r James, Duke of Ormond, Our Lieuten^t Grall and Grall Governo^r of that Our Kingdome of Ireland, Hee the said Ogilby and the pet^r, Willm Morgan, Did for Our Service, at a great Charge, build a Theatre and settle a Company of good Actors in Dublin furnishing them wth cloaths properties and scenes to the satisfaction of Our said Lieutenant the Nobility and other Our Loving Subjects; But the pet^r having further represented, That he and the said Company might be made more Serviceable to Us if Wee would be generously pleased to Grant him a New patent with such Additionall Clauses and Alterations as may constitute the Company under his Governm^t Servants to Our Selfe and Our Royall Consort, and enable him fully to Execute his Office and enjoy the benefit thereof, And therefore humbly praying that wee would accept of the Surrender of Our Lett^rs patents granted to the said John Ogilby for the Office of the Revells for two Lives, and to Grant him the pet^r Another for the Office of the Revells Dureing the naturall life of him the said William Morgan, Joseph Ashberry and Charles his Son, Confirming to them the powers priviledges and advantages granted to the said John Ogilby, and Constituting the Company under the pet^rs Governm^t Servants to Our selfe and Our Royall Consort with sure priviledges as are enjoyed by Thomas Killigrew Esqr his heires and Assignes and the Company under their Governm^t. Wee were graciously pleased to referre the Consideration of the whole matter to Our said Lieutenen^t of Ireland, Who hath made his Report thereupon in the words following.

May it pleas yor Ma^ty

In Obedience to yor Ma^ts Referrence of the 27th of March I have taken into Consideration the petition of William Morgan yor Ma^ts Cosmographer and Master of yor Revells in Ireland, and know that pursuant to yor Ma^ts former patent a Theatre was built and a Company of good Actors setled at Dublin and contynued under the Governm^t and care of Mr Ogilby and the pet^r, And am humbly of opinion yor Ma^ty may be graciously pleased to bestow upon them the Title of Servants to your Ma^ty and yor Royall Consort, Granting the pet^r in Ireland the priviledges conteined in Mr Killigrew's patent as Governo^r of yor Ma^{ts} Comedians here, with such Apt words as yor Ma^{ts} Attorney or Soll. Grall shall approve to explaine the powers, priviledges & advantages already granted him as Master of the Revells in Ireland equally with what is exercised & enjoyed by the Master of yor Ma^{ts} Revells in England, And I p^{r}sume it can be no p^{r}judice to yor Ma^{ts} Service to Gratifie the pet^{rs} care and diligence in accepting of the surrend^r of yor Ma^{ts} former Grant for two lives, giving him a New patent for the Office of the Revells Dureing the n[atu]rall life of him the said William Morgan Joseph Ashberry & Charles Ashberry as the pet^r humbly prayes. All wch is humbly submitted to yor Ma^{ts} good pleasure

Hampsted the 2d of June 1683   Ormonde

Wee are satisfied with the Report and opinion of Our said Lieuten^t and have accordingly thought fit hereby to signifie Our pleasure unto you That you accept of the Surrender of Our Lett^{rs} patents granted unto John Ogilby as aforesaid, and that in lieu thereof you cause New Lett^{rs} patents to be drawne with the advice of Our Councill Learned there and passed under the Great Seale of that Our Kingdome conteineing a Grant of the Office of Master of Our Revells and Masques in Our said Kingdome of Ireland Unto the said William Morgan his Exct^{rs} and Assignes for and dureing the naturall life of him the said William Morgan and of Joseph Ashberry and Charles Ashberry son of the said Joseph and the life of the longer liver of them, together with all fees profits priviledges advantages and emoluments whatsoever in as ample manner and forme as it hath been already granted to John Ogilby Esqr and as the now Master of the Revells in Our Kingdome of England or any other pson or psons formerly enjoying the said Office have lawfully received taken and enjoyed or ought to have received taken and enjoyed; The said Office to be Executed by the said William Morgan his Executo^{rs} or Assignes or his or their sufficient Deputy or Deputies dureing the lives of the said William Morgan and of Joseph Ashberry and Charles Ashberry aforesaid, As also with full power & authority to him the said William Morgan and his heires Exec^{rs} and Assignes to enjoy the benefit of the Theatre already built by John Ogilby and the said William Morgan in Dublin and to Erect and build One or more Theatre or Theatres in whatsoever place or places shall seem to him most fit and convenient either in Our Citty of Dublin or elsewhere in Our said Kingdome of Ireland on such ground as the said William Morgan his heires or Assignes to himselfe or themselves in Fee, and in the said Theatre already built,

and in such Theatre or Theatres so to be built & Erected as aforesaid
at all lawfull times (Except when Wee or Our Cheife Governo^r of
Our Kingdome of Ireland shall see cause to forbid the Acting of
playes) publickly to present and Act or cause to be presented and
Acted all Comedies Tragedies Operas and other Interludes of what
kind soever decent & becomeing and not profane & Obnoxious.
To have hold & enjoy the said Theatre or Theatres so built and
Erected or to be Erected and built as aforesaid Unto him the said
William Morgan his heires and Assignes for ever, Forbidding all
person and persons whatsoever that they nor any of them presume
to Erect or build any Theatre or Theatres Stage or Stages whatsoever within that Our Kingdome of Ireland, and therein or thereon
to present or Act any Comedies Tragedies Operas or other Interludes whatsoever without license from the said William Morgan
his Exec^{rs} or Assignes in writing under his or their hand & Seal
first had & Obteined; But with full power License & authority to
him the said William Morgan his heires and Assignes from time to
time to gather together, enterteine, Governe, priviledge & keep
such and so many players and persons to Exercise and Act Tragedies
Comedies Playes Operas and other performances on the Stage as
hee or they shall think fit & requisite for that purpose Which company shall be the Servants of Us and Our Dear Consort, and shall
consist of such Nomber as the said William Morgan his heires &
Assignes shall from time to time think meet and such persons to
contynue dureing the pleasure of the said William Morgan his
heires or Assignes from time to time to Act playes and Entertainem^{ts}
of the Stage of all sorts peaceably & quietly without the impediment
of any person or persons whatsoever, And that the said William
Morgan his heires and Assignes may take & receive such Sume &
Sumes of Money as have been usually taken or shall be thought
reasonable in regard of Scenes and Musick and such new Decorations as have not been formerly used, With power also to the said
William Morgan his heires and Assignes out of such Allowances to
the Actors or such other persons by him or them employed as hee
or they shall think fit, And all Scandalous or Mutinous persons to
be by him or them from time to time Ejected & disabled from
playing in the said Theatre or Theatres, And that noe person
deserting the company shall be received into any other company
without the consent and approbation of the said William Morgan
his heires or Assignes signified under his or their hands and Seales,
And with all other good and Usefull clauses for the better Governem^t
of the said company and Executeing the Office of Master of the

Revells, with mention of the powers and priviledges that are & have been from time to time Exercised and enjoyed by the Master of the Revells in England, and such other clauses as were granted to Thomas Killigrew Esqʳ for the Governement of Our company in London as farr as the same may bee accomodated to the wayes and Usages of Ireland. For the doeing whereof this shall be yoʳ warrant, And soe Wee bid you very heartily farewell. Given at Our Court at Whitehall the 28ᵗʰ day of November 1683 in the five and Thirtieth year of Our Reigne.

Entr. 5ᵗʰ Janʳʸ 168¾   By his Maᵗᵉ Comand
                                                        L. Jenkins

13. Power of attorney, dated 20 January 1683, given by William Morgan to Edward Corkey of Dublin to surrender Ogilby's patent of the Office. (Formerly preserved in the Public Record Office, Dublin, and copied in full by W. J. Lawrence before destruction by fire in 1922.)

Whereas his most excellent Matʸ by his letters pattents beareing date at Whitehall the nine and twentieth day of November last past directed to his Excellency Richard, Earl of Arran, lord deputy of his maties Kingdom of Ireland and to ye chiefe Governor or Governors thereof for ye tyme being hath been gratiously pleased to detail his acceptance of ye Pattent to John Ogilby Esq & his Assignes for ye office of Master of ye Revells in the Kingdome of Ireland and hath directed ye surrender thereof by William Morgan to be accepted and a new patent to bee passed as by ye said petition thereunto being had itt doth and may more fully appeare, Bee itt therefore known unto all whom itt doth and may concerne that in obedience to his maties comands and in pursuance of his maties gratious pleasure detailed in his letter aforesaid, I, William Morgan of ye Citty of London cosmographer to his most Gratious Maty and master of his majesties Revells &c, in yt kingdom doe surrender and yeild up the patent of master of ye Revells in Ireland granted to John Ogilby Esq and his Assignes and ye said William Morgan doe hereby Authorize, constitute and appoint my loveing friend Edward Corkey of Dublin Esquire my sufficient and lawfull attorney actually for me and in my name to surrender, give and yeild up the same, fully satisfieing and confirmeing whatsoever, &c, &c.

                                                        William Morgan

20 January 1683

Documents Relating to the Case of John Thurmond vs. the Patentee and Sharers of the Theatre Royal, Dublin: 1713

I

THE CASE OF JOHN THURMOND, / HUMBLY OFFER'D / TO HIS EXCIE THE LORD CHANCELLOR OF IRELAND

May it please your Excie.

Fourteen years ago, I was sent for from England by the Shearers of the Theatre of Dublin, to act upon the Stage for which I receiv'd 80 pounds, for my first years performance; and then for my Better Encouragement was admitted to a Share and Continued so for seven years following; after which I was obliged to leave the Kingdom.

But what I humbly offer to your Excie now is; that the present Shearers of the Theatre, about three months ago, Desir'd my son severall times to wright for me to Come for Dublin and I should be in the Share I formerly had; and the first play that I should act in should be for my Benefit, if I would accept of it for my yearly Play. I own I did not just at that time comply wth the Shearers offer, but soon after; seeing his Grace the Duke of Ormond; to whom I have the Honour of being very well known too, and receiv'd great marks of his favour, I inform'd his Grace I was willing to go for Dublin, his Grace was kind enough to assure me I should want no Encouragement that Stage would afford; upon wch I quitted Forty shillings a week & a Benefit Play once a year in London and have brought my Family in obediance to his Grace to Fix here.

But Mr Ashbury and the rest of the Shearers refuse me the Agreement they sent me three months ago, the reason they give for it is, they say they have oblidged themselves by an Article made since they writt to me, not to admitt any person into a Share unless they all Consent.

Therefore I humbly hope your Excie will be of the opinion that my Lord Duke of Ormond did not Design I shou'd be anyways Lessen'd from what I formerly had; and think it reasonable they should admitt me into a share.

[Endorsed, 'The Case of Mr. Thurmond—/ Mr. Ashbury to attend on Wednesday.']¹

II

THE CASE OF THE PATENTEE AND SHARERS OF THE THEATRE ROYALL, HUMBLY OFFER'D TO THEIR EXCIES THE LORDS JUSTICES OF IRELAND

May it please yoʳ Excies

The Theatre for severall years having labour'd under the severest Difficultys by the Chief Actors deserting it, amongst 'em Mr. Thurmond who is lately return'd (as he informs the Sharers) with a Recommendation from his Grace the Duke of Ormonde, to which the Sharers will at all times (as 'tis their Duty) pay the greatest Deference and profoundest Respect, Yet 'tis with utmost submission hop'd, That yoʳ Excies will please to take into yoʳ Consideration the following just Objections against his being a Sharer and the present unhappy Circumstances of the Company.

Imprs.—Mr. Thurmond did about Six years ago desert the Kingdom after having received his Benefit Play without acting in any of the other Sharers' Benefits, leaving 'em at that time involv'd in many grievous Debts, some of which at this day they unhappily labour under, and disjoynted their whole Stock of Plays for want of his Parts, which are since fill'd up and supply'd by Men of more Merit in the Theatricall Affairs, (viz.), Mr. Evans, Mr. Elrington, and Mr. Leigh.

That Mr. Thurmond did before his leaving the Kingdom pawn all the Dresses both antient and modern which he and his Son us'd to appear in and which were then in his possession, Most of which the Sharers at their own proper Cost have since redeemed.

That Mr. Thurmond did during the Cessation of the Theatres for the Death of King William appropriate to his own use a weekly Subscription of Severall Ladys of Quality, design'd for the Support of the Company, tho' Severall were at that time in very great Extremity.

---

¹ Petitions, Carton 268, no. 9893, Public Record Office, Dublin: destroyed by fire in 1922, but previously copied in full by W. J. Lawrence and preserved in his notes, Irish theatre collection, University of Cincinnati.

That Mr. Thurmond did for his better Encouragement to continue in the Kingdom receive a Days Pay from each Officer of Coll. Munden's and another Regiment then in Dublin, Yet after the Receipt of the said Subscriptions he quitted the Kingdome.

That Mr. Thurmond did in all things during his being a Sharer pursue his own private Ends to the mighty prejudice of the Company.

Tho' Mr. Thurmond is of little Use at present in the Theatre, for when Ever he appears in any materiall Character another Actor more Significant, perfect in the part must lye idle. Yet in obedience to his Grace's Recommendation the Sharers are willing to give him all the Encouragement they possibly can (vizt.) Sixty Pounds p. ann. which is the same that Mr. Leigh has by Agreemt.

That Mr. Thurmond in London had but Forty Shillings p. week for nine Months in the Year and proper Abatements out of the sd. Sallary for every day that a Play was not acted, by which means the sd. 40/- p. week seldom amounted to more than sixty Pounds p. ann.

That Mr. Thurmond was obliged to pay the Sum of Forty Three Pounds out of his Benefit for the Charge of each Play and Seldom or ever was known to have much more than the said sum of Forty Three Pounds in the House.

That the present Patentee and Sharers did mutually enter into articles and Bonds to continue in the Kingdom for the Diversion of the Nobility and Gentry of the Same, Which are humbly offered to yor Excies Perusall.

That through the slender Encouragemt and the constant heavy Charges of the Theatre the Sharers lye under many Debts and Difficulties, which yet they don't doubt to surmount by yor Excies Favour, and the Prospect of Happiness from this Glorious Peace, the prospect of which furnish'd 'em with Resolution to persevere in the Business in the worst of Times.

'Tis humbly hop'd That yor Excies in yor great judgments will not make void the Sharers Articles and Bonds, nor think Mr. Thurmond who has been absent Six years and is now wholly useless in that Affair has an equal pretence to the Profits of the Theatre with the Sharers who have continued in the Kingdom and have greatly impair'd their little Fortunes by endeavouring to support the Company.[1]

---

[1] The originals of this and the two following briefs were sold at Sotheby's, London, to Bertram Dobell in June 1906. At that time W. J. Lawrence made careful transcripts of all three documents. They are reproduced here from these transcripts in his Irish theatre collection, University of Cincinnati. The originals have since disappeared from record.

III

TO THEIR EXCELLENCIES THE LORDS JUSTICES OF IRELAND. THE MOST HUMBLE ANSWER OF JOHN THURMOND TO A PAPER LAID BEFORE YOUR EXCIES INTITULED THE CASE OF THE PATENTEE AND SHARERS OF THE THEATRE ROYAL IN DUBLIN

Tho' the said Thurmond is afflicted with the deepest Concern to think that any poor affair of his shd. so far as it has done already encroach on your Excellencys valuable time, yet because it is become soe necessary for him to clear his Reputation before he can think himself worthy of your Excellencys care and Protection, he Humbly begs leave to do the one that he may deserve the Comfortable Influence of the other, and without which he and his family must inevitably suffer.

To the Preamble and first part of the Charge the said Thurmond says:

That he was arrested by Mr. Ashbury just upon the receiveing the benefit of his Play, which so alarmed the rest of his Creditors that his House goods and wearing Apparell were immediately seiz'd by them and he himself forced to abscond, in which condition he made several overtures to the Company whereby he might be enabled to stay amongst them but with no Success, so that he was forced with great unwillingness to leave the Kingdom having first divided the profits of his Play as far as it would go amongst his Credrs, and was obliged to the Charity of some worthy Gentlemen for the Charges of his Journey, and he humbly hopes that this will not be imputed to him as a Desertion which was owing to his Partners neglect of him and the oppression of his Credrs. As to the Company's being then in Debt, it is presumed they are so still, toward the Payment whereof he is willing to give his utmost assistance and hopes he may be as capable of serving the Company as formerly tho' the Parts he used to Act may have been disposed of to others, whose merit he does not dispute, neither is he willing to attest his own, but humbly hopes he may be as acceptable to an Audience now as he has been formerly when none of those who were then here contested the precedency with him, And with the greatest deference to your Excellencys judgment he craves leave to add that there are very few if any Plays but which Requires more than three Persons to fill the Characters.

To the second Article the said Thurmond says:

That such of the Dresses as were in the said Thurmond's Custody at the time mentioned in the case were either given to the said Thurmond by some of the Quality or made at his own Expense and not paid for by the then sharers, and the same were seiz'd with the rest of the said Thurmond's goods when he was forced to abscond as aforesaid, and if the same have been since bought for the use of the Stage, the Sharers have had an Advantage by buying them at a low price and the loss has been only the said Thurmond's.

To the third Article the said Thurmond says:

That most of the sharers at the time of the death of King William had some Profession besides Playing or were known not to be in want of mony, the said Thurmond's Case being unhappily otherwise. Some of the Ladys of Quality did make a Present to him which matter was then Reflected on as it is now and upon Enquiry made the Ladys did then Declare that they designed the benefit to the said Thurmond alone which Mr. Estcourt who took on himself the trouble to Enquire into it, Testifyed to the rest of the sharers.

To the fourth Article the said Thurmond says:

That he knows of no days Pay Granted by the Officers of any Regiment for the purposes alleged but Confesses and can give undoubted proof of it that some mony was about that time paid into a Gentleman's hands to be applyed to the Payment of some of his Debts in Case he could be enabled to stay in the Kingdom or otherwise to be given to him to bear his Expences over into England.

The fifth Article of

The said Thurmond's pursuing his own Private ends is so general that he can only observe that considering the sharers have raked together so many Calumnys in the other parts of their charge, if they had the least semblance of one instance in this they would have told it, but he humbly begs leave to say that the contrary of that assertion is true, for his Excie the Lord Cutts having in many instances distinguished the said Thurmond above the rest of the sharers by frequent favours bestowed on him, did particularly at the said Thurmond's Request when the sharers laboured under as great difficultys as they had don at any time, Subscribe and Pay to the said Thurmond Twenty pounds and he Received by the like applicacon from his Excie the then Lord Chancellor Cox, and others of the Quality, forty pounds more which he brought to the common Stock and Divided with them.

To the sixth Article the said Thurmond says:

That the Proposition of makeing him Subservient to such as have Shewen by their Case how they would Treat him if they had him in their Power will be he humbly hopes an Inducement to your Excies to prevent it.

To the seventh and eighth Articles.

The said Thurmond Believes the Calculation of his Sallary in England to be true but says the insinuation of his receiveing but little benefit from his Play is false he having one year with another reced at least forty pounds p. ann. by that one Article and the profits by the Vacation Acting have been sometimes more beneficial than the Sallary would have been to him.

To the remaining part of the said Case the said Thurmond says:

That he knows not the nature of the Bonds and Articles therein mentioned but has heard the Same were Entered into since their sending for him over, and with a design to impose upon him, yet since they confess their having sent for him and that it is most true that he relyed on their performance and has removed himself and Family away from England he therefore humbly hopes your Excellencys will be of opinion that the said Bonds and Articles ought to be of no force against him.

The said Thurmond having herein answered the reasons given by the Sharers why he ought not to be received amongst them pursuant to their Agreement with all humility begs leave to add that what they have laid to his Charge if the same had been true, would in all probability have prevented them sending for him and that these Calumnys are raised at this Juncture with a Malicious Intent to render the favour graciously intended by the Duke of Ormonde of no Emolument to him, for while they can receive the advantages of Acting and the Summer Season advances they too well know that a Play will be of less benefit to him and his Circumstances will be the less Capable of being relieved by it.

But your Excies are the sole Judges of this affair in Confidence of whose great wisdom and goodness he keeps himself and Family in hopes that they shall not be a Prey to those with whom he yet must desire to live, tho' they have shewen themselves so much his Enemys.

IV

THE SHARERS' REPLY TO MR. THURMOND'S ANSWER TO THE PATENTEE AND SHARERS' CASE

With all Dutifull Submission humbly offered to their Excies
the Lords Justices of Ireland.

It is with the utmost Regret to the Sharers, in any Capacity to give y^r Excies the least Molestation to the great Buisiness of the Nation, yet in this affair they Humbly beg leave to prove the following just allegations against Mr. Thurmond, which they are ready to do by Oath, to every particular Paragraph herein incerted, and to clear themselves to y^r Excies of aspersing him falsely. That being one of the last Things the Sharers would upon any occasion be Guilty of to offer a malicious or false aspersion to y^r Excies Perusall.

Mr. Ashbury says That Thurmond being arrested by McKensie a Taylor, for the sum of fourteen Pounds sterl. for his own wearing apparell, and the said McKensie being Indebted to Mr. Ashbury, Thurmond made Application to Ashbury to release him out of the Bailiff's Hand, in whose Custody he was, promising if he would discount with McKensy for the said sum of Fourteen Pounds, he would in a limitted time, repay Mr. Ashbury without faile the aforesaid sum. Mr. Ashbury accepted the Offer and released him, but the time proposed being considerably elapsed, and no payment made, Mr. Ashbury did (upon hearing of Thurmond's Designe of quitting the Kingdome, under the pretence of going into the Country), take out an Action for the money, & the Bailiffs accordingly seized him, with his Bootes on, but Mr. Ashbury in a very little time released him again, at the Intercession of Evans & Griffith, two of the present Sharers, who promised to pay to Mr. Ashbury if Thurmond did not, the aforesaid Sum of fourteen Pounds, Thurmond neglecting to pay out of his Benefitt play any part of the said Debt, and soon after quitting the Kingdom, the said Sharers did since his Departure hence according to Promise, pay Thurmond's said debt of Fourteen Pounds to Mr. Ashbury.

That Mr. Thurmond's quitting the Kingdome was not occasioned by any neglect of his Partners for they had allowed him the Profitts of his Benefitt Play before any of their own were acted. That since Mr. Thurmond does not deny his Parts are disposed of to men of more Merit, it is humbly hoped y^r Excies will not think him of equall Service to the Company as formerly.

That Mr. Ashbury never esteemed Mr. Thurmond as the best Actor in the Company, but always gave the preferrence to others in their proper Characters.

That 'tis humbly presumed y^r Excies will please to think Three score Pounds p. ann., a sufficient Sallary to any person, who must be obliged to act fourth parts on the Irish Stage.

That the Dresses in Thurmond's Possession were not seized but pawned, particularly His Grace the Duke of Ormond's Birthday Suit, which His Grace did him the Honour to Order for his Wearing and never was heard of since. His Excie the Lord Cutts' Suit, was released for the sum of five Pounds at the sharers' Expence from Mrs. Smyth, A Roman Shape, Two Spanish shapes and a Modern Coat trim'd with Silver, all made at the Sharers' Expence, all pawn'd, the Roman shape redeemed from Mr. Bradshaw by the Sharers, the rest of the Dresses never heard of since.

That Thurmond hearing of a Subscription among severall Ladys of Quality, designed for the Support of the Company upon the Silence of King William's death, obliged Bowman the then Boxkeeper, to shew him where those Ladys lived, and received the Subscription, applying it to his own Use, tho' the Boxkeeper did believe he shared it with the Company, yet Mr. Ashbury declares he never received one Shilling of the same, nor Estcourt ever acquainted him, 'twas designed for the Use of Thurmond. That Mr. Thompson at whose House Capt. Negus in Coll. Munden's Regiment lodg'd, and severall of the Officers used, is ready to Testifye by Oath that he has often heard both Capt. Negus and the other Officers say, that each of 'em did Subscribe a days pay at the Request of Coll. Neville to enable Thurmond to continue in the Kingdom, and that Evans and Griffith who were acquainted with the said Officers, are willing to make Oath of the same, and that they do believe notwithstanding his Equivocation, that the said subscription of those Officers to be part of the money he acknowledges to have received from severall Gentlemen.

That the said Sharers in their Case were cautious of troubling yr Excies by Enumerating the many Instances they could Testifie of Thurmond's pursuing his private interest, rather than the Company's Good, yet now begg leave with all Humility to offer one, which his Excie the Lord Cutts did them the Honour to hear.—— That Mr. Thurmond and his Wife being allowed by the Company the sum of Twelve Pounds for making and Embellishing some Spanish Shapes for the play of the Island Princess, yet neither Thurmond nor his Wife would deliver up the Dresses the day that the Play was to be Acted, unless the Sharers would oblige themselves to pay him the sum of fifty Two Pounds for the same, tho' barely worth the sum agreed for, 'till upon Application being made to his Excie Lord Cutts, who comanded him to deliver the Shapes, and severely chid him for Endeavouring at so great an Imposition.

That his Excie the Lord Cutts did forbid Thurmond his sight upon his frequent Misbehaviour. That his Grace the Duke of Ormond upon his departure to England did the Sharers the Honour to recommend a Subscription to the then Lord Justices and Nobility of the Kingdome which they subscribed to for the Support of the Theatre, and not at the Request of Mr. Thurmond, as he Endeavours falsely to Intimate to y^r Excies in his answer, but was only desired by the Company to attend their Excies to receive the said Subscriptions, and was paid by the Sharers for doing the same.

That the sharers can prove by the Office Books in England that Mr. Thurmond did not clear by either of the plays that were acted for his Benefitt (vizt.) All for Love, and Venice Preserved, one shilling but at this Instant he remaines indebted to the Sharers in London for part of the forty Three Pounds, the Charge of each Night, and was often forced in the Vacation to stroll to Greenwich, where he received but little Encouragement for his Acting.

That the Sharers do acknowledge that they were under the necessity last November, by Mr. Leigh Threatening to leave the Kingdome, to propose an agreement to Mr. Thurmond's Son, for the bringing over of his father, which was seemingly consented to by the said son, yet after some time he broke the 'said Agreement with the Sharers, as severall Gentlemen can testifie, who were then present, by the Father's advise, as appeares both in Mr. Thurmond's Case and in a Letter to Griffith; the Sharers were obliged the Christmas following upon the breach of the sd. Thurmond's agreement, to Article for five years with Mr. Leigh, making an Addition to his Sallary and giving him Security for the same.

Yet some Misfortune as 'tis Conjectured having obliged Thurmond to quit London last April, 'tis presumed he made Interest to obtain His Grace the Duke of Ormond's Recommendation, to which the Sharers will at all times pay both in Inclination and Duty, their profoundest Respect, and are willing to Encourage Thurmond to the best of their ability as their Case expresses, not so much in Regard of his Merit in the Theatrical Affair, as in Honour to his Graces Letter of Recommendation.

That Mr. Thurmond's Family so often mentioned in his Answer in Hopes of Exciting y^r Excies Compassion to him, is only his Wife;

having no Children but his Son who is capable of providing for himself.

'Tis therefore with all Dutiful submission, humbly hoped that y^r Excies will oblige Mr. Thurmond to accept the sallary proposed (vizt.) Sixty Pounds p. ann. or to dispose of himself some other way, and not so far discourage the Patentee and Sharers, who have so long continued in the Kingdome, as to break their Bonds and Articles in favour of Thurmond; their being sevll. others in England, who have formerly been Sharers in the Theatre, and have like Mr. Thurmond unhandsomely quitted the same, would then endeavour by Sollicitations to be readmitted into their former Posts, tho' now as wholly useless as he in the affair, which would prove a mighty detrement to the Company in generall and the totall Subversion of the Constitution of the sharers. And the Patentee humbly conceives that if these Bonds and Articles are broke, none that he can make for the future can be of force enough to keep the Company together.

However, the Premises are entirely Submitted with all humble Resignation to y^r Excies Great Wisdomes and Judgment.

Plays Acted at the Dublin Theatres, 1637–1720

Dates in parentheses indicate years of known or probable performance

Acis and Galatea (1709)	Pierre Motteux
Agrippa, King of Alba: or, The False Tiberinus (*c.* 1666–*c.* 1669)	John Dancer
Alchemist, The (1637–8; *c.* 1670–*c.* 1684)	Ben Jonson
Atheist, The: or, The Second Part of the Soldier's Fortune (1686)	Thomas Otway
Bartholomew Fair (1670)	Ben Jonson
Belphegor: or, The Marriage of the Devil (*c.* 1677)	John Wilson
Bold Stroke for a Wife, A (1718–19)	Mrs. Susannah Centlivre
Cato (1713)	Joseph Addison
Comedy of Errors, The (*c.* 1670–*c.* 1680)	William Shakespeare
Comical History of Don Quixote, The, Parts 1 and 2 (1714)	Thomas D'Urfey
Comical Revenge, The: or, Love in a Tub (1698–9)	Sir George Etherege
Committee, The, (*c.* 1697; 1714)	Sir Robert Howard
Constant Couple, The: or, A Trip to the Jubilee (1704)	George Farquhar
Coronation, The (*c.* 1638)	James Shirley
Country Wife, The (*c.* 1698)	William Wycherley
Coy Shepherdess, The (1709)	Anthony Aston
Crafty Executors, The (1715–16)	Charles Shadwell
Disappointment, The: or The Mother in Fashion (1685)	Thomas Southerne
Don John: or, The Libertine (1685)	Thomas Shadwell
Drummer, The: or, The Haunted-House (1717)	Joseph Addison
Fatal Marriage, The: or, The Innocent Adultery (*c.* 1694)	Thomas Southerne
General, The (*c.* 1638)	author unknown
Hamlet (*c.* 1670–*c.* 1680)	William Shakespeare
Hasty Wedding, The: or, The Intrigueing Squire (1716–17)	Charles Shadwell
Henry VIII (*c.* 1674–*c.* 1682; 1694)	William Shakespeare

Henry IV, Parts 1 and *2* (*c.* 1670–*c.* 1680)	William Shakespeare
Indian Emperor, The: or, The Conquest of	
Mexico by the Spaniards (*c.* 1698)	John Dryden
Irish Gentleman, The (*c.* 1638)	author unknown
Irish Hospitality: or, Virtue Rewarded	
(1717–18)	Charles Shadwell
Island Princess, The: or, The	
Generous Portuguese (*c.* 1705)	Pierre Motteux
Jovial Crew, A: or, The Merry Beggars (*c.* 1687)	Richard Brome
Julius Caesar (*c.* 1670–*c.* 1676)	William Shakespeare
King Lear (*c.* 1670–*c.* 1680)	William Shakespeare
Landgartha (1639)	Henry Burnell
Love in a Hurry (1709)	Anthony Aston
Love's Crueltie (*c.* 1638)	James Shirley
Loyal Subject, The (1670)	John Fletcher
Macbeth (*c.* 1674–*c.* 1682; *c.* 1696–*c.* 1698)	William Shakespeare
Man of Mode, The: or, Sir Fopling Flutter	
(*c.* 1696–*c.* 1698; 1698–9)	Sir George Etherege
Masquerade, The (1717–18)	Charles Johnson
Merry Wives of Windsor, The	
(*c.* 1670–*c.* 1680)	William Shakespeare
Midsummer Night's Dream, A	
(*c.* 1670–*c.* 1680)	William Shakespeare
Nicomede (translated from Pierre Corneille) (1670)	John Dancer
Night Walker, The: or, The Little Thief	John Fletcher and
(*c.* 1639; 1684–5)	James Shirley
No Wit: No Help Like a Woman's	Thomas Middleton and
(1638–9)	James Shirley
Oedipus (1685)	John Dryden and Nathaniel Lee
Opportunitie, The (*c.* 1638)	James Shirley
Oroonoko: or, The Royal Slave (1698)	Thomas Southerne
Othello (1662; *c.* 1670–*c.* 1680;	
1691; 1692; 1696)	William Shakespeare
Peace Triumphant (1713)	author unknown
Philaster: or, Love Lies a-Bleeding	Francis Beaumont and
(*c.* 1697)	John Fletcher
Pilgrim, The (1709)	John Fletcher and Sir John Vanbrugh
Plotting Lovers, The: or, The	
Dismal Squire (1719–20)	Charles Shadwell
Pompey (translated from	
Pierre Corneille) (1663)	Mrs. Katherine Philips

Rival Queans, The: or,
    Alexander the Great (1713)   Colley Cibber
Rival Queens, The: or, The Death of
    Alexander the Great (1685; c. 1694)   Nathaniel Lee
Rosania: or, Love's Victory (1638)   James Shirley
Rotherick O'Connor, King of Connaught: or, The
    Distressed Princess (1719–20)   Charles Shadwell
Royal Master, The (1637)   James Shirley
St. Patrick for Ireland (1639)   James Shirley
St. Stephen's Green: or, The
    Generous Lovers (1699)   William Philips
Scornful Lady, The (c. 1697)   Francis Beaumont and
                          John Fletcher

Sham Prince, The: or, News from
    Passau (1718–19)   Charles Shadwell
She Would If She Could (1698–9)   Sir George Etherege
Spanish Wives, The (1707)   Mrs. Mary Griffith Pix
Squire of Alsatia, The (1698)   Charles Shadwell
Tamerlane (1711; 1714)   Nicholas Rowe
Timon of Athens (1714)   William Shakespeare
Toy, The (c. 1638)   author unknown
Troilus and Cressida (c. 1670–c. 1680)   William Shakespeare
Twelfth Night (c. 1670–c. 1680)   William Shakespeare
Vertue Betray'd: or, Anna Bullen (c. 1697)   John Banks
Volpone: or, The Fox (c. 1662)   Ben Jonson
Wit Without Money (c. 1639; 1662)   John Fletcher
Woman Captain, The (1713)   Thomas Shadwell
Woman is a Riddle (1718–19)   Christopher Bullock

APPENDIX D

Actors and Actresses at the Dublin Theatres, 1637–1720

Dates in parentheses indicate the years of known or probable affiliation

Andrews, Mr. (*c.* 1675–*c.* 1680).
Armiger, Edward (1637).
Ashbury, Joseph (1662–1720).
Ashbury, Mrs. Ann (1684–*post* 1720).
Aston, Anthony (1709; 1715).
Aston, Mrs. (1709; 1715).

Baker, Francis (*c.* 1670–85).
Barnes, Mr. (*c.* 1675–*c.* 1680).
Booth, Barton (1698–1700).
Bowen, William (1698–9; 1703–4).
Bowman, John (1707–9; 1714).
Bright, George (*c.* 1670–*c.* 1678).
Brown, T. (*c.* 1677).
Buckley, Richard (1694–*c.* 1716).
Buckley, Mrs. Elizabeth (1694–*post* 1700).
Butler, Mrs. Charlotte (1694–*c.* 1695).

Calvert, Nicholas (1662–5).
Cooke, William (1637–*c.* 1641).
Cotts, Mr. (*c.* 1675).
Cross, Miss (1698–1704).
Cudworth, Mr. (*c.* 1675–*c.* 1680).

Daugherty, George (*c.* 1707–*post* 1720).
Doggett, Thomas (1684–8).

Dumeney, Mrs. (*c.* 1709–*c.* 1716).
Dumott, Mr. (1716–*post* 1720).

Elliott, Mr. (*c.* 1698).
Elliott, Mrs. (*c.* 1698).
Elrington, Francis (1714–*post* 1720).
Elrington, Ralph (1717–*post* 1720).
Elrington, Thomas (1712–14; 1715–16; 1717–18; 1719–*post* 1720).
Estcourt, Richard (1694–1704).
Evans, John (1699–1709; 1710–14; 1715–18).

Farlow, Mr. (*c.* 1674).
Farquhar, George (1696–8; 1704).
Fitzgerald, Mrs. (*c.* 1707–*c.* 1716).
Freeman, John (*c.* 1675–82).

Giffard, Henry (1716–*post* 1720).
Giffard, Mrs. (Mary Lyddal) (1716–*post* 1720).
Goddard, Mr. (*c.* 1707).
Griffin, Philip (1699–1701).
Griffith, Thomas (1698–9; 1703–*c.* Feb. 1712; fall 1712–14; 1715–*post* 1720).

Hall, John (*c.* 1713–14).

Hallam, Adam (*c.* 1707–*post* 1720).

Hallam, Mrs. (*c.* 1714).

Hardican, Mrs. (*c.* 1684).

Harrison, Mrs. (*c.* 1698).

Haywood, Mrs. Elizabeth (1714–17).

Hook, Mrs. Mary (1698–1702).

Husband(s), Benjamin (1696–1700; 1714; 1718–*post* 1720).

Kaine, Mr. (*c.* 1675).

Kaine, Mrs. (*c.* 1675).

Keen, Theophilus (1696–1704).

Kendall, Mr. (*c.* 1707–*c.* 1716).

Knightly, Mrs. (*c.* 1698).

Layfield, Lewis (1719–*post* 1720).

Lee, George (*c.* 1675).

Leigh, John (*c.* 1709–14).

Leveridge, Richard (1699–1700).

Lisle, Jeremiah (*c.* 1670–*c.* 1688).

Longmore, Mr. (*c.* 1677–*c.* 1708).

Lyddal, Mr. (*c.* 1716–*post* 1720).

Lyddal, Mrs. (*c.* 1716–*post* 1720).

Lyddal, Mary (*c.* 1716–*post* 1720).

Lyddal, Nancy (*c.* 1716–*post* 1720).

Martin, Mrs. (*c.* 1698–1702; 1703–*post* 1720).

Minns, Mr. (*c.* 1714).

Moore, William (*c.* 1662–7).

Moreau, Anthony (*c.* 1719–*post* 1720).

Moreau, Mrs. (Miss Schoolding) (*c.* 1713–14; *c.* 1719–*post* 1720).

Norris, Henry (1693–9).

Norris, Mrs. Sarah (1693–9).

Norton, Hugh (1694–9).

Norton, Mrs. Mary (1694–9).

Oates, Mr. (*c.* 1714–15).

Osborne, Mrs. Margaret (1677–9).

Peer, William (*c.* 1670–*c.* 1679).

Perry, William (1637–41).

Pinkethman (Pinkiman), William (*c.* 1670–88).

Quin, James (*c.* 1713–15).

Richards, John (1662–76; 1682–8).

Richards, Mrs. (*c.* 1670–6; 1682–8).

Rogers, Mr. (1719–*post* 1720).

Schoolding, Mr. (1698–1714).

Schoolding, Mrs. (1698–1714).

Schoolding, Miss (*c.* 1713–14; 1719–*post* 1720).

Smeton, Mr. (*c.* 1674–*c.* 1682).

Smith, Henry (*c.* 1670–82).

Smith, Mrs. (*c.* 1670–*c.* 1700).

Thomas, Mr. (*c.* 1717).

Thurmond, John (1699–1708; 1713–15).

Thurmond, Mrs. Winifred (*c.* 1700–8).

Thurmond, John, Jr. (1712–15).

Thurmond, Mrs. John, Jr. (1712–15).

Totterdale, John (*c.* 1674–*c.* 1688).

Trefusis, Joseph (*c.* 1675–88; 1698–*c.* 1720).

Vanderbank, James (1716–*post* 1720).

Vanderbank, Mrs. (1716–*post* 1720).

Verbruggen, John (1707–8).

Wall, Mrs. (*c.* 1675).

Walmsley, Mr. (*c.* 1675–*c.* 1688).

Walmsley, Mrs. (*c.* 1680–*c.* 1688).

Waters, Miss (*c.* 1719).

Watson, John (*c.* 1713–*post* 1720).

Watson, John, Jr. (*c.* 1719).

Watson, Marmaduke (1682–*c.* 1688).

Weekes, Richard (1637).

Wilkins, Mrs. (1703–*c.* 1716).

Wilks, Robert (1688; 1691–3; 1694–9).

Wilks, Mrs. Elizabeth (1694–9).

Wilks, William (1714–15).

Williams, David (*c.* 1676).

Wilson, Miss (*c.* 1714–*c.* 1718).

Wolf, Mrs. (*c.* 1707).

Wolfe, Miss (*c.* 1719).

Yeoghny, Mr. (*c.* 1662–*c.* 1667).

Yoe, Millicent (*c.* 1684).

Bibliography

I. *Manuscripts*

'The Black Book of Kings Inns.' MS. 38, Library of Kings Inns, Dublin.

CROKER, THOMAS C. 'Recollections of Cork.' MS. 1206, Trinity College Library, Dublin.

DERING, SIR EDWARD, 2nd Bart. MS. Original Letterbook, 1661–5. University of Cincinnati Library, Cincinnati, Ohio.

DINELEY (DINGLEY), THOMAS. 'Observations in a Voyage Through the Kingdom of Ireland.' MS. 392, National Library of Ireland, Dublin.

DUNTON, JOHN. 'A Tour in Ireland: Observations on Ireland.' MS. Rawlinson D. 71, Bodleian Library, Oxford.

'Extracts from Old Books of Accounts, Tailors Guild, Dublin.' MS. De Rebus Eblanae 80, Gilbert Collection, Pearse Street Library, Dublin.

Great Britain. Public Record Office, London.

   MS. Domestic Entry Book.

   MS. Domestic Signet Office Papers.

   MS. Egmont Letters.

   MS. Patent Rolls, Charles II.

   MS. State Papers Domestic Entry Book.

   MS. State Papers, Ireland.

Ireland. Public Record Office, Dublin.

   MS. British Departmental Papers. (Destroyed by fire, 1922.)

   MS. Chancery Patent Rolls. (Destroyed by fire, 1922.)

   MS. Hearth Money Book (1685), St. John's Church, Dublin. (Destroyed by fire, 1922.)

   MS. Irish Parliamentary Papers. (Destroyed by fire, 1922.)

   MS. Signet Office Docket Books. (Destroyed by fire, 1922.)

   MS. Treasury Ledgers. (Destroyed by fire, 1922.)

The Lanesborough Manuscripts. MS. 879, Trinity College Library, Dublin.

LAWRENCE, WILLIAM J. Notebooks for a history of the Irish stage. University of Cincinnati Library, Cincinnati, Ohio.

LYNCH, JOHN. 'De Historia Ecclesiae Hiberniae.' MS. K. 6.15.16, Trinity College Library, Dublin.

MASON, WILLIAM MONCK. 'Collection for a History of the City of Dublin.' Egerton MS. 1773, British Museum, London.

—— 'Collection for a History of the Irish Stage.' Egerton MS. 1763, British Museum, London.

NIEMEYER, ALBERT. 'The Life and Works of the Earl of Roscommon.' Ph.D. dissertation (unpublished), 1933, Harvard College Library.

'The Principal Christenings and Burials in Dublin in the Seventeenth Century.' MS. 674, Trinity College Library, Dublin.

St. John's Church, Dublin. The Valuation Booke of the Parish of St. John's (1687). MS. 1477, no. 195, Trinity College Library, Dublin.

St. Werburgh's Church, Dublin.
  MS. Account Books, 1641–2.
  MS. Notes from St. Werburgh's Registry. MS. 104, National Library of Ireland, Dublin.
  MS. Parish Ratings.

Smock Alley Theatre, Dublin, prologues and epilogues. MS. English 674 F, Harvard College Library.

'Treasury Book of the City of Dublin, 1541–1612.' Muniment Room, City Hall, Dublin.

Trinity College Register. Muniment Room, Trinity College, Dublin.

WARE, ROBERT. 'The History and Antiquities of Dublin Collected from Authentic Records and the MSS. Collection of Sir James Ware.' MS. De Rebus Eblanae 74, 75, Gilbert Collection, Pearse Street Library, Dublin.

WILSON, JOHN. 'Belphegor.' Smock Alley Theatre, Dublin, prompt copy. MS. 827. 1, Folger Shakespeare Library, Washington, D.C.

II. *Printed Books and Articles*

Account Roll of the Priory of the Holy Trinity, Dublin, 1337–1346, with the Middle English Moral Play 'The Pride of Life' (from the original in the Christ Church Collection in the Public Record Office, Dublin). Ed. James Mills, M.R.I.A. Dublin, 1891.

ADAIR, PATRICK. *A True Narrative of the Rise and Progress of the Presbyterian Church in Ireland.* Belfast, 1866.

ADAMS, J. Q. *Chief Pre-Shakespearian Dramas.* Boston and New York, [1924].

An Answer to the Memoirs of Mrs. Billington. With the life and adventures of Richard Daly, Esq., and an account of the present state of the Irish Theatre. London, 1792.

ARBER, EDWARD. *A Transcript of the Registers of the Company of Stationers of London.* London, 1875–7. 5 v.

ASTON, ANTHONY. *The Coy Shepherdess.* Dublin, 1709.

AUBREY, JOHN. *'Brief Lives', chiefly of Contemporaries, set down by John Aubrey between the Years 1669 and 1696.* Ed. Andrew Clark. Oxford, 1898. 2 v.

BAKER, DAVID ERSKINE. *Biographica Dramatica, or A Companion to the Play-house.* London, 1813. 2 v.

BALD, R. C. 'Shakespeare on the Stage in Restoration Dublin.' *Publications of the Modern Language Association of America,* lvi (1941).

BALE, JOHN. 'The Vocation of John Bale to the Bishopric of Ossory in Ireland.' *The Harleian Miscellany,* vi. London, 1808–10. 10 v.

BARRINGTON, JONAH. *Personal Sketches of His Own Times.* London, 1827. 3 v.

BARTON, SIR D. PLUNKET. *Links between Ireland and Shakespeare.* Dublin, n.d.

BENTLEY, GERALD E. *The Jacobean and Caroline Stage.* Oxford, 1941. 2 v.

Bibliotheca Lindesiana: Royal Proclamations, 1485–1714. Oxford, 1910.

BOYLE, RICHARD, First Earl of Cork. *Lismore Papers*, 1st series. Ed. A. B. Grosart. London, 1886. 5 v.

—— *Lismore Papers*, 2nd series. Ed. A. B. Grosart. London, 1887–8. 5 v.

BOYLE, ROGER, Earl of Orrery. *The Dramatic Works*. London, 1739. 2 v.

—— *Dramatic Works of Roger Boyle, Earl of Orrery.* Ed. William Smith Clark II. Cambridge, Massachusetts, 1937. 2 v.

BRERETON, SIR WILLIAM. *Travels in Holland, The United Provinces, England, Scotland, and Ireland, 1634–1635.* Ed. Edward Hawkins. [London], 1844.

A Brief Character of Ireland. London, 1692.

BURGHCLERE, LADY WINIFRED. *The Life of James First Duke of Ormonde.* London, 1922. 2 v.

BURNELL, HENRY. *Landgartha.* Dublin, 1641.

Calendar of Ancient Records of Dublin. Ed. Sir John T. Gilbert. Dublin, 1889–1922. 17 v.

CHAMBERS, E. K. *The Elizabethan Stage.* Oxford, 1923. 4 v.

—— *The Mediaeval Stage.* Oxford, 1903. 2 v.

CHETWOOD, WILLIAM RUFUS. *A General History of the Stage.* London, 1749.

A Chronology of Some Memorable Accidents. Dublin, 1743.

CIBBER, COLLEY. *An Apology for the Life of Mr. C. Cibber with an Historical View of the Stage.* Ed. Edmund Bellchambers. London, 1822.

CIBBER, THEOPHILUS. *The Lives and Characters of the Most Eminent Actors and Actresses of Great Britain and Ireland.* Dublin, 1752.

COLUM, PADRAIC. 'An Irish Drama', *The Irish Independent,* Dublin, 8 December 1906.

CONCANEN, MATTHEW. *Miscellaneous Poems by Several Hands.* London, 1724.

—— *Poems upon Several Occasions.* Dublin, 1722.

CONGREVE, WILLIAM. *The Complete Works of William Congreve.* Ed. Montague Summers. London, 1923. 4 v.

COOPER, ELIZABETH. *The Life of Thomas Wentworth.* London, 1874. 2 v.

The Council Book of the Corporation of Youghal. Ed. Richard Caulfield. Guildford, Surrey, 1878.

[CURLL, EDMUND]. *The Life of that Eminent Comedian, Robert Wilks, Esq.* London, 1733.

D'ALTON, EDWARD ALFRED. *A History of Ireland.* London, 1906. 2 v.

DANCER, JOHN. *Agrippa.* London, 1675.

—— *Nicomede.* London, 1671.

DE CAVELLI, MARGUISE CAMPANA. *Les Derniers Stuarts à Saint Germain en Laye.* Paris, 1871.

A Description of the City of Dublin in Ireland. London, 1732.

DIBDIN, JAMES C. *The Annals of the Edinburgh Stage.* Edinburgh, 1888.

Dickson's Dublin Intelligencer.

Dictionary of National Biography.

DILLON, WENTWORTH, Earl of Roscommon. *Poems by the Earl of Roscommon.* London, 1717.

DIX, E. R. McCLINTOCK. *Catalogue of Early Dublin-Printed Books: 1661–1700.* Ed. C. Winston Dugan. Dublin, 1898–1905. 4 v.

DODDS, JOHN W. *Thomas Southerne, Dramatist*. New Haven, 1933.

DOWNES, JOHN. *Roscius Anglicanus*. Ed. Montague Summers. London, n.d.

Dublin Courant.

Dublin Gazette.

The Dublin Intelligence.

Dublin University Magazine.

Dublin Weekly Journal.

DUNTON, JOHN. *The Dublin Scuffle*. London, 1699.

EDMUNDSON, WILLIAM. *A Journal of the Life, Travels, Sufferings, and Labour in the Work of the Ministry, of that worthy elder and faithful servant of Jesus Christ, William Edmundson*. 3rd ed., Dublin, 1820.

ELLIOTT, REV. ANTHONY L. 'The Abbey of St. Thomas the Martyr', *The Journal of the Royal Society of Antiquaries of Ireland*, 5th series, ii (1892).

FALKINER, C. LITTON. *Illustrations of Irish History and Topography, Mainly of the Seventeenth Century*. London and New York, 1904.

—— 'The Phoenix Park: Its Origin and Early History', *Proceedings of the Royal Irish Academy*, 3rd series, vi.

FARQUHAR, GEORGE. *The Complete Works of George Farquhar*. Ed. Charles Stonehill. London, 1930. 2 v.

—— *Works*. Ed. Thomas Wilkes. Dublin, 1775. 3 v.

FLOOD, W. H. GRATTAN. *The History of Irish Music*. Dublin, 1913.

FLYNN, J. W. *Random Recollections of an Old Playgoer*. Cork, 1890.

Freeman's Journal, Dublin.

GARTH, SIR SAMUEL. *Prologue for the 4th of November, 1711. Being the anniversary of or the birth-day of the late King William*. London, [1711].

—— *The Prologue that was spoken At the Queen's Theatre in Dublin, on Tuesday the 4th of November, 1712*. Dublin, [1712].

GENEST, JOHN. *Some Account of the English Stage, From the Restoration in 1660 to 1830*. Bath, 1832. 10 v.

GILBERT, SIR JOHN T. *A History of the City of Dublin*. Dublin, 1854–9. 3 v.

[GILDON, CHARLES]. *The Lives and Characters of the English Dramatic Poets, Etc.*, First begun by Mr. Langbaine: improved and continued down to this time by a Careful Hand. London, 1699.

Great Britain. Historical Manuscripts Commission Reports.

The MSS. of the Earl of Ashburnham. London, 1881.

The MSS. of the Earl of Dartmouth. London, 1887–96. 3 v.

The MSS. of the Earl of Egmont. London, 1906–9. 2 v.

The MSS. of the Earl of Egmont. London, 1920–3. 3 v.

The MSS. of J. Eliot Hodgkin. London, 1897.

The MSS. of His Grace, The Duke of Portland. London, 1891–1931. 10 v.

The MSS. of Lord De l'Isle and Dudley. Preserved at Penshurst. London, 1925–42. 2 v.

The MSS. of the Marquis of Ormonde. London, 1895–9. 2 v.

The MSS. of the Marquess of Ormonde, new series. London, 1902–20. 8 v.

The MSS. of S. H. LeFleming. London, 1890.

Eighth Report. London, 1881.

Great Britain. Historical Manuscripts Commission Reports (*cont.*).
　Report XII, Appendix. London, 1891.
　Report LVII. London, 1936.
Great Britain. Public Record Office, London.
　Calendar of State Papers, Domestic Series.
　Calendar of State Papers Relating to Ireland, Preserved in the Public Record Office.
　Calendar of Treasury Books.
　Reports from the Commissioners . . . respecting the Public Records of Ireland.
　　London, 1821–5.
GWYNN, AUBREY. 'The Origins of the Anglo-Irish Theatre', *Studies* (Dublin),
　xxxviii (1939).
GWYNN, STEPHEN. *Dublin Old and New.* New York, 1938.
—— *A History of Ireland.* New York, 1923.
—— *Ireland.* New York, 1926.
HAMILTON, GUSTAVUS E. *An Account of the Honourable Society of King's Inns,*
　Dublin. Dublin, 1915.
HARBAGE, ALFRED. *Annals of English Drama: 975–1700.* Philadelphia, 1940.
Harding's Dublin Newsletter.
HARRIS, WALTER. *The History and Antiquities of the City of Dublin.* Dublin,
　1766.
HEAD, RICHARD. *Hic et Ubique; or, The Humours of Dublin.* London, 1663.
HERBERT, J. D. *Irish Varieties.* London, 1836.
The History of the Theatre Royal. Dublin, 1869.
HITCHCOCK, ROBERT. *An Historical View of the Irish Stage.* Dublin, 1788–94. 2 v.
HODGES, JOHN C. *William Congreve the Man.* New York, 1941.
HORE, EDMUND. 'Christmas in the Baronies of Forth and Bargy Eighty
　Years Ago', *The Wexford Independent,* December 1854.
HOTSON, LESLIE. *The Commonwealth and Restoration Stage.* Cambridge,
　Massachusetts, 1928.
HUGHES, SAMUEL C. *The Church of St. John the Evangelist.* Dublin, 1889.
—— *The Pre-Victorian Drama in Dublin.* Dublin, 1904.
Impartial Occurrences, Foreign and Domestic. Dublin.
Ireland. Public Record Office, Dublin.
　Deputy Keeper of the Public Records in Ireland, 57th Report. 1936.
　An Enrollment of the Number of Hearths in the City of Dublin, Revenue Ex-
　　chequer Presentations, &c., no. 14.
Ireland from the Flight of the Earls to Grattan's Parliament (1607–1782). Ed.
　James Carty. Dublin, 1949.
JOYCE, P. W. *A Social History of Ancient Ireland.* London, 1903. 2 v.
JOYCE, WESTON ST. JOHN. *The Neighbourhood of Dublin.* Dublin, 1912.
KAVANAGH, PETER. *The Irish Theatre.* Tralee, 1946.
KENNEDY, PATRICK. *The Banks of the Boro: a Chronicle of the County of Wexford.*
　Dublin, 1875.
'Kilkenny Corporation Records', *Journal of the Royal Historical and Archaeo-*
　logical Association of Ireland, 4th series, vi (1883–4).
LANGBAINE, GERARD. *An Account of the Early Dramatic Poets.* Oxford, 1691.

LAUDER, SIR JOHN, of Fountainhall. *Historical Selections from the Manuscripts: Vol. I. Historical Observations, 1680–1686.* Edinburgh: Printed for the Bannatyne Club, 1837.

The Laureate: Or, The Right Side of Colley Cibber, Esq. London, 1740.

LAW, HUGH A. *Anglo-Irish Literature.* Dublin, 1926.

LAWRENCE, WILLIAM J. 'Early English Stage and Theatre Lighting', *Stage Year Book,* 1927.

—— *The Elizabethan Playhouse,* 1st series. Stratford, 1912.

—— *The Elizabethan Playhouse,* 2nd series. Stratford, 1913.

—— 'Irish Players at Oxford and Edinburgh', *Dublin Magazine,* vii (1932).

—— 'New Light on the Old Dublin Stage'. *The New Ireland Review,* xxvi (1906).

LE BRAZ, A. *Essai sur l'histoire du theatre Celtique.* Paris, 1904.

LEFANU, ALICIA. *Memoirs of the Life and Writings of Mrs. Frances Sheridan.* London, 1824.

Liber Munerum Publicorum Hiberniae. London, 1824. 2 v.

The Life of James Quin, Comedian. London, 1887.

Lloyd's Newsletter, Dublin.

The London Gazette.

LONGFORD, CHRISTINE. *A Biography of Dublin.* London, 1936.

MACLYSAGHT, EDWARD. *Irish Life in the Seventeenth Century: After Cromwell.* London, 1939.

McMANAWAY, JAMES G. 'Additional Prompt-Books of Shakespeare from the Smock Alley Theatre', *Modern Language Review,* xlv (1950).

MACMANUS, M. J. *Irish Cavalcade (1550–1850).* London, 1939.

MANLY, JOHN M. *Specimens of the Pre-Shakespearean Drama.* Boston, 1897. 2 v.

MAXWELL, CONSTANTIA. *Dublin Under the Georges.* London, 1936.

—— *A History of Trinity College Dublin: 1591–1892.* Dublin, 1946.

Memoirs of the Life of Barton Booth, Esq. London, 1733.

Memoirs of the Life of Mr. Theophilus Keene. London, 1718.

Mercurius Musicus, London.

Mercurius Publicus, London.

MOLLOY, J. FITZGERALD. *The Romance of the Irish Stage.* London, 1897. 2 v.

MORRIS, HENRY. 'Irish Wake Games', *Journal of the Folklore of Ireland Society,* viii (1938).

MURRAY, JOHN TUCKER. *English Dramatic Companies: 1558–1642.* London, 1910. 2 v.

My Countrymen. By an Irishman. Edinburgh and London, 1930.

NAHM, M. C. *John Wilson's 'The Cheats'.* Oxford, 1935.

NASON, ARTHUR H. *James Shirley: Dramatist.* New York, 1915.

NICOLL, ALLARDYCE. *A History of English Drama, 1660–1900:* vol. i, *Restoration Drama, 1660–1700* (4th edition); vol. ii, *Early Eighteenth Century Drama* (3rd edition). Cambridge, 1952.

Non-Cycle Mystery Plays. Early English Text Society, London, 1909.

Notes and Queries.

O'BRIEN, GEORGE. *The Economic History of Ireland in the Seventeenth Century.* Dublin and London, 1919.

O'BRYAN, DANIEL. *Authentic Memoirs, or, The Life and Character of That Most Celebrated Comedian, Mr. Robert Wilks.* London, 1732.

O'CONNOR, G. B. *Elizabethan Ireland: Native and English.* Dublin, n.d.

OGILBY, JOHN. *The Relation of His Majestie's Entertainment Passing through the City of London, To His Coronation: with a Description of the Triumphal Arches, and Solemnity.* London, 1661.

O'KEEFFE, JOHN. *Recollections of the Life of John O'Keeffe, Written by Himself.* London, 1826. 2 v.

O'MAHONY, CHARLES. *The Viceroys of Ireland.* London, 1912.

PHILIPS, MRS. KATHERINE. *Letters from Orinda to Poliarchus.* London, 1705.

—— *Letters from Orinda to Poliarchus.* The Second Edition, with Additions. London, 1729.

—— *Poems.* London, 1678.

—— *Pompey.* London, 1678.

PHILIPS, WILLIAM. *St. Stephen's Green or The Generous Lovers.* Dublin, 1700.

PHILLIPS, SIR THOMAS. *Londonderry and the London Companies, 1609–27.* Belfast, 1928.

PHIPPS, SIR CONSTANTIN. *Sir Constantin Phipps's Address at Dublin Castle to the Mayor, Aldermen and Magistrates of the City of Dublin, on January 16, 1712–13.* Dublin, [1713].

PRIDEAUX, HUMPHREY. *Letters of Humphrey Prideaux, sometime Dean of Norwich, to John Ellis, sometime Under-Secretary of State, 1674–1722.* Ed. Edward Maunde Thompson. [London], Printed for the Camden Society, 1875.

PRIM, JOHN G. A. 'Olden Popular Pastimes in Kilkenny', *Transactions of the Kilkenny Archaeological Society,* ii (1852–3).

Register of the Privy Council of Scotland, 3rd series. London, 1915.

The Registers of St. John the Evangelist, Dublin: 1619 to 1699. Ed. James Mills. Dublin, 1906.

'A Retrospect of the Dublin Stage', *The Dublin Morning Post,* 18 October 1827.

ROSSI, MARIO M. *Pilgrimage in the West.* Tr. J. M. Hone. Dublin, 1933.

SEYMOUR, ST. JOHN D. *Anglo-Irish Literature: 1200–1582.* Cambridge, 1929.

SHADWELL, CHARLES. *Five New Plays.* London, 1720.

—— *The Works of Mr. Charles Shadwell.* Dublin, 1720. 2 v.

SHIRLEY, JAMES. *The Dramatic Works and Poems of James Shirley.* Ed. William Gifford and Alexander Dyce. London, 1833. 6 v.

The Shortest Way to Peace; or an Answer to a Prologue that was to be spoke at the Queen's Theatre in Dublin on the 5th of November, 1711. Dublin, [1711].

SMITH, CHARLES. *The Ancient and Present State of the County and City of Cork.* Dublin, 1774. 2 v.

SOUERS, PHILIP W. *The Matchless Orinda.* Cambridge, Massachusetts, 1931.

STEVENSON, ALLAN H. 'James Shirley and the Actors of the First Irish Theater', *Modern Philology,* xl (1942).

—— 'Shirley's Publishers', *The Library,* xxv (1944–5).

—— 'Shirley's Years in Ireland', *Review of English Studies,* xx (1944).

STOCKWELL, LA TOURETTE. *Dublin Theatres and Theatre Customs (1637–1820)*. Kingsport, Tennessee, 1938.

—— 'Lirenda's Miserie', *Dublin Magazine*, new series, v (1930).

—— 'New Light on the Werburgh-street Theatre', ibid., viii (1933).

STRICKLAND, W. G. *Dictionary of Irish Artists*. Dublin, 1913. 2 v.

STUBBS, W. C. 'The Weavers Guild', *Journal of the Royal Society of Antiquaries*, 6th series, ix (1919).

SUMMERS, MONTAGUE. *The Playhouse of Pepys*. New York, 1935.

—— *The Restoration Theater*. London, 1934.

SWIFT, JONATHAN. *The Correspondence of Jonathan Swift, D.D.* Ed. F. Elrington Ball. London, 1911. 6 v.

—— *The Poems of Jonathan Swift, D.D.* Ed. William E. Browning. London, 1910. 2 v.

—— *Satires and Personal Writings by Jonathan Swift*. Ed. William A. Eddy. London and New York, 1932.

THALER, ALWIN. *Shakespeare to Sheridan*. Cambridge, Massachusetts, 1922.

The Theatrical Remembrancer. London, 1788.

THORN-DRURY, G. *A Little Ark*. London, 1921.

TRAILL, H. D. *Lord Strafford*. London, 1899.

The Tricks of the Town laid open, or A Companion for Country Gentlemen. Dublin, n.d.

A Trip to Ireland, &c. Dublin, 1699.

USSHER, ARLAND. *The Face and Mind of Ireland*. New York, 1950.

VALLANCEY, CHARLES. *Collectanea de Rebus Hibernicis*. Dublin, 1770–1804. 6 v.

VANBRUGH, SIR JOHN. *The Complete Works of Sir John Vanbrugh*. Ed. Bonamy Dobrée and Geoffrey Webb. London, 1927. 4 v.

VAN LENNEP, WILLIAM. 'The Smock Alley Players of Dublin', *A Journal of English Literary History*, xiii (1946).

VICTOR, BENJAMIN. *The History of the Theatres of London and Dublin from 1730 to the Present Time*. London, 1761. 2 v.

WALKER, JOSEPH COOPER. 'An Historical Essay on the Irish Stage', *The Transactions of the Royal Irish Academy*, ii (1788).

WARBURTON, JOHN. *A History of the City of Dublin*. London, 1818. 2 v.

WARE, SIR JAMES. *Rerum Hibernicarum Annales*. Dublin, 1664.

WEBB, JOHN J. *The Guilds of Dublin*. Dublin, 1929.

—— *Municipal Government of Ireland: Medieval and Modern*. Dublin, 1918.

Whalley's Newsletter, Dublin.

[WILKES, THOMAS]. *A General View of the Stage*. London, 1759.

WOOD, ANTHONY. *The Life and Times of Anthony Wood*. Ed. Andrew Clark. Oxford, 1891–2. 2 v.

INDEX